PEARSON CUSTOM LIBRARY

PEARSON

ISBN 10: 1-269-77469-7
ISBN 13: 978-1-269-77469-7

Table of Contents

Culturally Responsive Schooling

Students show more interest in reading when the curriculum includes content that is relevant to their culture.

© Monkey Business/Fotolia

Unlike my grandmother, the teacher did not have pretty brown skin and a colorful dress. She wasn't plump and friendly. Her clothes were of one color and drab. Her pale and skinny form made me worry that she was very ill. . . . The teacher's odor took some getting used to also. Later I learned from the girls this smell was something she wore called perfume. The classroom . . . was terribly huge and smelled of medicine like the village clinic I feared so much. Those fluorescent light tubes made an eerie drone. Our confinement to rows of desks was another unnatural demand made on our active little bodies. . . . We all went home for lunch since we lived a short walk from the school. It took coaxing, and sometimes bribing, to get me to return and complete the remainder of the school day.

Joe Suina (1985, writing his impressions on entering school at age 6)

From Chapter 9 of *The Crosscultural, Language, and Academic Development Handbook: A Complete K–12 Reference Guide*, Fifth Edition. Lynne T. Díaz-Rico. Copyright © 2014 by Pearson Education, Inc. All rights reserved.

The narrative of this Pueblo youth illustrates two cultural systems in contact. Suina was experiencing a natural human reaction that occurs when a person moves into a new cultural situation—culture shock. He had grown up in an environment that had subtly, through every part of his life, taught him appropriate ways of behavior—for example, how people looked (their color, their size, their dress, their ways of interacting) and how space was structured (the sizes of rooms, the types of lighting, the arrangement of furniture). His culture had taught him what was important and valuable. The culture Suina grew up in totally enveloped him and gave him a way to understand life. It provided him with a frame of reference through which he made sense of the world.

Culture is so pervasive that often people perceive other cultures as strange and foreign without realizing that their own culture may be equally mystifying to others. Culture, though largely invisible, influences instruction, policy, and learning in schools. Members of the educational community accept the organization, teaching and learning styles, and curricula of the schools as natural and right, without realizing that these patterns are cultural. And the schools are natural and right for members of the culture that created them. As children of nondominant cultures enter the schools, however, they may find the organization, teaching and learning styles, and curricula to be alien, incomprehensible, and exclusionary.

Unfortunately, teachers—who, with parents, are the prime acculturators of society—often have little training regarding the key role of culture in teaching and learning. Too often, culture is incorporated into classroom activities in superficial ways—as a group of artifacts (baskets, masks, distinctive clothing), as celebrations of holidays (Cinco de Mayo, Martin Luther King, Jr. Day), or as a laundry list of stereotypes and facts (Asians are quiet; Hispanics are family-oriented; Arabs are Muslims). Teachers who have a more insightful view of culture and cultural processes are able to use their understanding to

Table 1   The Skills and Responsibilities of the Intercultural Educator

Understand Culture and Cultural Diversity
Explore key concepts about culture.
Investigate ourselves as cultural beings.
Learn about students' cultures.
Recognize how cultural adaptation affects learning.
Strive for Equity in Schooling
Detect unfair privilege.
Combat prejudice in ourselves and others.
Fight for fairness and equal opportunity.
Promote Achievement with Culturally Responsive Schooling
Respect students' diversity.
Work with culturally supported facilitating or limiting attitudes and abilities.
Sustain high expectations for all students.
Marshal parental and community support for schooling.

Source: Díaz-Rico (2000).

move beyond the superficial and to recognize that people live in characteristic ways. They understand that the observable manifestations of culture are but one aspect of the cultural web—the intricate pattern that weaves and binds a people together. Knowing that culture provides the lens through which people view the world, teachers can look at the "what" of a culture—the artifacts, celebrations, traits, and facts—and ask "why."

Teachers in the twenty-first century face a diverse student population that demands a complicated set of skills to promote achievement for all students. As intercultural educators, teachers understand culturally responsive schooling and can adapt instruction accordingly. Table 1 outlines the skills and responsibilities of the intercultural educator. This chapter addresses culturally responsive schooling and the struggle to achieve equity in schooling. This chapter also includes using culturally responsive pedagogy to promote student achievement.

Understanding Culture and Cultural Diversity

As an initial step in learning about the complexity of culture and how the culture embodied within the school affects diverse students, the following sections examine the nature of culture. Knowledge of the deeper elements of culture—beyond superficial aspects such as food, clothing, holidays, and celebrations—can give teachers a crosscultural perspective that allows them to educate students to the greatest extent possible. These deeper elements include values, belief systems, family structures and child-rearing practices, language and nonverbal communication, expectations, gender roles, and biases—all the fundamentals of life that affect learning.

The Nature of Culture

Does a fish understand water? Do people understand their own culture? Teachers are responsible for helping to pass on cultural knowledge through the schooling process. Can teachers step outside their own culture long enough to see how it operates and to understand its effects on culturally diverse students? A way to begin is to define culture.

The term *culture* is used in many ways. It can refer to activities such as art, drama, and ballet or to items such as pop music, mass media entertainment, and comic books. The term *culture* can be used for distinctive groups in society, such as adolescents and their culture. It can be used as a general term for a society, such as the "French culture." Such uses do not, however, define what a culture is. As a field of study, culture is conceptualized in various ways (see Table 2).

The definitions in Table 2 have common factors but vary in emphasis. The following definition of culture combines the ideas in Table 2:

> Culture is the explicit and implicit patterns for living, the dynamic system of commonly agreed-upon symbols and meanings, knowledge, belief, art, morals, law, customs, behaviors, traditions, and/or habits that are shared and make up the total way of life of a people, as negotiated by individuals in the process of constructing a personal identity.

Table 2 Definitions of Culture

Definition	Source
The sum total of a way of life of a people; patterns experienced by individuals as normal ways of acting, feeling, and being	Hall (1959)
That complex whole that includes knowledge, belief, art, morals, law, and custom, and any other capabilities acquired by humans as members of society	Tylor (in Pearson, 1974)
Mental constructs in three basic categories: *shared knowledge* (information known in common by members of the group), *shared views* (beliefs and values shared by members of a group), and *shared patterns* (habits and norms in the ways members of a group organize their behavior, interaction, and communication)	Snow (1996)
Partial solutions to previous problems that humans create in joint mediated activity; the social inheritance embodied in artifacts and material constituents of culture as well as in practices and ideal symbolic forms; semi-organized hodgepodge of human inheritance. Culture is exteriorized mind and mind is interiorized culture	Cole (1998)
Frames (nationality, gender, ethnicity, religion) carried by each individual that are internalized, individuated, and emerge in interactions	Smith, Paige, and Steglitz (1998)

Postmodern writers have added much to the study of the interplay between culture and the individual by emphasizing the importance of performativity: People act out the roles in culture that display the identities they wish to have known, and they often do this at odds to, or in defiance of, the surrounding ambiance. Moreover, people in the post-modern world take on temporary identities and then shrug off identities that no longer fit. Therefore one must add another paragraph to the preceding definition of culture:

> To understand culture, one must look beyond the obvious to understand how values, codes, beliefs and social relations are continually being reshaped by shifting parameters of place, identity, history, and power. Rather than individuals being excluded for differing from cultural norms, people with dissonant, flexible, complex, and hybrid racial and ethnic identities struggle to generate new meanings within accommodating contexts as they use experimentation and creativity to rework existing configurations of knowledge and power and thus extend the possibilities of being human, even in the face of an uncertain outcome.

The important idea is that culture involves both observable behaviors and intangibles such as beliefs and values, rhythms, rules, and roles. The concept of culture has evolved over the last fifty years away from the idea of culture as an invisible, patterning force to that of culture as an active tension between the social "shortcuts" that make consensual society possible and the contributions and construction that each individual creates while living in society. Culture is not only the filter through which people see the world but also the raw dough from which each person fashions a life that is individual and satisfying.

Because culture is all-inclusive, it includes all aspects of life. Snow (1996) listed a host of components (see Table 3).

Cultures are more than the mere sum of their traits. There is a wholeness about cultures, an integration of the various responses to human needs. Cultures cannot be taught merely by examining external features such as art and artifacts. For example, a

Table 3 Components of Culture

Daily Life			
Animals	Hobbies	Medical care	Sports
Clothing	Housing	Plants	Time
Daily schedule	Hygiene	Recreation	Traffic and transport
Food	Identification	Shopping	Travel
Games	Jobs	Space	Weather
The Cycle of Life			
Birth	Divorce	Rites of passage	
Children	Friends	Men and women	
Dating/mating	Old age		
Marriage	Funerals		
Interacting			
Chatting	Functions in communication	Parties	
Eating	Gifts	Politeness	
Drinking	Language learning	Problem solving	
Society			
Business	Education	Government and politics	Science
Cities	Farming	Languages and dialects	Social problems
Economy	Industry	Law and order	
The Nation			
Holidays	Cultural borrowing	National issues	
Geography	Famous people	Stereotypes	
History			
Creative Arts			
Arts	Genres	Music	
Entertainment	Literature	Television	
Philosophy, Religion, and Values			

Source: Based on Snow (1996).

teacher who travels to Japan may return laden with kimonos and chopsticks, hoping these objects will document Japanese culture. But to understand the culture, that teacher must examine the living patterns and values of the culture that those artifacts represent.

Key Concepts about Culture

Despite the evolving definitions of culture, theorists agree on a few central ideas. These concepts are first summarized here and then treated with more depth.

Culture Is Universal. Everyone in the world belongs to one or more cultures. Each culture provides templates for the rituals of daily interaction: the way food is served, the way children are spoken to, the way needs are met. These templates are an internalized way to organize and interpret experience. All cultures share some universal characteristics. The manner in which these needs are met differs.

Culture Simplifies Living. Social behaviors and customs offer structure to daily life that minimizes interpersonal stress. Cultural patterns are routines that free humans from endless negotiation about each detail of living. Cultural influences help unify a society by providing a common base of communication and common social customs.

Culture Is Learned in a Process of Deep Conditioning. Cultural patterns are absorbed unconsciously from birth, as well as explicitly taught by other members. Culture dictates how and what people see, hear, smell, taste, and feel, and how people and events are evaluated. Cultural patterns are so familiar that members of a culture find it difficult to accept that other ways can be right. As cultural patterns are learned or acquired through observation and language, seldom are alternatives given. The fact that cultural patterns are deep makes it difficult for the members of a given culture to see their own culture as learned behavior.

Culture Is Demonstrated in Values. Every culture deems some beliefs and behaviors more desirable than others, whether these be about nature, human character, material possessions, or other aspects of the human condition. Members of the culture reward individuals who exemplify these values with prestige or approval.

Culture Is Expressed Both Verbally and Nonverbally. Although language and culture are closely identified, the nonverbal components of culture are equally powerful means of communication about cultural beliefs, behaviors, and values. Witness the strong communicative potential of the obscene gesture! In the classroom, teachers may misunderstand a student's intent if nonverbal communication is misinterpreted.

Example of Concept *Nonverbal Miscommunication*

Ming was taught at home to sit quietly when she was finished with a task and wait for her mother to praise her. As a newcomer in the third grade, she waited quietly when finished with her reading assignment.	Mrs. Wakefield impatiently reminded Ming to take out a book and read or start another assignment when she completed her work. She made a mental note: "Ming lacks initiative."

Societies Represent a Mix of Cultures. The patterns that dominate a society form the *macroculture* of that society. In the United States, European American traditions and cultural patterns have largely determined the social behaviors and norms of formal institutions. Within the macroculture, a variety of *microcultures* coexist, distinguished by characteristics such as gender, socioeconomic status, ethnicity, geographical location, social identification, and language use.

Generational experiences can cause the formation of microcultures. For example, the children of Vietnamese who immigrated to the United States after the Vietnam War often became native speakers of English, separating the two generations by language. Similarly, Mexicans who migrate to the United States may find that their children born in the United States consider themselves "Chicanos."

Individuals who grow up within a macroculture and never leave it may act on the assumption that their values are the norm. When encountering microcultures, they may be unable or unwilling to recognize that alternative beliefs and behaviors are legitimate within the larger society.

Culture Is Both Dynamic and Persistent. Human cultures are a paradox—some features are flexible and responsive to change, and other features last thousands of years without changing. Values and customs relating to birth, marriage, medicine, education, and death seem to be the most persistent, for humans seem to be deeply reluctant to alter those cultural elements that influence labor and delivery, marital happiness, health, life success, and eternal rest.

Culture Is a Mix of Rational and Nonrational Elements. Much as individuals living in western European post-Enlightenment societies may believe that reason should govern human behavior, many cultural patterns are passed on through habit rather than reason. People who bring a real tree into their houses in December—despite the mess it creates—do so because of centuries-old Yule customs. Similarly, carving a face on a hollow pumpkin is not a rational idea. Those who create elaborate altars

---

Did You Know? **The Persistence of Cultural Values** The Sarmatians, like their neighbors the Scythians, were nomadic people who lived just north of the Black Sea in ancient times. They had one outstanding trait in particular—a unique love of their horses, such that graves were almost always found with horse bones, bridles, and other accoutrements buried next to the human remains. Thousands of years later, in the twentieth century, their descendants, the Ossetians, waged a fierce cultural skirmish with government officials of the Union of Soviet Socialist Republics (USSR). The issue? The Ossetians insisted on killing a man's horse when he died and burying it with the corpse. The Soviets mandated that it was a crime to waste the People's resources. For many years, subterfuge persisted—a deceased man's horse mysteriously would become sick or disabled and had to be shot, and graves would be reopened in the dead of night to accommodate one more body. (More information at www.ossetians.com/eng.)

Did You Know? Extreme dedication to the concept of standardized testing is deeply ingrained in Chinese parents. Government officials in the Sui dynasty (circa 605 CE) began a competitive examination system that later in the Tang dynasty attracted candidates from all over the country. Test-takers hoped that by attaining a high score on the examination they might qualify for positions of power and influence in the civil service of imperial government. Do students today complain about the rigors of "test week"? Scholars taking the imperial exams were often locked in bare, isolated cells, or in cubicles with other candidates, taking twenty-four to seventy-two hours to complete a test that covered military strategy, civil law, revenue and taxation, agriculture, and geography, as well as works by Confucius and some of his disciples. (Read more about China's Imperial examinations: www.sacu.org/examinations.html.)

in their homes or take food to the grave of a loved one for the Mexican celebration of Day of the Dead do so because of spiritual beliefs.

Cultures Represent Different Values. The fact that each culture possesses its own particular traditions, values, and ideals means that actions can be judged only in relation to the cultural setting in which they occur. This point of view has been called *cultural relativism*. In general, the primary values of human nature are universal—for example, few societies condone murder. However, sanctions relating to actions may differ.

Attempting to impose "international" standards on diverse peoples with different cultural traditions causes problems. This means that some cardinal values held by teachers in the United States are not cultural universals but instead are values that may not be shared by students and their families. For example, not all families value children's spending time reading fiction; some may see this as a waste of time. Some families may not see value in algebra or higher mathematics; others might consider art in the classroom to be unimportant.

Even Diverse Societies Have a Mainstream Culture. The term *mainstream culture* refers to those individuals or groups who share values of the dominant macroculture. In the United States, this dominant or core culture is primarily shared by members of the middle class. Mainstream American culture is characterized by the following values (Gollnick & Chinn, 2006):

- Individualism and privacy
- Independence and self-reliance
- Equality
- Ambition and industriousness
- Competitiveness
- Appreciation of the good life
- Perception that humans are separate from and superior to nature

Culture Affects People's Attitudes toward Schooling. For many individuals, educational aspiration affects the attitude they have toward schooling: what future job or profession they desire, the importance parents ascribe to education, and the investment in education that is valued in their culture. Cultural values also affect the extent to which families are involved in their children's schooling and the forms this involvement takes.

Adapted Instruction

Working with Attitudes toward Schooling

In working with diverse students, teachers will want to know:

- What educational level the student, family, and community desire for the student
- What degree of assimilation to the dominant culture (and to English) is expected and desired

Culture Governs the Way People Learn. Any learning that takes place is built on previous learning. Students have learned the basic patterns of living in the context of their families. They have learned the verbal and nonverbal behaviors appropriate for their gender and age and have observed their family members in various occupations and activities. The family has taught them about love and about relations between friends, kin, and community members. They have observed community members cooperating to learn in a variety of methods and modes. Their families have given them a feeling for music and art and have shown them what is beautiful and what is not. Finally, they have learned to use language in the context of their homes and communities. They have learned when questions can be asked and when silence is required. They have used language to learn to share feelings and knowledge and beliefs. Culture appears to influence learning styles, the way individuals select strategies, and the way they approach learning (Shade & New, 1993).

The culture that students bring from the home is the foundation for their learning. Although certain communities exist in relative poverty—that is, they are not equipped with middle-class resources—poverty should not be equated with cultural deprivation. Every community's culture incorporates vast knowledge about successful living. Teachers can utilize this cultural knowledge to organize students' learning in schools.

Example of Concept   *Culturally Specific Learning Styles*

Students can acquire knowledge by means of various learning modalities, which are often expressed in culturally specific ways. The Navajo child is often taught by first observing and listening, and then taking over parts of the task in cooperation with and under the supervision of an adult. In this way, the child gradually learns all the requisite skills. Finally, the child tests himself or herself privately—failure is not seen by others, whereas success is brought back and shared. The use of speech in this learning process is minimal (Phillips, 1978).

In contrast, acting and performing are the focus of learning for many African-American children. Children observe other individuals to determine appropriate behavior and to appreciate the performance of others. In this case, observing and listening culminates in an individual's performance before others (Heath, 1983b). Reading and writing may be primary learning modes for other cultures such as traditionally educated Asian students.

Investigating Ourselves as Cultural Beings

The Personal Dimension

For intercultural educators, self-reflection is vital. By examining their own attitudes, beliefs, and culturally derived beliefs and behaviors, teachers begin to discover what has influenced their value systems. Villegas and Lucas (2002) summarized this self-reflection in eight components (see Table 4).

Table 4 Components of the Personal Dimension of Intercultural Education

Component	Description
Engage in reflective thinking and writing.	Awareness of one's actions, interactions, beliefs, and motivations—or racism—can catalyze behavioral change.
Explore personal and family histories by interviewing family members.	Exploring early cultural experiences can help teachers better relate to individuals with different backgrounds.
Acknowledge group membership.	Teachers who acknowledge their affiliation with various groups in society can assess how this influences views of, and relationships with, other groups.
Learn about the experiences of diverse groups by reading or personal interaction.	Learning about the histories of diverse groups—from their perspectives—highlights value differences.
Visit students' families and communities.	Students' home environments offer views of students' connections to complex cultural networks.
Visit or read about successful teachers.	Successful teachers of children from diverse backgrounds provide exemplary role models.
Appreciate diversity.	Seeing difference as the norm in society reduces ethnocentrism.
Participate in reforming schools.	Teachers can help reform monocultural institutions.

Source: Based on Villegas and Lucas (2002).

CULTURAL SELF-STUDY:

Self-Exploration Questions

- Describe yourself as a preschool child. Were you compliant, curious, adventuresome, goody-goody, physically active, nature loving? Have you observed your parents with other children? Do they encourage open-ended exploration, or would they prefer children to play quietly with approved toys? Do they encourage initiative?
- What was the knowledge environment like in your home? What type of reading did your father and mother do? Was there a time when the members of the family had discussions about current events or ideas and issues? How much dissent was tolerated from parental viewpoints? Were children encouraged to question the status quo? What was it like to learn to talk and think in your family?
- What kind of a grade-school pupil were you? What is your best memory from elementary school? What was your favorite teacher like? Were you an avid reader? How would you characterize your cognitive style and learning style preferences? Was the school you attended ethnically diverse? What about your secondary school experience? Did you have a diverse group of friends in high school?
- What is your ethnic group? What symbols or traditions did you participate in that derived from this group? What do you like about your ethnic identity? Is there a time now when your group celebrates its traditions together? What was the neighborhood or community like in which you grew up?
- What was your experience with ethnic diversity? What were your first images of race or color? Was there a time in your life when you sought out diverse contacts to expand your experience?
- What contact do you have now with people of dissimilar racial or ethnic backgrounds? How would you characterize your desire to learn more? Given your learning style preferences, how would you go about this?

Cultural Self-Study

Self-study is a powerful tool for understanding culture. A way to begin a culture inquiry is by investigating one's personal name. For example, ask, "Where did I get my name? Who am I named for? In which culture did the name originate? What does the name mean?" Continue the self-examination by reviewing favorite cultural customs—such as holiday traditions, home décor, and favorite recipes. More difficult self-examination questions address the mainstream U.S. values of individual freedom, self-reliance, competition, individualism, and the value of hard work. Ask, "If someone in authority tells me to do something, do I move quickly or slowly? If someone says, 'Do you need any help?' do I usually say, 'No, thanks. I can do it myself'? Am I comfortable promoting myself (e.g., talking about my achievements in a performance review)? Do I prefer to work by myself or on a team? Do I prefer to associate with high achievers and avoid spending much time with people who do not work hard?" These and other introspective questions help to pinpoint cultural attitudes. Without a firm knowledge of one's own beliefs and behaviors, it is difficult to contrast the cultural behaviors of others. However, the self-examination process is challenging and ongoing. It is difficult to observe one's own culture.

Learning about Students' Cultures

Teachers can use printed, electronic, and video materials, books, and magazines to help students learn about other cultures. However, the richest source of information is local—the life of the community. Students, parents, and community members can provide insights about values, attitudes, and habits. One method of learning about students and their families, ethnographic study, has proved useful in learning about the ways that students' experiences in the home and community compare with the culture of the schools.

Ethnographic Techniques

Ethnography is an inquiry process that seeks to provide cultural explanations for behavior and attitudes. Culture is described from the insider's point of view, as the classroom teacher becomes not only an observer of the students' cultures but also an active participant (Erickson, 1977). Parents and community members, as well as students, become sources for the gradual growth of understanding on the part of the teacher.

For the classroom teacher, ethnography involves gathering data in order to understand two distinct cultures: the culture of the students' communities and the culture of the classroom. To understand the home and community environment, teachers may observe and participate in community life, interview community members, and visit students' homes. To understand the school culture, teachers may observe in a variety of classrooms, have visitors observe in their own classrooms, audio- and videotape classroom interaction, and interview other teachers and administrators.

Observations. The classroom teacher can begin to observe and participate in the students' cultures, writing up field notes after participating and perhaps summing up the insights gained in an ongoing diary that can be shared with colleagues.

Such observation can document children's use of language within the community; etiquettes of speaking, listening, writing, greeting, and getting or giving information; values and aspirations; and norms of communication.

When analyzing the culture of the classroom, teachers might look at classroom management and routines; affective factors (students' attitudes toward activities, teachers' attitudes toward students); classroom talk in general; and nonverbal behaviors and communication. The thoughts and intentions of the participants can also be documented.

Interviews. Structured interviews use a set of predetermined questions to gain specific kinds of information. Unstructured interviews are more like conversations in that they can range over a wide variety of topics, many of which the interviewer would not necessarily have anticipated. As an outsider learning about a new culture, the classroom teacher would be better served initially using an unstructured interview, beginning with general questions and being guided in follow-up questions by the interviewee's responses. The result of the initial interview may in turn provide a structure for learning more about the culture during a second interview or conversation. A very readable book about ethnography and interviewing is *The Professional Stranger: An Informal Introduction to Ethnography* (Agar, 1980).

Home Visits. Home visits are one of the best ways in which teachers can learn what is familiar and important to their students. The home visit can be a social call or a brief report on the student's progress that enhances rapport with students and parents. Scheduling an appointment ahead of time is a courtesy that some cultures may require and provides a means for the teacher to ascertain if home visits are welcome. Dress should be professional. The visit should be short (twenty to thirty minutes) and the conversation positive, especially about the student's schoolwork. Viewing the child in the context of the home provides a look at the parent–child interaction, the resources of the home, and the child's role in the family. One teacher announces to the class at the beginning of the year that she is available on Friday nights to be invited to dinner. Knowing in advance that their invitation is welcomed, parents and children are proud to act as hosts.

Example of Concept *A Home Visit*

Home visits can be an effective way for a teacher not only to demonstrate accessibility and interest to students and their families, but also to learn about the family and the context in which the student lives.

One teacher announced to her class that she would be available on Friday evenings to be invited to eat in students' homes. That set of a bit of competition! Students passed the "request for invitation" to their families, and she was booked solidly from fall through the winter holidays. When she would begin class on Monday mornings with thanks to the host student, and describe the tastiest part of the menu, eyes would sparkle with the memory of having had a special guest at home.

Students as Sources of Information. Students generally provide teachers with their initial contact with other cultures. Teachers who are good listeners offer students time for shared conversations by lingering after school or opening the classroom during lunchtime. Teachers may find it useful to ask students to map their own neighborhood. This is a source of knowledge from the students' perspectives about the boundaries of the neighborhood and surrounding areas.

Parents as Sources of Information. Parents can be sources of information in much the same way as their children. The school may encourage parent participation by opening the library once a week after school. This offers a predictable time during which parents and teachers can casually meet and chat. Parents can also be the source for information that can form the basis for classroom writing. Using the Language Experience Approach, teachers can ask students to interview their parents about common topics such as work, interests, and family history. In this way, students and parents together can supply knowledge about community life.

Community Members as Sources of Information. Community members are a rich source of cultural knowledge. Much can be learned about a community by walking or driving through it, or stopping to make a purchase in local stores and markets. One teacher arranged to walk through the neighborhood with a doctor whose office was located there. Other teachers may ask older students to act as tour guides. During these visits, the people of the neighborhood can be sources of knowledge about housing, places where children and teenagers play, places where adults gather, and sources of food, furniture, and services.

Through community representatives, teachers can begin to know about important living patterns of a community. A respected elder can provide information about the family and which members constitute a family. A community leader may be able to contrast the community political system with the city or state system. A religious leader can explain the importance of religion in community life. Teachers can also attend local ceremonies and activities to learn more about community dynamics.

The Internet. Websites proliferate that introduce the curious to other cultures. Webcrawler programs assist the user to explore cultural content using keyword prompts.

Participating in Growth Relationships. Self-study is only one means of attaining self-knowledge. Teachers who form relationships with individuals whose backgrounds differ from their own, whether teacher colleagues or community members, can benefit from honest feedback and discussions that help to expand self-awareness. Intercultural educators are not free from making mistakes when dealing with students, family and community members, and colleagues whose culture differs from their own. The only lasting error is not learning from these missteps or misunderstandings.

Sociocultural Consciousness. Villegas and Lucas (2007) invite teachers who were raised in middle-class, monolingual communities to develop a "sociocultural consciousness" (p. 31) that impels them to examine the role of schools in both perpetuating and challenging social inequities. Understanding the role that differential distribution of wealth and power plays in school success helps teachers to commit to the ethical obligation of helping all students learn.

How Cultural Adaptation Affects Learning

As immigrants enter American life, they make conscious or unconscious choices about which aspects of their culture to preserve and which to modify. When cultures meet, they affect each other. Cultures can be swallowed up (*assimilation*), one culture may adapt to a second (acculturation), both may adapt to each other (*accommodation*), or they may coexist (*pluralism or biculturalism*). Contact between cultures is often not a benign process. It may be fraught with issues of prejudice, discrimination, and misunderstanding. Means of mediation or resolution must be found to alleviate cultural conflict, particularly in classrooms.

Fears about Cultural Adaptation. Pryor (2002) captured the nature of immigrant parents' concerns about their children's adjustment to life in the United States:

> In the United States, some immigrant parents live in fear that their children will be corrupted by what they believe to be the materialistic and individualistic dominant culture, become alienated from their families, and fall prey to drugs and promiscuity. Their fears are not unfounded, as research shows that the longer that immigrants live in the United States, the worse their physical and mental health becomes. . . . One Jordanian mother stated, "I tell my son (who is 8 years old) not to use the restroom in school. I tell him he might catch germs there that he could bring home, and make the whole family ill. I really am afraid he may get drugs from other kids in the restroom." (p. 187)

Many immigrant parents are overwhelmed with personal, financial, and work-related problems; they may have few resources to which to turn for help. In the process of coming to terms with life in a foreign country, they may be at odds with the assimilation or acculturation processes their children are experiencing, causing family conflict.

Example of Concept *Holding on to Sikh Heritage in the United States*

Sikhs began coming to the United States in large numbers in the 1980s because of religious persecution in India, gradually numbering about 500,000 across America. Sikh communities across North America began to realize that their children needed to acquire Punjabi in order to maintain their religious practice (Sikhism is the world's fifth largest religion). Now there are about 150 *gurdwaras,* or Sunday schools, to teach how to speak and write Punjabi and maintain the culture and values of the Sikh religion.

According to Jasdeep Singh, who has two young sons who attend weekly classes, his parents' generation has their ties to India to support their ethnic identity. But young people need more. "I think my generation is the one that's actually seen the value of Punjabi schools." (Abdulrahim, 2011, p. AA3)

Assimilation. When members of an ethnic group are absorbed into the dominant culture and their culture gradually disappears in the process, they are said to assimilate. *Cultural assimilation* is the process by which individuals adopt the behaviors, values, beliefs, and lifestyle of the dominant culture. *Structural assimilation* is participation in the social, political, and economic institutions and organizations of mainstream society. It is structural assimilation that has been problematic for many immigrants. Teachers may strive to have students assimilate culturally but be blind to the fact that some of their students will not succeed because of attitudes and structures of the dominant society.

Acculturation. When individuals adapt effectively to the mainstream culture, they are said to *acculturate*. To acculturate is to adapt to a second culture without necessarily giving up one's first culture. Some researchers have emphasized the importance of acculturation for success in school.

Schools are the primary places in which children of various cultures learn about the mainstream culture. Sometimes culture is taught explicitly as a part of the ELD curriculum (Seelye, 1984). According to Cortés (2013):

> Acculturation of students should be a primary goal of education because it contributes to individual empowerment and expands life choices. However, this acculturation should be additive, not subtractive. Subtractive acculturation can disempower by eroding students' multicultural abilities to function effectively within both the mainstream and their own ethnic milieus, as well as in their relations with those of other cultural backgrounds. But today even traditional additive acculturation is not enough. For our multicultural twenty-first century, education should strive to develop student multicultural capacities by embracing what I call "multiculturation," the blending of *multiple* and *acculturation*.

Accommodation. A two-way process, accommodation happens when members of the mainstream culture change in adapting to a minority culture, the members of which in turn accept some cultural change as they adapt to the mainstream. Thus, accommodation is a mutual process. To make accommodation a viable alternative in schools, teachers need to demonstrate that they are receptive to learning from the diverse cultures in their midst, and they also need to teach majority students the value of "interethnic reciprocal learning" (Gibson, 1991).

 Example of Concept   *Accommodating Students' Culture*

[I]n non-Indian* classes students are given opportunities to ask the teacher questions in front of the class, and do so. Indian students are given fewer opportunities for this because when they do have the opportunity, they don't use it. Rather, the teacher of Indians allows more periods in which she is available for individual students to approach her alone and ask their questions where no one else can hear them. (Philips, 1972, p. 383)

*Native American

Pluralism. Assimilation, not acculturation, was the aim of many immigrants who sought to become part of the melting pot. More recently, minority groups and their advocates have begun to assert that minority and ethnic groups have a right, if not a responsibility, to maintain valued elements of their ethnic cultures. This *pluralist* position is that coexistence of multicultural traditions within a single society provides a variety of alternatives that enrich life in the United States. Pluralism is the condition in which members of diverse cultural groups have equal opportunities for success, in which cultural similarities and differences are valued, and in which students are provided cultural alternatives. Integration creates the conditions for cultural pluralism. Merely mixing formerly isolated ethnic groups does not go far enough, because groups rapidly unmix and resegregate.

Biculturalism. Being able to function successfully in two cultures constitutes biculturalism. Darder (1991) defined *biculturalism* as

> a process wherein individuals learn to function in two distinct sociocultural environments: their primary culture, and that of the dominant mainstream culture of the society in which they live. It represents the process by which bicultural human beings mediate between the dominant discourse of educational institutions and the realities they must face as members of subordinate cultures. (pp. 48–49)

What is it like to be bicultural in the United States? Bicultural people are sometimes viewed with distrust. An example is the suspicion toward Japanese Americans during World War II and the resulting internment. Parents may also feel threatened by their bicultural children. Appalachian families who moved to large cities to obtain work often pressured their children to maintain an agrarian, preindustrial lifestyle, a culture that is in many ways inconsistent with urban environments (Pasternak, 1994). Similarly, families from rural Mexico may seek to maintain traditional values after immigrating to the United States even as their children adopt behaviors from the U.S. macroculture. The process of becoming bicultural is not without stress, especially for students who are expected to internalize dissimilar, perhaps conflicting, values.

Cultural Congruence. In U.S. schools, the contact of cultures occurs daily. In this contact, the congruence or lack thereof between mainstream and minority cultures has lasting effects on students. Students from families whose cultural values are similar to those of the European-American mainstream culture may be relatively advantaged in schools, such as children from those Asian cultures who are taught that students sit quietly and attentively. In contrast, African American students who learn at home to project their personalities and call attention to their individual attributes (Gay, 1975) may be punished for efforts to call attention to themselves during class.

Teachers, who have the responsibility to educate students from diverse cultures, find it relatively easy to help students whose values, beliefs, and behaviors are congruent with U.S. schooling but often find it difficult to work with others. The teacher who can find a common ground with diverse students will promote their further education.

Stages of Individual Cultural Contact. Experiencing a second culture causes emotional ups and downs. Reactions to a new culture vary, but there are distinct stages in the process of experiencing a different culture (Brown, 2007). These same emotional stages can occur for students. The intensity will vary depending on the degree of similarity between home and school culture, the individual child, and the teacher.

The first state, *euphoria*, may result from the excitement of experiencing new customs, foods, and sights. This may be a "honeymoon" period in which the newcomer is fascinated and stimulated by experiencing a new culture.

The next stage, *culture shock*, may follow euphoria as cultural differences begin to intrude. The newcomer is increasingly aware of being different and may be disoriented by cultural cues that result in frustration. Deprivation of the familiar may cause a loss of self-esteem. Depression, anger, or withdrawal may result.

The final stage, *adaptation to the new culture*, may take several months to several years. Long-term adjustment can take several forms. Ideally, the newcomer feels capable of negotiating most new and different situations. On the other hand, individuals who do not adjust as well may feel lonely and frustrated. A loss of self-confidence may result. Eventually, successful adaptation results in newcomers being able to actively express themselves and to create a full range of meaning in the situation.

Example of Concept   *Diagnose Your Vulnerability to Culture Shock*

The *Intercultural Effectiveness Scale (IES)* is a self-assessment available from the Kozai Group (http://www.intercultural.org/kozai.php) that "evaluates competencies critical for effective interaction with people from different cultures." Those who take this self-assessment receive a diagnostic booklet that explains which self-reported personality strengths and challenges might lead to more or less success when interacting with other cultures. According to the website of the Intercultural Communication Institute, "[The *IES*] is useful in crosscultural and diversity courses to increase awareness and self-analysis for improvement."

Source: Printed with permission of The Intercultural Communication Institute. (2013). The Intercultural Effectiveness Scale (IES). Online at www.intercultural.org/kozai.pho.

Striving for Equity in Schooling

Teachers who were themselves primarily socialized in mainstream American culture may not be aware of the challenges faced by individuals from nondominant cultures as they strive to succeed in U.S. schools. Bonilla-Silva (2003) contended that European Americans have developed powerful rationalizations and justifications for contemporary racial inequality that exculpate them from responsibility for the status of people of color. This constitutes a new racial ideology he called "color-blind racism" (p. 2), which is a way of committing or participating in racist practices while not believing that oneself is racist (also called "racism without racists" [p. 1] and "new racism" [p. 3]).

To create school environments that are fair for all students, teachers need to achieve clarity of vision (Balderrama & Díaz-Rico, 2005) about the social forces that advantage some members of society and disadvantage others. This work entails recognizing that society is becoming increasingly polarized, moving toward a vast separation between the rich and the poor. Class and racial privilege, prejudice, and unequal opportunity are barriers to success. Awareness of unfair practices is the first step toward remedy.

Detecting Unfair Privilege

For European American middle-class teachers to accept the work of achieving equity in education, they must at some point examine their own complicity in the privileges of being white and middle class in a society predicated on inequity. *Privilege* is defined as the state of benefiting from special advantages, favors, or rights accorded to some, to the exclusion of others. McIntosh's (1996) article "White Privilege and Male Privilege" is a useful tool for exploring the advantage experienced by those who are white, male, or middle-class in order to become aware of the many social advantages they have reaped at the expense of those who are nonwhite, non-middle-class, or female. Figure 1 presents some of the privileges that the dominant race/class/gender enjoys.

Fighting for Fairness and Equal Opportunity

Schools in the United States have not been level playing fields for those of nonmainstream cultures. Teachers can remedy this in both academic and extracurricular areas. According to Manning (2002), teachers should

> consider that all learners deserve, ethically and legally, equal access to curricular activities (i.e., higher-level mathematics and science subjects) and opportunities to participate in all athletic activities (i.e., rather than assuming all students of one race will play on the basketball team and all students of another race will play on the tennis or golfing teams). (p. 207)

Cultural fairness can extend to the social and interpersonal lives of students, those daily details and microinteractions that also fall within the domain of culture. Teachers who invest time to get to know their students, as individuals as well as cultural beings, address issues of fairness through a personal commitment to equality of treatment and opportunity.

Figure 1   The Privileges of the Dominant Race/Class/Gender

I can rent or purchase housing in an affordable, desirable area, with neighbors who will be neutral or pleasant to me.
My children will see their race represented in curricular materials.
When I purchase, my skin color does not suggest financial instability.
I can criticize our government without being seen as a cultural outsider.
"The person in charge" is usually a person of my race.
Traffic cops do not single me out because of my race.
My behavior is not taken as a reflection on my race.
If my day is going badly, I need not suspect racial overtones in each negative situation.
I can imagine many options—social, political, or professional—without wondering if a person of my race would be allowed to do what I want to do.

Source: Adapted from McIntosh (1996).

Establishing a Climate of Safety

Many students live in terror of school because they are bullied. Bullying is an issue of power, and those who lack power and social capital—such as immigrants—are often targets. English learners may suffer from racial and ethnic stereotyping; cultural and language barriers and concerns over legal status may lead to many incidents not being reported to authorities. Classroom discussion about current or historical events involving immigrant communities can also help prevent bullying by humanizing those groups to other students.

Gay, lesbian, bisexual, and transgender (GLBT) students also report a high level of being bullied. According to a 2009 survey of more than 7,200 middle- and high-school students, nearly eighty-five percent of LGBT students say they are verbally harassed, and forty percent report physical harassment because of their sexual orientation (Kosciw, Greytak, Díaz, & Bartkiewicz, 2010). GLBT teens commit suicide at three to four times the rate of other students. Almost eighty percent of teens say their teachers do little or nothing to stop anti-LGBT bullying when they see it. Reece-Miller (2010) calls the gay, lesbian, bisexual, transgender, and queer/questioning (LGBTQ) students "the silent minority," whose needs are largely ignored in K–12 schools.

Educators have a legal responsibility to respond to students' bullying one another. If a student is teased because of perceived sexual orientation, "Some teachers and principals don't get involved. This might seem like an issue best left out of the classroom, but there's a population of gay, lesbian, bisexual and transgender (GLBT) students who feel unsafe at school" (Martin, 2011, p. 9).

Educators can create safe schools for GLBTIQ (now including "intersex") students:

- Establish a student club ("gay-straight alliance") where students can talk about issues related to sexual orientation.
- Provide anti-bullying training, emphasizing GLBT issues.
- Develop the presence of supportive staff (who are not necessarily GLBTIQ themselves).
- Include GLBTIQ figures in the curriculum. (Martin, 2011)

Example of Concept   *Reducing Verbal Emotional Violence*

Tired of battling students' verbal put-downs of one another in his eighth-grade social studies classroom, John Ash led a discussion on what it felt like to both send and receive put-downs. Using definitions, examples, and student input, Ash showed students how to identify and react to this kind of verbal violence.

In less than a month, Ash had drastically reduced the incidents of verbal violence in his classroom. "Some people think 'safe' refers only to physical safety," he said. "But it also means emotional safety. If I don't provide an environment where students are safe emotionally, how much learning do you think will occur?" (Moorman & Haller, 2011)

Combating Prejudice in Ourselves and Others

If diversity is recognized as a strength, educators will "avoid basing decisions about learners on inaccurate or stereotypical generalizations" (Manning, 2002, p. 207). Misperceptions about diversity often stem from prejudice.

The Dynamics of Prejudice. One factor that inhibits cultural adaptation is prejudice. Prejudice takes various forms: excessive pride in one's own ethnic heritage, country, or culture so that others are viewed negatively; *ethnocentrism*, in which the world revolves around oneself and one's own culture; a prejudice against members of a certain racial group; and stereotypes that label all or most members of a group. All humans are prejudiced to some degree, but it is when people act on those prejudices that discriminatory practices and inequalities result.

A closer look at various forms of prejudice, such as racism and stereotyping, as well as resulting discriminatory practices can lead to an understanding of these issues. Teachers can then be in a position to adopt educational methods that are most likely to reduce prejudice.

Example of Concept   *Xenophobia in U.S. History*

Sutherland (1989) described the Centennial of 1876, which was held in Philadelphia:

> [T]he Centennial impressed everyone. Its 167 buildings and 30,000 exhibits covered 236 acres in Fairmount Park. The Main Exhibition Building, housing the principal exhibits of manufactured products and scientific achievements, measured 1,800 feet long and 464 feet wide, the largest building in the world.... [A] total of thirty-five foreign nations provided exhibits or entertainment in one form or another.... [W]herever they went on the fairgrounds, visitors saw and heard xenophobic expressions of prejudice. Foreign-looking people of all races and nationalities, were they Orientals, Turks, Slavs, Egyptians, or Spaniards, were "followed by large crowds of idle boys, and men, who hooted and shouted at them as if they had been animals of a strange species." (pp. 263, 264, 268)

Racism. Racism is the view that a person's race determines psychological and cultural traits—and, moreover, that one race is superior to another. Racism can also be cultural when one believes that the traditions, beliefs, languages, artifacts, music, and art of other cultures are inferior. On the basis of such beliefs, racists justify discriminating against or scapegoating other groups. As important as is the facet of symbolic violence that racism represents, of equal importance is the fact that goods and services are distributed in accordance with such judgments of unequal worth.

Racism is often expressed in hate crimes, which are public expressions of hostility directed at specific groups or individuals. These may take the form of harassment (scrawling graffiti on people's homes; pelting houses with eggs; burning crosses on lawns; children playing in yards being subjected to verbal taunts; hate-filled e-mails sent to individuals or groups; swastikas carved into public textbooks, school desks, or other property; etc.) or, at the extreme, assaults and murder directed toward minitories. Schools are often prime sites in which hate crimes are committed. This fact underscores the urgency of educators' efforts to understand and combat racism.

Example of Concept

Racial Tension—Differing Points of View

When racial tensions erupted between Black and Asian students at South Philadelphia High School, Asian students shared their concerns about the events at a news conference with community advocates. They charged that school security guards did not protect them. In turn, the security spokesman said, "What gets lost in all of this is the fact that the school, the community, and the students have worked hard over the past two years to foster a positive learning environment."

Through a translator, ninth-grader Chaofei Zheng said that he wants to get an education, make friends, and improve his English; that there are nice students at the school and he doesn't understand the reason for the attacks that sent several Asian students to a hospital.

Amina Velazquez, a senior who is Black and Puerto Rican, said that Asian students tend to stay within their own groups, making it hard to get to know them. Valazquez, a member of student government, suggested that if Asian students participated in more activities, they would be further integrated into the school community. She noted that for some, language barriers make interaction difficult.

Superintendent Michael Silverman had a fourth viewpoint. The racial tension "started in the community and came to school—I don't know how you separate the school from the community." (Matheson, 2009, Associated Press, (www.accessmylibrary.com /article-1G1-213640674/us-school-racial-tensions .html)

Teaching against Racism. Students and teachers alike must raise awareness of racism in the attempt to achieve racial equality and justice. Actively listening to students in open discussion about racism, prejudice, and stereotyping can increase teachers' understanding of how students perceive and are affected by these concepts. School curricula can be used to help students be aware of the existence and impact of racism. Science and health teachers can debunk myths surrounding the concept of race. Content-area teachers can help students develop skills in detecting bias.

Adapted Instruction

How to Interrupt Oppressive Behavior

Essential tools in the effort to promote equity in the classroom and school environment are the skills that work toward social justice. All too frequently students join in mockery or discriminatory behaviors because they cannot stand up to peer pressure—instead, they turn away, or they "go with the crowd." In such situation, students can "act toward" social justice in the following ways:

• Interrupting the behavior by voicing disapproval: "I don't think that's funny."

• Interrupting and educating others by explaining why the behavior is wrong.

• Supporting others who are proactive by siding with them physically or verbally.

• Replacing hurtful behaviors by initiating and organizing opposite, proactive responses. (McClintock, 2000)

Stereotypes. Often resulting from racist beliefs, stereotypes are preconceived and oversimplified generalizations about a particular ethnic or religious group, race, or gender. The danger of stereotyping is that people are not considered as individuals but are categorized with all other members of a group. A stereotype can be favorable or unfavorable, but, whether it is positive or negative, the results are negative: The perspective on an entire group of people is distorted.

Example of Concept — *Comparisons within a Cultural Group*

Mrs. Abboushi, a third-grade teacher, discovers that her students hold many misconceptions about the Arab people. Her goal becomes to present them with an accurate and more rounded view of the Arab world. She builds background information by using a world map on which the students identify the countries featured in the three books they will read: *Ibrahim* (Sales, 1989), *The Day of Ahmed's Secret* (Heide & Gilliland, 1990), and *Nadia, the Willful* (Alexander, 1983).

After reading and interactively discussing the books, students are divided into groups of four, each receiving a copy of one of the books. Students prepare a Cultural Feature Analysis chart that includes the cultural features, setting, character and traits, family relationships, and message. Groups share their information and Mrs. Abboushi records the information on a large chart. During the follow-up discussion, students discover that not all Arabs live the same way, dress the same way, or look the same way. They recognize the merging of traditional and modern worlds, the variability in living conditions, customs and values, architecture, clothing, and modes of transportation (Diamond & Moore, 1995, pp. 229–230).

Adapted Instruction

Antiracist Activities and Discussion Topics

- Recognize racist history and its impact on oppressors and victims.
- Understand the origins of racism and why people hold racial prejudices and stereotypes.
- Be able to identify racist images in the language and illustrations of books, films, television, news media, and advertising.
- Identify specific ways of developing positive interracial contact experiences.
- Extend the fight against racism into a broader fight for universal human rights and respect for human dignity.

Source: Bennett (2003, pp. 370–373).

Programs to Combat Prejudice and Racism. The Southern Poverty Law Center distributes Teaching Tolerance magazine, a free resource sent to over 600,000 educators twice a year that provides antibias strategies for K–12 teachers. Carnuccio (2004) describes the Tolerance.org website, a web project of the Southern Poverty Law Center (available at www.splcenter.org), as an "extremely informative resource":

The project has done an excellent job of collecting and disseminating information on the advantages of diversity.... The site features pages designed specifically for children, teens, teachers, and parents. *Planet Tolerance* has stories for children to read and listen to and games for them to play. Teens can find ideas on how to bring diverse groups together in their schools. Teachers' pages feature articles, films and books to order, lesson ideas, and a forum in which to share ideas with other teachers. The pamphlet *101 Tools for Tolerance* suggests a variety of ideas for community, workplace, school, and home settings. *Parenting for Tolerance* offers ways for parents to guide their children to develop into tolerant adults. (p. 59)

Example of Concept   *Combating Anti-Muslim Bias*

In the wake of the 2001 World Trade Center bombings, the 2.5 million Muslims in the United States have reported widespread negative bias. Educators have taken the lead in combatting this bias.

Southeastern Michigan is a richly diverse area that includes a large Arab American community. But in this divided region, kids from different backgrounds rarely meet. For the past twenty years, the group Generation of Promise has chosen sixty high-school juniors for a ten-month program that gives them the opportunity to showcase their culture and learn about others.

"We attempt to take students who are leaders in those communities, who can influence their peer groups, and expose them to that diversity in a real, intimate way," says Christine Geoghegan, director of Generation of Promise. That can happen through trips to a mosque in Dearborn or by attending a Shabbat dinner at the home of a Jewish student.

In 2010, Maya Edery, an Israeli American, was paired with Mohamad Idriss, a native of Lebanon who is Muslim. They have become close friends.

"You can coordinate the most sophisticated program," says Geoghegan. "But what changes people is people—access to relationships they're otherwise not having." (www.tolerance .org/magazine/number-39-spring-2011/feature/ combating-anti-muslim-bias)

Institutional Racism. "[T]hose laws, customs, and practices that systematically reflect and produce racial inequalities in American society" (Jones, 1981) constitute institutional racism. Classroom teaching that aims at detecting and reducing racism may be a futile exercise when the institution itself—the school—promotes racism through its policies and practices, such as underreferral of minority students to programs for gifted students or failing to hire minority teachers in classrooms where children are predominantly of minority background.

Classism. In the United States, racism is compounded with classism, the distaste of the middle and upper classes for the lifestyles and perceived values of the lower classes. Although this classism is often directed against linguistic and cultural minorities—a typical poor person in the American imagination is urban, black, and young, either a single teen mother or her offspring—portraying poverty that way makes it easier to stigmatize the poor (Henwood, 1997).

Classism has engendered its own stereotype against poor European Americans—for example, the stereotyped European American indigent who is called, among other things, "White trash" (Wray & Newitz, 1997). Poor whites, who outnumber poor minorities, may bear the brunt of a "castelike" status in the United States as much as linguistic and cultural minorities do.

Discrimination. Discriminatory practices tend to legitimize the unequal distribution of power and resources between groups defined by such factors as race, language, culture, gender, and/or social class. Blatant discrimination, in which differential education for minorities is legally sanctioned, may be a thing of the past, but discrimination persists. De facto segregation continues; most students of color are still found in substandard schools. Schools with a high percentage of minority enrollment tend to employ faculty who have less experience and academic preparation. Teachers may communicate low expectations to minority students. The "hidden curriculum" of tracking and differential treatment results in schools that perpetuate the structural inequities of society. Thus, school becomes a continuation of the discrimination experienced by minorities in other institutions in society (Grant & Sleeter, 1986).

In the past, those in power often used physical force to discriminate. With the spread of literacy, the trend moved away from the use of physical force toward the use of shame and guilt. The school plays a part in this process. The values, norms, and ideology of those in power are taught in the school. Skutnabb-Kangas (1981, 1993) called this *symbolic-structural violence*. Direct punishment is replaced by self-punishment, and the group discriminated against internalizes shame associated with cultural differences. The emotional and intellectual bonds of internalized injustice make the situation of minorities more difficult.

Example of Concept   *Avoiding "Microaggressions"*

Teachers may be unaware of the effect of their interactions with students from underrepresented groups. Derald Wing Sue's *Microaggressions in Everyday Life: Race, Gender, and Sexual Orientation* (2010) offers an analysis of how careless, unintended slights and inadvertent social cues can take massive tolls on the psychological well-being and academic achievement of minority groups. (*Hint:* Never sigh, "Oh, boy…" in frustration when teaching a group of African American youth.)

Reducing Interethnic Conflict

If interethnic conflict occurs, taking immediate, proactive steps to resolve the conflict is necessary. Table 5 presents a scenario in which conflict resolution is needed and describes a twelve-skill approach to mediation.

Johnson and Johnson (1979, 1994, 1995) emphasized the usefulness of cooperative, heterogeneous grouping in the classroom in the resolution of classroom conflict. Explicit training for elementary students in negotiation and mediation procedures has proved effective in managing conflict, especially when such programs focus on safely expressing feelings, taking the perspective of the other, and providing the rationale for diverse points of view (Johnson, Johnson, Dudley, & Acikgoz, 1994).

Table 5 Applying a Twelve-Skill Approach to Interethnic Conflict

Scenario: A group of four European American girls in tenth grade had been making fun of Irena and three of her friends, all of whom were U.S.-born Mexican Americans. One afternoon Irena missed her bus home from high school, and the four girls surrounded her when she was putting books in her locker. One girl shoved a book out of the stack in her hands. Irena shoved her back. Just then, a teacher came around the corner and took Irena to the office for discipline. The assistant principal, Ms. Nava, interviewed Irena to gain some background about the situation. Rather than dealing with Irena in isolation, Ms. Nava waited until the next day, called all eight of the girls into her office, and applied the twelve-skill approach to conflict resolution.

Skill	Application of Skills to Scenario
1. The win–win approach: Identify attitude shifts to respect all parties' needs.	Ms. Nava asked each girl to write down what the ideal outcome of the situation would be. Comparing notes, three of the girls had written "respect." Ms. Nava decided to use this as a win–win theme.
2. Creative response: Transform problems into creative opportunities.	Each girl was asked to write the name of an adult who respected her and how she knew it was genuine respect.
3. Empathy: Develop communication tools to build rapport. Use listening to clarify understanding.	In turn, each girl described what she had written above. The other girls had to listen, using eye contact to show attentiveness.
4. Appropriate assertiveness: Apply strategies to attack the problem not the person.	Ms. Nava offered an opportunity for members of the group to join the schools' Conflict Resolution Task Force. She also warned the group that another incident between them would result in suspension.
5. Cooperative power: Eliminate "power over" to build "power with" others.	Each girl was paired with a girl from the "other side" (cross-group pair) to brainstorm ways in which teens show respect for one another.
6. Managing emotions: Express fear, anger, hurt, and frustration wisely to effect change.	Ms. Nava then asked Irena and the girl who pushed her book to tell their side of the incident without name-calling.
7. Willingness to resolve: Name personal issues that cloud the picture.	Each girl was asked to name one underlying issue between the groups that this incident represented.
8. Mapping the conflict: Define the issues needed to chart common needs and concerns.	Ms. Nava mapped the issues by writing them on a wall chart as they were brought forth.
9. Development of options: Design creative solutions together.	Still in the cross-group pairs from step 5 above, each pair was asked to design a solution for one of the issues mapped.
10. Introduction to negotiation: Plan and apply effective strategies to reach agreement.	Ms. Nava called the girls into her office for a second day. They reviewed the solutions that were designed and made a group plan for improved behavior.
11. Introduction to mediation: Help conflicting parties to move toward solutions.	Each cross-group pair generated two ideas for repair if the above plan failed.
12. Broadening perspectives: Evaluate the problem in its broader context.	The eight girls were asked if racial conflict occurred outside their group. Ms. Nava asked for discussion: Were the same issues they generated responsible for this conflict?

Source: Based on www.crnhq.org.

Especially critical is the role of a mediator in establishing and maintaining a balance of power between two parties in a dispute, protecting the weaker party from intimidation, and ensuring that both parties have a stake in the process and the outcome of mediation. In contrast, those programs that teach about "group differences,"

Example of Concept *Conflict Resolution in New Jersey*

Real estate development in the West Windsor–Plainsboro School District in the 1980s and 1990s brought into one rural area a population that was diverse in income, culture, race, and ethnicity. Increasing incidents of racial unrest in the schools and in the community at large caused school administrators to set into motion a program of conflict resolution in K–12 classrooms. Among its components were the following:

- A peacemaking program at the elementary level to teach children how to solve problems without resorting to aggression
- Training for middle school students in facilitating positive human relations
- A ninth-grade elective course in conflict resolution
- An elective course for grade 11 and 12 students to prepare student mediators for a peer-mediation center
- An annual "human relations" retreat for student leaders and teachers that encouraged frank and open conversations about interpersonal and race relations

- A planned welcome program for newcomers at the school to overcome feelings of isolation
- A minority recruitment program for teachers
- Elimination of watered-down, nonrigorous academic courses in lieu of challenging courses, accompanied by a tutoring program for academically underprepared high-school students

Within three years, the number of incidences of vandalism, violence, and substance abuse in the school district was reduced considerably. The people of West Windsor and Plainsboro "accomplished much in their quest to rise out of the degradation of bigotry" (Bandlow, 2002, pp. 91–92; Prothrow-Smith, 1994).

involve exhortation or mere verbal learning, or are designed directly for "prejudice reduction" are usually not effective.

Educators should not assume that cultural contact entails cultural conflict. Perhaps the best way to prevent conflict is to include a variety of cultural content and make sure the school recognizes and values cultural diversity. If conflict does occur, however, there are means to prevent its escalation. Teachers should be aware of conflict resolution techniques before they are actually needed.

Adapted Instruction

Resolving Conflicts in the Classroom

- Resolve to be calm in the face of verbalized anger and hostility.
- To defuse a problem, talk to students privately, encouraging the sharing of perceptions on volatile issues. Communicate expectations that students will be able to resolve their differences.
- If confrontation occurs, set aside a brief period for verbal expression. Allow students to vent feelings as a group.
- Do not tolerate violence or personal attacks.

Promote Achievement with Culturally Responsive Schooling

Intercultural educators who understand students' cultures can design instruction to meet children's learning needs. They invite students to learn by welcoming them, making them feel that they belong, and presenting learning as a task at which students can succeed. Teaching styles, interaction patterns, classroom organization, curricula, and involvement with parents and the community are factors within the teacher's power to adapt.

The intercultural educator uses culturally responsive schooling practices to promote the school success of culturally and linguistically diverse (CLD) students. As Richards, Brown, and Forde (2004) stated, "In a culturally responsive classroom, effective teaching and learning occur in a culturally supported, learner-centered context, whereby the strengths students bring to school are identified, nurtured, and utilized to promote student achievement" (n.p.).

The four major components of culturally responsive schooling that promote achievement (see Table 1) are as follows.

- Respect students' diversity.
- Work with culturally supported facilitating or limiting attitudes and abilities.
- Sustain high expectations for all students.
- Marshal parental and community support for schooling.

This section examines each of these components in turn.

Respecting Students' Diversity

Traditionally, educators have used the word *diversity* to denote racial differences. However, today's school population is diverse in a number of ways: academic ability, multiple intelligences, learning styles, thinking styles, gender, attitudes, culture and ethnicity, socioeconomic status, home language, and developmental readiness (Kagan, 2007). Differentiated instruction has come to mean the responsibility that teachers must assume in diversifying classroom practices to ensure that individual students will succeed.

Differentiated instruction involves first assessing students to get to know them in a variety of ways. Then, instructional components must be diversified. Differentiated instruction is an approach in which teachers assess students to determine how they differ on an array of characteristics and then modify instruction to honor that diversity. Ongoing assessment helps teachers maintain a flexible understanding of students' needs.

Acknowledging Students' Differences. Imagine a classroom of thirty students, each with just one unique fact, value, or belief on the more than fifty categories presented in Table 3. Culture includes diversity in values, social customs, rituals, work and leisure activities, health and educational practices, and many other aspects of life. Each of these can affect schooling and are discussed in the following sections, including ways that teachers can respond to these differences in adapting instruction.

Values are "beliefs about how one ought or ought not to behave or about some end state of existence worth or not worth attaining" (Bennett, 2003, p. 64). Values are particularly important to people when they educate their young, because education is a primary means of transmitting cultural knowledge.

Example of Concept

Teacher Whose Values Nurture Latino/as

Teachers play an indispensable part within the learning environment of the school. They engage and nurture student learning via a variety of social and personal situations. . . . Inherent in this process is the teacher's ideology as reflected in the pedagogical practices that the teacher exemplifies. The desired pedagogical practices will most likely include her or his curricular understandings embedded within constructs of diversity; pluralism; integrated pedagogy; knowledge acquisition and learning; first and second language acquisition and learning; academic content; democratic understandings; social justice; and . . . the new millennium of technology, multicomplex information systems, multicultural communications, and global collaboration and competition.

. . . Latinos/as need to be respected for whom they are and for what they bring to school. Unquestionably, Latino/a students need to be connected socially, emotionally, and academically to their schools. Latina/o students must experience teachers and a school curriculum that accepts them for whom they are and encourages them to grow to whom they can become. . . . Teachers and the schools that support them are prepared to do right by their students by daring to love and care genuinely for their students, their historicities, and their ethnicities.

—Rudolfo Chávez Chávez (1997, n.p.)

Social customs cause people to lead very different daily lives. These customs are paced and structured by deep habits of using time and space. For example, *time* is organized in culturally specific ways.

Example of Concept

Cultural Conceptions about Time

Adela, a Mexican American first-grade girl, arrived at school about twenty minutes late every day. Her teacher was at first irritated and gradually exasperated. In a parent conference, Adela's mother explained that braiding her daughter's hair each morning was an important time for the two of them to be together, even if it meant being slightly late to school. This family time presented a value conflict with the school's time norm.

Other conflicts may arise when teachers demand abrupt endings to activities in which children are deeply engaged or when events are scheduled in a strict sequence. In fact, schools in the United States are often paced very strictly by clock time, whereas family life in various cultures is not regulated in the same manner. Moreover, teachers often equate speed of performance with intelligence, and standardized tests are often a test of rapidity. Many teachers find themselves in the role of "time mediator"—helping the class to adhere to the school's time schedule while working with individual students to help them meet their learning needs within the time allotted.

Adapted Instruction

Accommodating Different Concepts of Time and Work Rhythms

- Provide students with choices about their work time and observe how time spent on various subjects accords with students' aptitudes and interests.

- If a student is a slow worker, analyze the work rhythms. Slow yet methodically accurate work deserves respect; slow and disorganized work may require a peer helper.

- If students are chronically late to school, ask the school counselor to meet with the responsible family member to discuss a change in morning routines.

Space is another aspect about which social customs differ according to cultural experience. Personal space varies: In some cultures, individuals touch one another frequently and maintain high degrees of physical contact; in other cultures, touch and proximity cause feelings of tension and embarrassment. The organization of the space in the classroom sends messages to students: how free they are to move about the classroom, how much of the classroom they "own," how the desks are arranged. Both the expectations of the students and the needs of the teacher can be negotiated to provide a classroom setting in which space is shared.

Adapted Instruction

Accommodating Different Concepts of Personal Space

- If students from the same culture and gender (one with a close personal space) have a high degree of physical contact and neither seems bothered by this, the teacher does not have to intervene.

- The wise teacher accords the same personal space to students no matter what their culture (e.g., does not touch minority students more or less than mainstream students).

Some *symbolic systems* are external, such as dress and personal appearance. For example, a third-grade girl wearing makeup is communicating a message that some teachers may consider an inappropriate indicator of premature sexuality, although makeup on a young girl may be acceptable in some cultures. Other symbolic systems are internal, such as beliefs about natural phenomena, luck and fate, vocational expectations, and so forth.

Each culture incorporates expectations about the proper ways to carry out *rites, rituals, and ceremonies*. School ceremonies—for example, assemblies that begin with formal markers such as the Pledge of Allegiance and a flag salute—should have nonstigmatizing alternatives for those whose culture does not permit participation.

Adapted Instruction

Culturally Influenced School Dress Codes

- Boys and men in some cultures (e.g., rural Mexico) wear hats; classrooms need to have a place for these hats during class time and provision for wearing the hats during recess.
- Schools that forbid "gang attire" yet permit privileged students to wear student council insignia (i.e., sweaters with embroidered names) should forbid clique-related attire for all.
- A family–school council with representatives from various cultures should be responsible for reviewing the school dress code on a yearly basis to see if it meets the needs of various cultures.
- Permission for religious garb (e.g., Islamic head scarves, Sikh ritual knives, Hassidic dress) should be a part of the school dress code.

Rituals in some elementary classrooms in the United States are relatively informal. For example, students can enter freely before school and take their seats or go to a reading corner or activity center. Students from other cultures may find this confusing if they are accustomed to lining up in the courtyard, being formally greeted by the principal or head teacher, and then accompanied in their lines as they enter their respective classrooms.

Rituals are also involved in parent conferences. Greeting and welcome behaviors, for example, vary across cultures. The sensitive teacher understands how parents expect to be greeted and incorporates some of these behaviors in the exchange.

Crosscultural variation in *work and leisure activities* is a frequently discussed value difference. Young people, particularly those in the U.S. mainstream-culture middle class, are trained to use specific tools of play, and their time is structured to attain skills (e.g., organized sports, music lessons). In other cultures, such as that of the Hopi Nation in Arizona, children's playtime is relatively unstructured, and parents do not interfere with play. Cultures also vary in the typical work and play activities expected of girls and of boys. All these values have obvious influence on the ways children work and play at school.

Adapted Instruction

Accommodating Diverse Ideas about Work and Play

- Many high-school students arrange class schedules in order to work part time. If a student appears chronically tired, a family–teacher conference may be needed to review priorities.
- Many students are overcommitted to extracurricular activities. If grades suffer, students may be well advised to reduce activities to regain an academic focus.
- Plagiarism in student work may be due to unclear conceptions about the permissability of shared work.
- Out-of-school play activities such as birthday parties should not be organized at the school site, such as passing out invitations that exclude some students.

Health and medicine practices involve deep-seated beliefs, because the stakes are high: life and death. When students come to school with health issues, teachers need to react in culturally compatible ways. Miscommunication and noncooperation can result when teachers and the family view health and disease differently. For example, community health practices, such as the Cambodian tradition of coining (in which a coin is dipped in oil and then rubbed on a sick person's back, chest, and neck), can be misinterpreted by school officials who, seeing marks on the child, call Child Protective Services.

Adapted Instruction

Health and Hygiene Practices

- Families who send sick children to school or, conversely, keep children home at the slightest ache may benefit from a conference with the school nurse.
- All students can profit from explicit instruction in home and school hygiene.

The *economic, legal, political,* and *religious institutions* that support and govern family and community life have an influence on behavior and beliefs. Interwoven into U.S. institutions are religious beliefs and practices. In the United States, religious practices are heavily embedded but formally bounded: witness the controversy over Christmas trees in schools but the almost universal cultural and economic necessity for increased consumer spending at the close of the calendar year.

Schools in the U.S. have been responsive to the need for sensitivity about events they sponsor that seem to be too closely tied to religious holidays. In fact, the role of religion in the schools is often fiercely debated. The Anti-Defamation League discusses issues of religion in the public schools at the website http://archive.adl.org/religion_ps_2004/teaching.asp. A few guidelines include the following: Religious symbols may be used as teaching aids in the classroom, but may not be used as classroom decoration; music, art, literature, and drama with religious themes may be included in the curriculum, provided that their overall effect does not endorse religion; and school assemblies or concerts may include religious music or drama as long as that inclusion does not appear to endorse religion over non-religion, or one religion over another.

Religious beliefs underlie other cultures even more fundamentally. Immigrants with Confucian religious and philosophical beliefs, for example, subscribe to values that mandate a highly ordered society and family through the maintenance of proper social relationships. In Islamic traditions, the Koran prescribes proper social relationships and roles for members of society. When immigrants with these religious beliefs encounter the largely secular U.S. institutions, the result may be that customs and cultural patterns are challenged, fade away, or cause conflict within the family.

Adapted Instruction

Muslim Students in the ELD Classroom

Muslim students from all over the world are appearing in U.S. classrooms, ranging from Bosnian, Somalian, and Afghani refugees in K–12 schools to Malaysians, Bangladeshis, Fijians, and Saudis in university classrooms. These students visit or immigrate from societies that could not be more diverse—cosmopolitan versus rural, progressive versus traditional, multilingual versus monolingual cultures. What they share as Muslims is a frame of reference in which religion plays a significant, public role in society, with spiritual matters playing a larger role in daily discourse than is encouraged in the secular West. Moreover, gender separation is deep and abiding.

Teachers are urged to approach controversial issues with tact and consideration. As far as coeducational activities, it is best to begin by including students in large mixed-gender groups rather than in mixed-gender pairs to allow students time to adjust to working in close proximity with strangers of the opposite sex. (Schmitt, 2009)

Students come to school already steeped in the learning practices of their own family and community. They come with *educational expectations,* but many of the organizational and teaching practices of the school may not support the type of learning to which students are accustomed. Teachers who can accommodate students' proclivities can gradually introduce student-centered practices while supporting an initial dependence on the teacher's direction.

Did You Know? Polynesian students coming from the South Pacific may have experienced classroom learning as a relatively passive activity. They expect teachers to give explicit instruction about what to learn and how to learn it and to carefully scrutinize homework daily. When these students arrive in the United States and encounter teachers who value creativity and student-centered learning, they may appear passive as they wait to be told what to do (Funaki & Burnett, 1993).

Teachers who seek to understand the value of education within the community can interview parents or community members.

Adapted Instruction

Accommodating Culturally Based Educational Expectations

- Classroom guests from the community can share methods for teaching and learning that are used in the home (e.g., modeling and imitation, didactic stories and proverbs, direct verbal instruction).

- Children from cultures that expect passive interaction with teachers (observing only) can be paired with more participatory peers to learn to ask questions and volunteer.

Cultures differ in the *roles* people play in society and the *status* accorded to these roles. For example, in the Vietnamese culture, profoundly influenced by Confucianism, the father ranks below the teacher, who ranks only below the king. Such a high status is not accorded to teachers in U.S. society, where, instead, medical doctors enjoy this type of prestige. Such factors as gender, social class, age, occupation, and education level influence the manner in which status is accorded to various roles. Students' perceptions about the roles possible for them in their culture affect their school performance.

Immigrants to the United States often come from cultures in which men and women have rigid and highly differentiated *gender roles*. The gender equality that is an ostensible goal in classrooms in the United States may be difficult for students of these cultures. For example, parents may spend much time correcting their sons' homework while ascribing little importance to their daughters' schoolwork.

To enlighten students about the achievements of women, Martínez's *500 Years of Chicana Women's History (500 Años de la Mujer Chicana)* is an invaluable reference for English-learner classrooms, especially those with Spanish-English bilingual skills. Text and pictures featuring social and political issues over the long history of Mexican American women's struggles will fascinate and enlighten English learners, provoking rich discussions and writing.

Sexual identification is also a part of gender issues. Gay, lesbian, or bisexual adolescents who face a hostile school climate or undergo harassment, and/or verbal or physical abuse may become truant, drop out, or resort to suicide or substance abuse (Nichols, 1999).

Adapted Instruction

Gender-Role Expectations

- Monitor tasks performed by boys and girls to ensure they are the same.
- Make sure that boys and girls perform equal leadership roles in cooperative groups.
- If families in a given community provide little support for the scholastic achievement of girls, a systematic effort on the part of school counselors and administrators may be needed to help families accommodate their beliefs to a more proactive support for women.

The belief that education can enhance *social economic class status* is widespread in the dominant culture of the United States, but individuals in other cultures may not have similar beliefs. In general, individuals and families at the upper-socioeconomic-status levels are able to exert power by sitting on college, university, and local school boards and thus determining who receives benefits and rewards through schooling. However, middle-class values are those that are generally incorporated in the culture of schooling. The social class values that children learn in their homes largely influence not only their belief in schooling but also their routines and habits in the classroom.

Adapted Instruction

The Influence of Social Class on Schooling

- Students who are extremely poor or homeless may need help from the teacher to store possessions at school.
- A teacher who receives an expensive gift should consult the school district's ethics policies.
- A high grade on a school assignment or project should not depend on extensive family financial resources.

In various cultures, expectations about *age-appropriate activities* for children and the purpose of those activities differ. Middle-class European Americans expect children to spend much of their time playing and attending school rather than performing tasks similar to those of adults. Cree Indian children, on the other hand, are expected from an early age to learn adult roles, including contributing food to the family. Parents may criticize schools for involving children in tasks that are not related to their future participation in Cree society (Sindell, 1988).

Cultures also differ in their criteria for moving through the various (culturally defined) life cycle changes. An important stage in any culture is the move into adulthood, but the age at which this occurs and the criteria necessary for attaining adulthood vary according to what *adulthood* means in a particular culture.

Adapted Instruction

Accommodating Beliefs about Age-Appropriate Activities

- Child labor laws in the United States forbid students from working for pay before a given age. However, few laws govern children working in family businesses. If a child appears chronically tired, the school counselor may need to discuss the child's involvement in the family business with a responsible family member.
- Cultural groups in which girls are expected to marry and have children at the age of fifteen or sixteen (e.g., Hmong) may need access to alternative schools.

In the United States, *occupation* very often determines income, which in turn is a chief determinant of prestige in the culture. Students thus may not see all occupations as desirable for them or even available to them and may have mixed views about the role education plays in their future occupation.

Some cultural groups in the United States are engaged in a voluntary way of life that does not require prolonged schooling (e.g., the Amish). Other groups may be involuntarily incorporated into U.S. society and relegated to menial occupations and ways of life that do not reward and require school success (e.g., Hispanics in the Southwest). As a result, they may not apply academic effort (Ogbu & Matute-Bianchi, 1986).

Example of Concept   *Collaborative Relationships*

Conchas (2006) studied the Medical Academy at Baldwin High School (California), a school-within-a-school that prepares students for careers in health-related occupations. A positive learning environment connected students and teachers across race, gender, and class differences. Both immigrant and U.S.-born Latinos formed a strong sense of belonging and identification with other students in the program; strong collaborative relationships led to academic success.

Adapted Instruction

Occupational Aspirations

- At all grade levels, school subjects should be connected with future vocations.
- Teachers should make available at every grade an extensive set of books on occupations and their requirements, and discuss these with students.
- Role models from minority communities can visit the classroom to recount stories of their success. Successful professionals and businesspeople can visit and explain how cultural diversity is supported in their place of work.

Child-rearing practices have wide implications for schools. Factors such as who takes care of children, how much supervision they receive, how much freedom they have, who speaks to them and how often, and what they are expected to do affect their behavior on entering schools. Many of the misunderstandings that occur between teachers and students arise because of different expectations about behavior, and these different expectations stem from early, ingrained child-rearing practices.

Because the largest group of English learners in California is of Mexican ancestry, teachers who take the time to learn about child-rearing practices among Mexican immigrants can help students adjust to schooling practices in the United States. An excellent source for this cultural study is *Crossing Cultural Borders* (Delgado-Gaitan & Trueba, 1991).

As the numbers of school-provided breakfasts and lunches increase, *food preferences* are an important consideration. Furthermore, teachers who are knowledgeable about students' dietary practices can incorporate their students' background knowledge into health and nutrition instruction.

Besides customs of what and when to eat, eating habits vary widely across cultures, and "good" manners at the table in some cultures are inappropriate or rude in others. For example, Indochinese consider burping, lip smacking, and soup slurping to be common behaviors during meals, even complimentary to hosts. Cultural relativity is not, however, an excuse for poor or unhygienic eating, and teachers do need to teach students the behaviors that are considered good food manners in the U.S. mainstream context.

Adapted Instruction

Dealing with Food Preferences

- In addition to knowing in general what foods are eaten at home, teachers will want to find out about students' favorite foods, taboo foods, and typical foods.

- Eating lunch with students—even on a by-invitation basis—can provide the opportunity to learn about students' habits.

- If a student's eating habits alienate peers, the teacher may need to discuss appropriate behaviors.

In many cultures, *arts and crafts* performed at home—such as food preparation; sewing and weaving; carpentry; home building and decoration; religious and ritual artistry for holy days, holidays, and entertaining—are an important part of the culture that is transmitted within the home. Parents also provide an important means of access to the humanities and the visual and performing arts of their cultures. The classroom teacher draws on the resources of the community and then shares these with all the members of the classroom.

Example of Concept *Preserving Traditional Vietnamese Music*

Lac Hong is the largest group in the United States that promotes traditional Vietnamese performing arts. Children as young as four begin singing traditional folk songs, eventually learning to play the moon-shaped lute (*dan nguyet*), the one-stringed monochord (*dan bau*), or the sixteen-string zither (*dan tranh*). Classes are led by Mai Nguyen, a former music professor from the Saigon National Conservatory, who immigrated to Orange County, California, at the end of the Vietnam War.

"The students are not just learning music," Nguyen says, "they are learning culture—and the culture is still alive." (Tran, 2008, p. B3)

Educating Students about Diversity. Both mainstream students and CLD students benefit from education about diversity, not only cultural diversity but also diversity in ability, gender preference, and human nature in general. This engenders pride in cultural identity, expands the students' perspectives, and adds cultural insight, information, and experiences to the curriculum.

Did You Know? James Banks (1994) explained the difference between studying the cultures of other countries and the cultures within the United States. According to Banks, teachers may implement a unit on the country of Japan but avoid teaching about Japanese internment in the United States during World War II (Brandt, 1994).

Global and Multicultural Education. ELD teachers—and mainstream teachers who teach English learners—can bring a global and multicultural perspective to their classes.

> Language teachers, like teachers in all other areas of the curriculum, have a responsibility to plan lessons with sensitivity to the racial and ethnic diversity present in their classrooms and in the world in which their students live. . . . [Students] can learn to value the points of view of many others whose life experiences are different from their own. (Curtain & Dahlberg, 2004, p. 244)

Table 6 lists some cultural activities that Curtain and Dahlberg recommended for adding cultural content to the curriculum.

The goal of multicultural education is to help students "develop cross-cultural competence within the American national culture, with their own subculture and within and across different subsocieties and cultures" (Banks, 1994, p. 9). Banks introduced a model of multicultural education that has proved to be a useful way of assessing the approach taken in pedagogy and curricula. The model has four levels, represented in Table 7 with a critique of strengths and shortcomings taken from Jenks, Lee, and Kanpol (2002).

There is a clear distinction between multiculturalism and globalism, although both are important features of the school curriculum: "Globalism emphasizes the cultures and peoples of other lands, and multiculturalism deals with ethnic diversity within the United States" (Ukpokodu, 2002, pp. 7–8).

Table 6 Sample Cultural Activities for Multicultural Education

Activity	Suggested Implementation
Visitors and guest speakers	Guests can share their experiences on a variety of topics, using visuals, slides, and hands-on materials.
Folk dances, singing games, and other kinds of games	Many cultures can be represented; cultural informants can help.
Field trips	Students can visit neighborhoods, restaurants, museums, or stores that feature cultural materials.
Show-and-tell	Students can bring items from home to share with the class.
Read books about other cultures	Age-appropriate fiction or nonfiction books can be obtained with the help of the school or public librarian.
Crosscultural e-mail contacts	Students can exchange cultural information and get to know peers from other lands.

Source: Curtain and Dahlberg (2004).

Nieto and Bode (2008) make the point that multicultural education does more than merely celebrate diversity:

> [M]ulticultural education does not simply involve the affirmation of language and culture. Multicultural education confronts not only issues of difference but also issues of power and privilege in society. This means challenging racism and other biases as well as the inequitable structures, policies, and practices of schools and, ultimately, of society itself. Affirming language and culture can help students become successful and

Table 7 Banks's Levels of Multicultural Education, with Critique

Level	Description	Strengths	Shortcomings
Contributions	Emphasizes what minority groups have contributed to society (e.g., International Food Day, bulletin board display for Black History Month).	Attempts to sensitize the majority white culture to some understanding of minority groups' history.	May amount to "cosmetic" multiculturalism in which no discussion takes place about issues of power and disenfranchisement.
Additive	Adding material to the curriculum to address what has been omitted (reading *The Color Purple* in English class).	Adds to a fuller coverage of the American experience, when sufficient curricular time is allotted.	May be an insincere effort if dealt with superficially.
Transformative	An expanded perspective is taken that deals with issues of historic, ethnic, cultural, and linguistic injustice and equality as a part of the American experience.	Students learn to be reflective and develop a critical perspective.	Incorporates the liberal fallacy that discussion alone changes society.
Social action	Extension of the transformative approach to add students' research/action projects to initiate change in society.	Students learn to question the status quo and the commitment of the dominant culture to equality and social justice.	Middle-class communities may not accept the teacher's role, considering it as provoking students to "radical" positions.

Source: Model based on Banks (1994); strengths and shortcomings based on Jenks, Lee, and Kanpol (2002).

well-adjusted learners, but unless language and cultural issues are viewed critically through the lens of equity and social justices, they are unlikely to have a lasting impact in promoting real change. (pp. 4–5)

Similar to Banks's superficial-to-transformative continuum is that of Morey and Kilano (1997). Their three-level framework for incorporating diversity identifies as "exclusive" the stereotypical focus on external aspects of diversity (what they called the four *f*'s: food, folklore, fun, and fashion); "inclusive," the addition of diversity into a curriculum that, although enriched, is fundamentally the same structure; and "transformed," the curriculum that is built on diverse perspectives, equity in participation, and critical problem solving. Howard (2007) has suggested that a transformative approach to diversity has five basic phases: building trust, engaging personal culture, confronting issues of social dominance and social justice, transforming educational practices, and engaging the entire school community. Thus, it is clear that pouring new wine—diversity—into old bottles—teacher-centered, one-size-fits-all instruction—is not transformative.

In general, research suggests that substantive changes in attitudes, behaviors, and achievement occur only when the entire school environment changes to demonstrate a multicultural atmosphere. Parents are welcomed in the school, and programs are instituted that permit interactions between students of different backgrounds. In such schools, all students learn to understand cultures different from their own. Minority students do not internalize negativity about their culture and customs. Cooperative learning groups and programs that allow interaction between students of diverse backgrounds usually result in fewer incidents of name-calling and ethnic slurs as well as in improved academic achievement (Nieto & Bode, 2008).

It is not easy for culturally and linguistically diverse (CLD) students to maintain pride in their cultures if these cultures suffer low status in the majority culture. Students feel conflict in this pride if their culture is devalued. When the languages and cultures of students are highly evident in their schools and teachers refer to them explicitly, they gain status. Schools that convey the message that all cultures are of value—by displaying explicit welcome signs in many languages, by attempts to involve parents, by a deliberate curriculum of inclusion, and by using affirmative action to promote hiring of a diverse faculty—help to maintain an atmosphere that reduces interethnic conflict.

Example of Concept   *Action Research for Curricular Change*

Diane Red and Amy Warner are two fourth-grade teachers who are dissatisfied with the four-week unit on "Explorers" in the social studies curriculum. They were concerned that the unit was too focused on the European viewpoint and did not adequately represent the perspectives of the indigenous people of the Americas. They modified the readings to include books that presented a range of perspectives on Columbus. In an action research project, they asked students to tally the number of times in each book that Europeans were pictured versus the native Tainos or Caribs from the islands where Columbus landed, and used the tallies as data in their research. In the modified lessons, they used K-W-L charts, and included many opportunities for discussion. Their "action research" focused on gathering evidence to evaluate the success of their "renovated" approach.

Source: Nolan and Hoover (2008).

How the Identity of a Young Child Is Affected by Learning a New Language. Researchers who study English learners within a critical and sociocultural perspective view the individual as socially situated within a network of social relations, using language as a social practice. Within this matrix, language helps to forge a complex identity that changes over time and space. Litowitz (1997) queried the teacher's role in creating these identities: It is important to reexamine not only "what we are asking the learner to *do* but whom we are asking the learner to *be*" (p. 479).

Identity is affected by the child's linguistic and social capital. Children of the socioeconomic elite are granted an advantage toward school success by the ability to establish a school-success-supported identity, including the attraction of peers that share the advantage of similar capital. Day (2002) studied the social relationships of a Punjabi-speaking English learner in a Canadian elementary school, showing the critical role his relationships played in the identities he could negotiate and the access, participation, and opportunities for language learning he could therefore gain. Similarly, Gutierrez (1994) studied three different classrooms in which the contexts for learning were constructed differently, leading to differential access to learning on the part of Latino elementary children.

English learners are particularly challenged when asked to negotiate a dual-language environment. In a two-year study of four Mandarin/English bilingual students in a California school, McKay & Wong (1996) traced how students actively used flexible identities to position and reposition themselves, to resist positioning, and to set up "counter-discourses" that shaped their investment toward learning English. In a similar study, Hunter (1997) analyzed the multiple and often contradictory positioning of Roberto, a Portuguese/English bilingual child, whose identity in relation to school expectations often conflicted with his identity among peers, and the effect this had on his second-language acquisition.

Validating Students' Cultural Identity. "An affirming attitude toward students from culturally diverse backgrounds significantly impacts their learning, belief in self, and overall academic performance" (Villegas & Lucas, 2002, p. 23). Cultural identity—that is, having a positive self-concept or evaluation of oneself and one's culture—promotes self-esteem. Students who feel proud of their successes and abilities, self-knowledge, and self-expression, and who have enhanced images of self, family, and culture, are better learners.

Oakes and Lipton (2007) believe that students should view their cultural identities as integral to their school success, not as something they must "overcome":

> Perhaps schools' greatest challenge is to create a school culture that supports college attendance for students whose lives do not conform to [the profile of a person with high scores on standardized tests, whose parents went to college, whose main language is mainstream, unaccented English, and who have middle-class perspectives and financial support]. The school culture must position college success as expected and inevitable not just for students who change [identities] or for students who are exceptions to stereotypes, but for students who have no need or no intention to slight their family's background and culture as they acquire skills and knowledge that are genuinely useful for college success. (p. 354)

Of course, the most powerful sense of self-esteem is the result not solely of one's beliefs about oneself but also of successful learning experiences. Practices of schooling that damage self-esteem, such as tracking and competitive grading, undermine authentic cooperation and sense of accomplishment on the part of English learners.

Classroom Practices That Validate Identity. Díaz-Rico (2008) suggested that through observations, shared conversations during lunchtime or before or after school, and group participation, teachers can gain understanding about various individuals and their cultures. Teachers can also ask students to interview their parents about common topics such as work, interests, and family history and then add a reflective element about their relationship and identification with these aspects of their parents' lives.

Adolescents acquire identities through sociocultural groups, such as language and cultural groups, as well as through activities in which they engage (athletics, band, computers, gangsta, goth). They are also labeled by schools (students in honors or special education, English learners, "at-risk," "leaders"). These identities may influence school behavior, as some groups pressure members not to invest in school success, but rather to adopt resistance or apathetic attitudes.

Example of Concept

Students' Co-creation of Pro-School-Success Identities

Willet (1995) described three female first-grade English learners, Nahla (an immigrant from Palestine), Etham (a native of the Maldive Islands), and Yael (a native Israeli), who were allowed to sit together during their daily thirty-minute pull-out ELD class. In contrast, a fourth student, Xavier, a Mexican American, was placed between two English-speaking girls who did not help him because he was a boy. Over the year of Willett's study, the three girls solidified identities as good students by cooperating and supporting one another, whereas Xavier became more reliant on the teacher and gained the reputation of a needy, dependent child. In this way, the social environment was a factor in the creation of identity.

Example of Concept

A School-Compatible Identity

Julie, a five-year-old child of Polish-speaking immigrant parents (in Canada), was able to form relationships with other kindergarten children by making a set of allies among children who would stick up for her when another child attempted to subordinate her or to exclude her from co-play activities. Moreover, she was able to create alliances with adults in her classroom by obeying key conventions of the schoolroom: She was silent upon adult command, moved smoothly through transitions between activities, showed adept use of tools such as scissors and paste, and often greeted adults who entered the classroom with excited smiles and hugs. Together, these behaviors resulted in adults attributing to her the personality of a pleasant and easygoing child—a "nice little girl"—and she was deemed "ready" for grade 1. She was then recommended for promotion—whereas some other English learners in the same class were not (Toohey & Norton, 2003).

Instructional Materials That Validate Identity. Classroom texts are available that offer literature and anecdotal readings aimed at the enhancement of identity and self-esteem. *Identities: Readings from Contemporary Culture* (Raimes, 1996) includes readings grouped into chapters titled "Name," "Appearance, Age, and Abilities," "Ethnic Affiliation and Class," "Family Ties," and so forth. The readings contain authentic text and may be best used in middle- or high-school classes.

A book that is useful for a comparison of Asian cultural values with those of mainstream American culture is Kim's (2001) *The Yin and Yang of American Culture*. This book presents a view of American culture—its virtues and vices—from an Eastern perspective and may stimulate discussion on the part of students. *Exploring Culturally Diverse Literature for Children and Adolescents* (Henderson & May, 2005) helps readers understand how stories are tied to specific cultural and socio-political histories, opening readers' minds to literature written from the "insider's" versus the "outsider's" point of view.

Promoting Mutual Respect among Students. The ways in which we organize classroom life should make children feel significant and cared about—by the teacher and by one another. Classroom life should, to the greatest extent possible, prefigure the kind of democratic and just society we envision and thus contribute to building that society. Together, students and teachers can create a "community of conscience," as educators Asa Hillard and George Pine call it (Christensen, 2000, p. 18).

Mutual respect is promoted when the curriculum includes multiple points of view and when students are given the chance to genuinely talk to one another about topics that concern them. The instructional conversation is a discourse format that encourages in-depth conversation.

Example of Concept   *A Cultural Heritage Project*

Promoting research projects is a way for students to participate in school in ways related to their personal identities. One teacher based a unit plan on this standard from the Michigan Curriculum Standard from Social Studies: *Students will gain knowledge about the past to construct meaningful understandings of our diverse cultural heritage.* In this unit, students were to compare two aspects of cultural heritage from information obtained from the Internet, culminating in an individual report on a favorite artist or inventor as

well as a group PowerPoint presentation and simulated interview with the historical figure.

The Puerto Rican group compared Ladislao Martinez and Alvin Medina, one traditional and one contemporary *cuatro* (folk guitar) player. They contrasted the two players, drawing on sound clips that included current musical favorites. A rich context of time and place gave each participant a personal connection to the topic (Conley, 2008).

Adapting to Students' Culturally Supported Facilitating or Limiting Attitudes and Abilities

A skilled intercultural educator recognizes that each culture supports distinct attitudes, values, and abilities. These may facilitate or limit the learning situation in U.S. public schools. For example, the cultures of Japan, China, and Korea, which promote high academic achievement, may foster facilitating behaviors, such as the ability to listen and follow directions; attitudes favoring education and respect for teachers and authorities; attitudes toward discipline as guidance; and high-achievement motivation. However, other culturally supported traits may hinder adjustment to the U.S. school, such as lack of experience participating in discussions; little experience with independent thinking; strong preference for conformity, which inhibits divergent thinking; and distinct sex-role differentiation, with males more dominant.

Example of Concept   *Overcoming Reluctance to Participate Orally*

Asian students are more likely to speak up in class when the participation is structured, such as in a debate that has definite rules for whose turn it is to talk. Unstructured class discussions in which one must aggressively promote one's turn may make many Asian students feel anxious and uncomfortable,

because this does not mirror the home environment, where often students speak only when requested to do so by a parental authority (Tateishi, 2007–2008). Small-group discussion with leaders whose task is to involve all members can be a means of conducting classroom talk.

Similarly, African American family and cultural values that encourage independent action, self-sufficiency, and imagination and humor may facilitate adjustment to the classroom, but dialect speakers with limited experiences with various types of Standard English patterns may be hindered. The Mexican American cultural values that encourage cooperation, the affectionate and demonstrative parental relationships, children assuming mature social responsibilities such as child care and translating family matters from English to Spanish, and an eagerness to try out new ideas may all facilitate classroom success. On the other hand, such attitudes as depreciating education after high school, especially for women; explicit sex-role stereotyping favoring limited vocational roles for women; and dislike of competition may go against classroom practices and hinder classroom success (Clark, 1983).

Cooperation versus Competition. Triandis (1995) stated that the most important difference between cultures that can be identified in schools is the contrast between individualist and collectivist value systems. Traditional U.S. classrooms mirror middle-class European American values of competition: Students are expected to do their own work; are rewarded publicly through star charts, posted grades, and academic honors; and are admonished to do their individual best. In the Cree Indian culture, however, children are raised in a cooperative atmosphere, with siblings, parents, and other kin sharing food as well as labor (Sindell, 1988). In the Mexican American culture, interdependence is a strength; individuals have a commitment to others, and all decisions are made together. Those who are successful have a responsibility to others to help them succeed.

Because about seventy percent of the world's population lives in a collectivist culture (including Native Americans, Native Hawaiians, Latin American, African Americans, Asians, and Arab groups), according to Tileston and Darling (2008), it is probably wiser for teachers to emphasize interdependence among students rather than aggressive and competitive competition. Some balance must be achieved in the classroom between the individual competitive culture of the dominant U.S. culture and the collaborative preferences of students from group-oriented, cooperative cultures.

The Use of Language. In learning a second language, students (and teachers) often focus on the form. Frequently ignored are the ways in which that second language is used. The culture that underlies each language prescribes distinct patterns and conventions about when, where, and how to use the language (see Labov, 1972). Heath's (1983b) *Ways with Words* noted that children in "Trackton," an isolated African American community in the South, were encouraged to use spontaneous verbal play, rich with metaphor, simile, and allusion. In contrast, the children of "Roadville," a lower-middle-class European American community in the South, used language in more restricted ways, perhaps because of habits encouraged by a fundamentalist religious culture. Heath contrasted language usage in these two cultures: verbal and nonverbal communication (the "said" and the "unsaid"), the use of silence, discourse styles, the nature of questions, and the use of oral versus written genres.

Both *verbal and nonverbal means* are used to communicate. More than sixty-five percent of the social meaning of a typical two-person exchange is carried by nonverbal cues (Birdwhistell, 1974). *Kinesic* behavior, including facial expressions, body movements, postures, and gestures, can enhance a message or constitute a message in itself. *Paralanguage*—the nonverbal elements of the voice—is an important aspect of speech that can affirm or belie a verbal message. *Proxemics*, the communication of interpersonal distance, varies widely across cultures. Last but not least, *olfactics*—the study of interpersonal communication by means of smell—constitutes a factor that is powerful yet often overlooked.

People throughout the world employ *silence* in communicating. As with other language uses, however, silence differs dramatically across cultures. In the United States, silence is interpreted as expressing embarrassment, regret, obligation, criticism, or sorrow (Wayne in Ishii & Bruneau, 1991). In Asian cultures, silence is a token of respect. Particularly in the presence of the elderly, being quiet honors their wisdom and expertise. Silence can also be a marker of personal power. In many Native American cultures, silence is used to create and communicate rapport in ways that language cannot.

Intercultural differences exist in *asking and answering questions*. In middle-class European American culture, children are exposed early on to their parents' questioning. While taking a walk, for example, a mother will ask, "See the squirrel?" and, later, "Is that a squirrel? Where did that squirrel go?" The questions are asked to stimulate conversation and to train children to focus attention and display knowledge. In the Inuit culture, on the other hand, adults do not question children or call their attention to objects and events in order to name them (Crago, 1993).

Responses to questioning differ across cultures. Students from non-Western cultures may be reluctant to attempt an answer to a question if they do not feel they can answer absolutely correctly. Students do not share the European-American value of answering questions to the best of their ability regardless of whether that "best" answer is absolutely correct or not.

Cultures may differ in *discourse styles* that influence conversations: the way conversations open and close, the way people take turns, the way messages are repaired to make them understandable, and the way in which parts of the text are set aside. These differences in discourse are stressful for second-language learners. Multiply this stress by the long hours children spend in school, and it is no wonder that English learners may feel subjected to prolonged pressure.

Example of Concept   *Classroom Discourse Patterns*

Discourse in the classroom can be organized in ways that involve children positively, in ways that are culturally compatible. A group of Hawaiian children, with the help of an encouraging and participating adult, produced group discourse that was co-narrated, complex, lively, imaginative, and well connected. Group work featured twenty-minute discussions of text in which the teacher and students mutually participated in overlapping, volunteered speech and in joint narration (Au & Jordan, 1981).

In contrast, Navajo children in a discussion group patterned their discourse after the adults of their culture. Each Navajo student spoke for an extended period with a fully expressed statement, and other students waited courteously until a clear end was communicated. Then another took a similar turn. In both communities, children tended to connect discourse with peers rather than with the teacher functioning as a central "switchboard." If the teacher acted as a central director, students often responded with silence (Tharp, 1989a).

Adapted Instruction

How Students Tell You They Don't Understand

Arabic (men): *Mish fahem*
Arabic (women): *Mish fahmeh*
Armenian: *Yes chem huskenur*
Chinese (Cantonese): *Ngoh m-ming*
Chinese (Mandarin): *Wo bu dung*
Persian: *Man ne'me fah'mam*
Japanese: *Wakarimasen*

Korean: *Juh-neun eehae-haji mot haget-ssum-nida*
Russian: *Ya nye ponimayu*
Spanish: *No comprendo*
Vietnamese: *Toi khong hieu*
Yiddish: *Ikh veys nikht*

In addition to ways to say "I don't understand" in 230 languages, J. Runner's webpage has translations in many languages for the following phrases: "Hello, how are you?" "Welcome," "Good-bye," "Please," "Thank you," "What is your name?" "My name is . . . ," "Do you speak English?" "Yes," and "No." There is also a link to Internet Language Resources; see www.elite.net/~runner/jennifers/understa.htm.

Source: Runner (2000).

Oral versus written language creates learning differences. Orality is the foundation of languages. Written expression is a later development. In fact, of the thousands of reported languages in use, only seventy-eight have a written literature (Edmonson, 1971). Research has suggested that acquiring literacy involves more than learning to read and write. Thinking patterns, perception, cultural values, communication style, and social organization can be affected by literacy (Ong, 1982; Scribner & Cole, 1978).

In studying oral societies, researchers have noted that the structure and content of messages tend to be narrative, situational, and oriented toward activity or deeds, although abstract ideas such as moral values are often implicit. In contrast, the style of literacy is conceptual rather than situational. Words are separate from the social context of deeds and events, and abstract ideas can be extracted from written texts. In an oral society, learning takes place in groups because narration must have an audience. This contrasts with a literate society, in which reading and writing can be solitary experiences. In an oral society, much reliance is placed on memory, as this is the principal means of preserving practices and traditions (Ong, 1982).

Example of Concept   ## Characteristics of One Oral Culture

Hmong immigrants in the United States demonstrate the comparative disadvantage faced by individuals from an oral culture when expected to perform in a literate environment. Hmong individuals may become frustrated in the abstract world of school. The very concept of independent study is alien to this culture because learning always occurs in community groups. Learning among strangers and doing homework, a solitary endeavor, run counter to traditional group practices and may distance children from their families. As Hmong children become literate and engage in independent study, parents may become disturbed over the loss of centrality and power in their children's lives, which may produce family tension (Shuter, 1991).

Participation Styles. The way teachers are taught to teach is a reflection of the expectations of U.S. culture. Teachers raised in a mainstream culture have elements of that culture embedded in their personal teaching approach. The selection of a particular teaching method reflects cultural values more than it argues for the superiority of the method. Some of these elements may need to be modified to meet the needs of students from other cultures. The accompanying Example of Concept illustrates the way the culturally preferred participation style of one group of students differed from their teachers'.

Example of Concept   *Culturally Preferred Participation Styles*

In classrooms on the Warm Springs (Oregon) Reservation, teacher-controlled activity dominated. All the social and spatial arrangements were created by the teacher: where and when movement took place; where desks were placed and even what furniture was present in the room; and who talked, when, and with whom. For the Warm Springs students, this socialization was difficult. They preferred to wander to various parts of the room, away from the lesson; to talk to other students while the teacher was talking; and to "bid" for one another's attention rather than that of the teacher.

For the Native American children, the small-reading-group structure in which participation is mandatory, individual, and oral was particularly ill fitting. They frequently refused to read aloud, did not utter a word when called on, or spoke too softly to be audible. On the other hand, when students controlled and directed interaction in small-group projects, they were much more fully involved. They concentrated completely on their work until it was completed and talked a great deal to one another in the group. Very little time was spent disagreeing or

arguing about how to go about a task. There was, however, explicit competition with other groups.

A look at the daily life of the Warm Springs children revealed several factors that would account for their willingness to work together and their resistance to teacher-directed activity. First, they spend much time in the company of peers with little disciplinary control from older relatives. They also spend time in silence, observing their elders and listening without verbal participation. Speech seems to be an optional response rather than a typical or mandatory feature of interaction. One last characteristic of community life is the accessibility and openness of community-wide celebrations. No single individual directs and controls all activity, and there is no sharp distinction between audience and performer. Individuals are permitted to choose for themselves the degree of participation in an activity. Schooling became more successful for these students when they were able to take a more active part.

Source: Adapted from Philips (1972, pp. 370–394).

Teacher–Student Interactions. The teacher–student relationship is culturally mandated in general ways, although individual relationships vary. Students who have immigrated may bring with them varying notions of teacher–student interactions. For example, in some cultures, learning takes place in an absolutely quiet classroom where the teacher is in complete control and authority is never questioned. In other cultures, students talk among themselves and are able to engage with teachers in cooperative planning. Attitudes toward authority, teacher–student relationships, and teacher expectations of student achievement vary widely. Yet the heart of the educational process is in the interaction between teacher and student. This determines the quality of education the student receives.

Adapted Instruction

Encouraging Positive Relationships

Although it may appear daunting to be able to accommodate the various teacher–student relations represented by different cultural groups in a classroom, there are several ways teachers can learn about their students to provide a learning environment.

- Express care and respect equally to all students.
- Openly communicate acceptance of students and be accessible to them.
- In classroom discussions and in private, encourage students to talk about their expectations for learning.

Source: Adapted from Lemberger (1999).

Example of Concept

"Retooling" to Improve Teacher–Student Relationships

Even teachers of color find they need to "retool" their practice when assigned to a classroom of culturally and linguistically diverse students. An African American teacher who taught for many years in a predominantly white suburban school said, "When I first found myself teaching classes of mostly black kids, I went home frustrated every night because I knew I wasn't getting through to them, and they were giving me a hard time. It only started getting better when I finally figured out that I had to re-examine everything I was doing" (Howard, 2007, p. 17).

To learn more about a student's actions for reactions in the context of their cultural backgrounds, teachers might pause for a reflection:

- If a student's background is very different from my own, what cultural assumptions do I bring to the situation that may be impeding my understanding of the student?
- What is it that I need to understand about this student's background that might be affecting the situation?
- How might speaking with the student's family help to further my cultural understanding?

Classroom Organization. The typical organization of U.S. classrooms is that of a teacher-leader who gives assignments or demonstrates to the students, who act as audience. Teacher presentations are usually followed by some form of individual study. Learning is then assessed through recitation, quizzes, or some other performance. Small-group work, individual projects, or paired learning require distinct participation structures, ways of behaving and speaking. Learning how to behave in these settings may require explicit cultural adaptation. Many students new to U.S. classrooms have never before taken part in group problem solving, story retelling, or class discussion. Such activities entail social as well as linguistic challenges. Teachers can help students by providing clear instructions and ample models, by calling on more self-confident students first, and by assigning self-conscious students minor roles at first in order not to embarrass them. Teachers who are sensitive to varying cultural styles organize other means for students to demonstrate language and content knowledge, and they act as observers and guides rather than directors or controllers of student activity.

Example of Concept   *Class Discussions*

A Vietnamese student who moved to the United States describes his reaction to a class discussion:

> As a student in Vietnam, I learned not to ask questions, not to raise my hand, or to have much contact with the teacher. I listened, took notes, and memorized the material. The teacher was always right. Imagine my surprise when I entered a U.S. classroom and listened as my classmates talked, argued, and discussed! The teacher encouraged discussion and even listened to what the students had to say. This felt very different to me.

Source: Dresser (1993, p. 120).

Curriculum. Many aspects of the school curriculum are highly abstract and contain themes and activities for which many CLD students have little referent. Some teachers, rather than finding ways in which students can become familiar with academically challenging content, are quick to devise alternative activities of lower academic worth. Research on Alaska Native education suggests a number of abuses perpetrated in the name of "being sensitive to children's cultural backgrounds." Teachers often exempt Alaska Native students from standards applicable to other students. For example, they assign an essay on "Coming to the City from the Village" as a substitute for a research paper. Too many lessons are created featuring stereotypic content (kayaks and caribou) that demonstrates a shallow cultural relevance (Kleinfeld, 1988).

Avoiding bias means more than using "politically correct" terminology that does not incorporate prejudice. It also means protecting the authenticity of sources. Reese (2007) comments on the distortions often displayed when children are presented with literature about Native Americans: Indians are portrayed either as savages, or on the other extreme, as poetic, romantic figures with a message about living in harmony with the earth. Reese, a Pueblo Indian, calls for literature that reflects the heterogeneity of the Native American experience in ways that counter culturally and historically inaccurate mythmaking. She offers valuable guidelines for evaluating and selecting Native American literature for classroom use, especially featuring markers of cultural authenticity.

Example of Concept   *The Eurocentric Curriculum*

What is a Eurocentric perspective, and why is that limiting for today's students? Because the United States began as a set of British colonies, many perspectives published even in contemporary textbooks reflect a European point of view. For example, in geography, Europe and the United States are centered side-by-side, with the rest of the world at the margins. Parts of the world are named according to their position relative to Europe, for example, the "Middle East" (Hernandez, 2001). Students may become depressed when their native countries and regions play so small a role in the curricula and texts, and the world of information does not include their issues and perspectives.

In her article "Educating Teachers for Cultural and Linguistic Diversity: A Model for All Teachers," Parla (1994) discussed issues related to the multicultural classroom and includes information on cultural sensitivity, linguistic diversity, and teaching strategies that can help teachers grow in their understanding of cultural issues and translate that understanding into classroom practice. The article can be found at www.ncela.gwu.edu/files/rcd/BE022361/Educating_Teachers_For_Cultural.pdf.

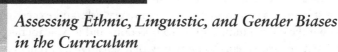

Adapted Instruction

Assessing Ethnic, Linguistic, and Gender Biases in the Curriculum

The following checklist can help teachers assess the extent to which ethnic, linguistic, and gender biases exist in the curriculum:

- What groups are represented in texts, discussion, and bulletin board displays? Are certain groups invisible?
- Are the roles of minorities and women presented in a separate manner from other content, isolated or treated as a distinct topic?
- Are minorities (and women) treated in a positive, diversified manner, or stereotyped into traditional or rigid roles?
- Are the problems faced by minorities presented in a realistic fashion, with a problem-solving orientation?
- Is the language used in the materials inclusive, or are biased terms used, such as masculine forms (*mankind, mailman*)?
- Does the curriculum foster appreciation of cultural diversity?
- Are experiences and activities other than those common to middle-class European American culture included?

Sustaining High Expectations for All Students

Jussim (1986) offered a general framework for the relationship between teacher expectations and student achievement. Teachers develop initial expectations based on a student's reputation, on previous classroom performance, or on stereotypes about racial, cultural, and linguistic groups. These expectations form the basis for differential treatment of students and for the rationalization for such treatment. Students, in turn, react to this differential treatment in ways that confirm the teacher's expectations. Thus, teachers have a high degree of effect on student achievement: Student effort and persistence are shaped, in part, by students' perception of the teacher's expectations.

Expecting high achievement from English learners and communicating these expectations require specific educational programs that draw attention to the hidden curriculum of the school, quality of interaction between teachers and students, diverse learning styles, the use of the community as a resource, and a commitment to democratic ideals in the classroom (Gollnick & Chinn, 2006).

Assessing Students' Ability and Achievement Validly. A major responsibility of the intercultural educator is to ensure that students' abilities are truly developed by instructional experiences. Many students' abilities are underestimated because their second-language skills do not adequately convey their talents. Sometimes unfamiliarity with the students' culture compounds the language barrier.

Challenging Students to Strive for Excellence as Defined by Their Potential. Teachers tread a fine line between expecting too much of their students, causing frustration on students' part through stress and overwork, and expecting too little by watering down the curriculum, leading to boredom and low academic achievement. Ongoing formative assessment, combined with a sensitive awareness of students' needs and a willingness to be flexible, helps the teacher to monitor and adjust the instructional level to students' abilities.

Teachers' behavior varies with the level of expectation held about the students. Students of whom much is expected are given more frequent cues and prompts to respond to, are asked more and harder questions, are given a longer time to respond, are encouraged to provide more elaborate answers, and are interrupted less often (Good & Brophy, 1984). Teachers tend to be encouraging toward students for whom they have high expectations. They smile at these students more often and show greater warmth through nonverbal responses such as leaning toward the students and nodding their heads as students speak (Woolfolk & Brooks, 1985). The online report *Expectations and Student Outcomes* (Cotton, 1989) is a useful resource in learning about how expectations are communicated to students.

Students' responses to teacher expectations seem to be highly influenced by cultural background and home discourse patterns. Some cultures encourage students to set internal standards of worth, and peer pressure devalues dependence on teachers for approval.

Motivating Students to Become Active Participants in Their Learning. Learner autonomy is a key element of constructivist learning—teachers help students to construct new knowledge, providing scaffolds between what students already know and what they need to learn. Learner autonomy occurs when learners feel that studying is taking place due to their own volition. This autonomy is the basis for self-managed, self-motivated instruction. Such autonomy must be supported in a systematic way by the teacher and curriculum in order for the learner to benefit.

Educators acknowledge that it is impossible to teach learners everything they need to know while they are in class. Therefore, a major aim of classroom instruction should be to equip learners with learning skills they can employ on their own. These include the following:

- Efficient learning strategies
- Identification of their preferred ways of learning
- Skills needed to negotiate the curriculum
- Encouragement to set their own learning objectives
- Support for learners to set realistic goals and time frames
- Skills in self-evaluation (Nunan, 1989, p. 3)

Student autonomy is at risk in the climate of coercive adherence to standardized test scores as the sole criterion of effective instruction. Certainly there is a place for choice in topics and freedom to voice divergent views as the core of democratic schooling (see Giroux & McLaren, 1996).

Encouraging Students to Think Critically. An important aspect of schooling in a democracy is the ability to think for oneself, analyze ideas, separate fact from opinion, support opinions from reading, make inferences, and solve problems. The ability to think critically can enhance self-understanding and help students approach significant issues in life with analytical skills. This includes critical thinking, preparing students to be problem solvers who can analyze, evaluate, synthesize, and design when offered real-life situations—students who can make connections between divergent ideas and face the world with compassion and empathy (Mintz & Yun, 1999). An organized introduction to this complex field, presenting lesson plans that have been remodeled to include critical thinking strategies, is available from www.critical thinking.org/pages/index-of-articles/1021/.

Critical thinking includes the ability to look for underlying assumptions in statements, to detect bias, to identify illogical connections between ideas, and to recognize attempts to influence opinion by means of propaganda. These skills are fundamental to the clear thinking required of autonomous citizens in a democracy.

Helping Students Become Socially and Politically Conscious. "Sociocultural consciousness means understanding that one's way of thinking, behaving, and being is influenced by race, ethnicity, social class, and language" (Kea, Campbell-Whatley, & Richards, 2004, p. 4). Students as well as teachers need to have clarity of vision about their sociocultural identities and their role in the institutions that maintain social and economic distinctions based on social class and skin color.

Political and social consciousness is hard-won. It requires teachers to offer students a forum in which to discuss social and political events without partisan rancor; to investigate issues in the national and local press that have possible multiple perspectives; and to find a way to support students' voices about their lives and feelings.

Bulletin boards on which student writing can be posted, weekly current event discussions, and class newsletters are projects that can encourage autonomous student thinking, writing, and discussion.

An excellent resource for student projects in the community, including those that deal with social justice issues, is Lewis's *The Kid's Guide to Social Action: How to Solve the Social Problems You Choose—And Turn Creative Thinking into Positive Action*. This book explains how to organize students to carry out projects such as having a proclamation issued, circulating a petition, and calling public officials—important ways that students can become involved in social issues and influence public policy in a democracy.

This chapter has emphasized the profound influence of culture on people's perceptions, feelings, and actions, and the variety of ways in which individuals experience contact with other cultures. Let us revisit briefly Joe Suina, the Pueblo youth whose contact with school created cultural conflict for him. How could the school have been more accommodating? Ideally, Suina's teacher would be a Pueblo Indian and would share his culture. Classrooms in a Pueblo school would resemble the home, with intimate spaces and furniture designed for student comfort. If these conditions are not feasible, a non-Pueblo teacher would accommodate to the ways of the students in the same way that students are expected to accommodate to the school.

Teachers can play an important role in learning about their students' communities and cultures and in reducing the culture shock between home and school by working actively toward the creation of culturally responsive instruction. The best way for a teacher to understand culture is first to understand himself or herself and the extent to which mainstream U.S. cultural values are explicitly or implicitly enforced during instruction. A teacher who understands his or her own teaching and learning styles can then ask to what extent each student is similar or dissimilar. This goes a long way toward understanding individual differences. The key for the intercultural educator is to be sensitive, flexible, and open.

LEARNING MORE

Further Reading

Victor Villaseñor's *Rain of Gold* (1992) is a fascinating history of his family's experience as Mexican immigrants to southern California. Read the book and identify passages that illustrate the following Mexican values: the importance of religion, the woman as center of home and family, respect for the mother, protection of women's virtue, the ideal woman as pure, how to be a man, the role of the man as protector of the family, the importance of tradition, respect for life, death as a part of life, respect for work, respect for learning, importance of honor, and acceptance of passion as a part of life.

Web Search

Explore the Southern Poverty Law Center's website at www.splcenter.org. The most current issue of *Teaching Tolerance,* the organization's magazine for teachers, is available to read online, and by clicking other buttons you can discover ideas and resources for teachers, parents, teens, and children. Also investigate www.tolerance.org. This site also provides invaluable information for teachers, parents, teens, and children. Share your findings with your colleagues and plan how to incorporate some of the lessons and ideas from this site into your overall school plan.

Exploration

Ask several educators how they celebrate the birthday of Dr. Martin Luther King, Jr. on the legal holiday of his birth. Find a commemoration in your area and attend. How does this stimulate you to follow the ideals of Dr. King?

Collaboration

View the movie *Stand and Deliver*, which is about the success of Jaime Escalante, the outstanding mathematics teacher at Garfield High School in Los Angeles. Watch the scene two or three times in which a grandmother comes to Escalante's house. Role-play with a friend the elaborate greeting ritual with which Mr. Escalante warmly welcomes the elderly woman. Discuss with a friend or classmate a form of greeting that might be appropriate for an elderly family member who visits a classroom.

MyEducationLab™

The Importance of Culture

In this video, teachers and other English-learner education experts discuss the role of culture in the process of second language acquisition, especially as it plays out in classroom interactions among students and teachers. Various aspects of culture are highlighted, including what people do, think, and believe about what constitutes appropriate ways to interact in the classroom; cultural norms concerning the meaning of eye contact, gestures, and facial expressions; and how much distance to maintain from others during conversations. The importance of learning about and validating students' home cultures is emphasized.

To access the video, go to MyEducationLab (www.myeducationlab.com), choose the Díaz-Rico text, and log in to MyEducationLab for English Language Learners. Select the topic Diversity, and watch the video entitled "The Importance of Culture."

Answer the following questions:

1. How would you define "culture"? Provide three examples of how it applies to classroom interactions and student learning.

2. The video emphasizes learning about and validating students' home cultures. Describe several ways you can modify instruction to better involve students' families and their resources.

3. In the video, mention is made of the friction and emotional stress that may occur when cultural norms are violated. Identify one specific cultural aspect that might be a source of friction or stress due to differences between home and school norms. How might you resolve the issue while at the same time respecting the home culture?

4. How can teachers promote tolerance by integrating home and school learning experiences? How can teachers solicit the help of parents as cultural mediators.

REFERENCES

Abdulrahim, R. (2011). Holding on to Sikh heritage in the U.S. *Los Angeles Times,* May 7, AA3.

Agar, M. (1980). *The professional stranger: An informal introduction to ethnography.* Orlando, FL: Academic Press.

Alexander, S. (1983). *Nadia, the willful.* New York: Dial.

Au, K., & Jordan, C. (1981). Teaching reading to Hawaiian children: Finding a culturally appropriate solution. In H. Trueba, G. Guthrie, & K. Au (Eds.), *Culture and the bilingual classroom: Studies in classroom ethnography* (pp. 139–152). Rowley, MA: Newbury House.

Bandlow, R. (2002). Suburban bigotry: A descent into racism and struggle for redemption. In F. Schultz (Ed.), *Annual editions: Multicultural education 2002–2003* (pp. 90–93). Guilford, CT: McGraw-Hill/Dushkin.

Banks, J. (1994). *An introduction to multicultural education.* Boston: Allyn & Bacon.

Bennett, C. (2003). *Comprehensive multicultural education: Theory and practice* (5th ed.). Boston: Allyn & Bacon.

Birdwhistell, R. (1974). The language of the body: The natural environment of words. In A. Silverstein (Ed.), *Human communication: Theoretical explorations* (pp. 203–220). Hillsdale, NJ: Erlbaum.

Bonilla-Silva, E. (2003). *Racism without racists: Color-blind racism and the persistence of racial inequality in the United States.* Lanham, MD: Rowman & Littlefield.

Brandt, R. (1994). On educating for diversity: A conversation with James A. Banks. *Educational Leadership, 51,* 28–31.

Carnuccio, L. M. (2004). Cybersites. *Essential Teacher, 1*(3), 59.

Christensen, L. (2000). *Reading, writing, rising up: Teaching about social justice and the power of the written word.* Milwaukee, WI: Rethinking Schools.

Clark, B. (1983). *Growing up gifted: Developing the potential of children at home and at school* (2nd ed.). Columbus, OH: Merrill.

Cole, M. (1998, April 16). *Cultural psychology: Can it help us think about diversity?* Presentation at the annual meeting of the American Educational Research Association, San Diego.

Conchas, G. Q. (2006). *The color of success: Race and high-achieving urban youth.* New York: Teachers College Press.

Cotton, K. (1989). *Expectations and student outcomes.* Retrieved April 6, 2005, from educationnorthwest.org/webfm_send/562.

Crago, M. (1993). Communicative interaction and second language acquisition: An Inuit example. *TESOL Quarterly, 26*(3), 487–506.

Curtain, H., & Dahlberg, C. A. (2004). *Language and children—Making the match: New languages for young learners, grades K–8.* Boston: Allyn & Bacon.

Darder, A. (1991). *Culture and power in the classroom.* New York: Bergin and Garvey.

Day, E. M. (2002). *Identity and the young English learner.* Clevedon, UK: Multilingual Matters.

Delgado-Gaitan, C., & Trueba, H. (1991). *Crossing cultural borders: Education for immigrant families in America.* London: Falmer Press.

Diamond, B., & Moore, M. (1995). *Multicultural literacy.* White Plains, NY: Longman.

Díaz-Rico, L. T. (2000). Intercultural communication in teacher education: The knowledge base for CLAD teacher credential programs. *CATESOL Journal, 12*(1), 145–161.

Dresser, N. (1993). *Our own stories.* White Plains, NY: Longman.

Edmonson, M. (1971). *Lore: An introduction to the science of fiction.* New York: Holt, Rinehart and Winston.

Funaki, I., & Burnett, K. (1993). *When educational systems collide: Teaching and learning with Polynesian students.* Presentation at the annual conference of the Association of Teacher Educators, Los Angeles.

Gay, G. (1975, October). Cultural differences important in education of black children. *Momentum,* 30–32.

Gibson, M. (1991). Minorities and schooling: Some implications. In M. Gibson & J. Ogbu (Eds.), *Minority status and schooling. A comparative study of immigrant and involuntary minorities* (pp. 357–381). New York: Garland.

Giroux, H., & McLaren, P. (1996). Teacher education and the politics of engagement: The case for democratic schooling. *Harvard Educational Review, 56*(3), 213–238.

Good, T., & Brophy, J. (1984). *Looking in classrooms* (3rd ed.). New York: Harper & Row.

Grant, C. A., & Sleeter, C. (1986). *After the school bell rings.* Philadelphia: Falmer Press.

Hall, E. (1959). *The silent language*. New York: Anchor Books.

Heath, S. (1983b). *Ways with words*. Cambridge, UK: Cambridge University Press.

Heide, F., & Gilliland, J. (1990). *The day of Ahmed's secret*. New York: Lothrop, Lee, & Shepard.

Henderson, D., & May, J. (2005). *Exploring culturally diverse literature for children and adolescents*. Boston: Pearson.

Henwood, D. (1997). Trash-o-nomics. In M. Wray, M. Newitz, & A. Newitz, (Eds.), *White trash: Race and class in America* (pp. 177–191). New York: Routledge.

Hernandez, H. (2001). *Multicultural education: A teacher's guide to linking context, process, and content* (2nd ed.). Upper Saddle River, NJ: Merrill Prentice Hall.

Howard, G. R. (2007). As diversity grows, so must we. *Educational Leadership, 64*(6), 16–22.

Johnson, D. W., Johnson, R. T., Dudley, B., & Acikgoz, K. (1994). Effects of conflict resolution training on elementary school students. *Journal of Social Psychology, 134*(6), 803–817.

Jones, J. (1981). The concept of racism and its changing reality. In B. Bowser & R. Hunt (Eds.), *Impacts of racism on white Americans* (pp. 27–49). Beverly Hills, CA: Sage.

Jussim, L. (1986). Self-fulfilling prophecies: A theoretical and integrative review. *Psychological Review, 93*(4), 429–445.

Kagan, S. (2007). *Differentiated instruction* (smart card). San Clemente, CA: Kagan Publishing.

Kea, C., Campbell-Whatley, G. D., & Richards, H. V. (2004). *Becoming culturally responsive educators: Rethinking teacher education pedagogy*. National Center for Culturally Responsive Educational Systems. Retrieved January 29, 2005, from www.nccrest.org/publications .html.

Kleinfeld, J. (1988, June). Letter to the editor. *Harvard Education Letter, 4*(3).

Kosciw, J. G., Greytak, E. A., Díaz, E. M., & Bartkiewicz, M. J. (2010). *The 2009 National School Climate Survey: The experiences of lesbian, gay, bisexual and transgender youth in our nation's schools*. New York: Gay, Lesbian and Straight Education Network.

Labov, W. (1972). *Sociolinguistic patterns*. Philadelphia: University of Pennsylvania Press.

Litowitz, B. (1997). Just say no: Responsibility and resistance. In M. Cole, Y. Engeström, & O. Vasquez (Eds.), *Mind, culture, and activity* (pp. 473–484). New York: Cambridge University Press.

Manning, M. L. (2002). Understanding diversity, accepting others: Realities and directions. In F. Schultz (Ed.), *Annual editions: Multicultural education 2002/2003* (pp. 206–208). Guilford, CT: McGraw-Hill/Dushkin.

Martin, D. (2011). The safe zone. *California Educator, 15*(6), 9–13.

Matheson, K. (2009). School's racial tension boils over into fights. Online at http://www.access mylibrary.com/article-1G1-213640674/us-school-racial-tensions.html.

McClintock, M. (2000). How to interrupt oppressive behavior. In M. Adams, W. J. Blumenfeld, R. Casteñeda, H. W. Hackman, M. L. Peters, & X. Zúñiga, *Readings for diversity and social justice* (pp. 483–485). New York and London: Routledge.

McIntosh, P. (1996). White privilege and male privilege: A personal account of coming to see correspondences through work in women's studies. In M. Anderson & P. Collins (Eds.), *Race, class, and gender: An anthology* (2nd ed., pp. 76–87). Belmont, CA: Wadsworth.

McKay, S., & Wong, S. (1996). Multiple discourses, multiple identities: Investment and agency in a second-language learning among Chinese adolescent immigrant students. *Harvard Educational Review, 66*(3), 577–609.

Mintz, E., & Yun, J. T. (1999). *The complex world of teaching: Perspectives from theory and practice*. Cambridge, MA: Harvard Educational Review.

Moorman, C., & Haller, T. (2011). *A safe and orderly environment*. National Education Association. Online at www.nea.org/tools/a-safe-and-orderly-environment.html.

Morey, A., & Kilano, M. (1997). *Multicultural course transformation in higher education: A broader truth*. Boston: Allyn & Bacon.

Nichols, S. L. (1999). Gay, lesbian, and bisexual youth: Understanding diversity and promoting tolerance in schools. *The Elementary School Journal, 99*(5), 505–519.

Nolan, J. F., & Hoover, L. A. (2008). *Teacher supervision & evaluation* (2nd ed.). Hoboken, NJ: Wiley.

Nunan, D. (1989). *Designing tasks for the communicative classroom*. Cambridge, UK: Cambridge University Press.

Ong, W. (1982). *Orality and literacy*. London: Methuen.

Parla, J. (1994). Educating teachers for cultural and linguistic diversity: A model for all teachers. *New York State Association for Bilingual Education Journal, 9,* 1–6. Retrieved February 7, 2005, from www.ncela.gwu.edu/pubs/nysabe/vol9/model.htm.

Pasternak, J. (1994, March 29). Bias blights life outside Appalachia. *Los Angeles Times,* A1, A16.

Philips, S. (1972). Participant structures and communicative competence: Warm Springs children in community and classroom. In C. Cazden, V. John, & D. Hymes (Eds.), *Functions of language in the classroom* (pp. 370–394). New York: Teachers College Press.

Phillips, J. (1978). College of, by, and for Navajo Indians. *Chronicle of Higher Education, 15,* 10–12.

Prothrow-Smith, D. (1994, April). Building violence prevention into the classroom. *The School Administrator, 8*(12), 8–12.

Pryor, C. B. (2002). New immigrants and refugees in American schools: Multiple voices. In F. Schultz (Ed.), *Annual editions: Multicultural education 2002/2003* (pp. 185–193). Guilford, CT: McGraw-Hill/Dushkin.

Raimes, A. (Ed.). (1996). *Identities: Readings from contemporary culture.* Boston: Houghton Mifflin.

Reece-Miller, P. C. (2010). An elephant in the classroom: LGBTQ students and the silent minority. In M. C. Fehr & D. E. Fehr (Eds.), *Teach boldly: Letters to teachers about contemporary issues in education* (pp. 67–76). New York: Peter Lang.

Reese, D. (2007). Proceed with caution: Using Native American folktales in the classroom. *Language Arts, 84*(3), 245–256.

Runner, J. (2000). *"I don't understand" in over 230 languages.* Retrieved April 8, 2005, from www.elite.net/~runner/jennifers/understa.htm.

Sales, F. (1989). *Ibrahim.* New York: Lippincott.

Schmitt, T. L. (2009). Working together: Bringing Muslim students into the ESL classroom. *TESOL Intercultural Communication Interest SectionNewsletter, 7*(3). Online at www.tesol.org/s_tesol/tc/documents/3_2010_schmitt.pdf.

Scribner, S., & Cole, M. (1978). Literacy without schooling: Testing for intellectual effects. *Harvard Educational Review, 48,* 448–461.

Seelye, H. (1984). *Teaching culture.* Lincolnwood, IL: National Textbook Company.

Shade, B., & New, C. (1993). Cultural influences on learning: Teaching implications. In J. Banks & C. Banks (Eds.), *Multicultural education: Issues and perspectives.* Boston: Allyn & Bacon.

Shuter, R. (1991). The Hmong of Laos: Orality, communication, and acculturation. In L. Samovar & R. Porter (Eds.), *Intercultural communication: A reader* (6th ed., pp. 270–276). Belmont, CA: Wadsworth.

Sindell, P. (1988). Some discontinuities in the enculturation of Mistassini Cree children. In J. Wurzel (Ed.), *Toward multiculturalism.* Yarmouth, ME: Intercultural Press.

Smith, S. L., Paige, R. M., & Steglitz, I. (1998). Theoretical foundations of intercultural training and applications to the teaching of culture. In D. L. Lange, C. A. Klee, R. M. Paige, & Y. A. Yershova (Eds.), *Culture as the core: Interdisciplinary perspectives on culture teaching and learning in the language curriculum* (pp. 53–91). Minneapolis, MN: Center for Advanced Research on Language Acquisition, University of Minnesota.

Snow, D. (1996). *More than a native speaker.* Alexandria, VA: Teachers of English to Speakers of Other Languages.

Sutherland, D. E. (1989). *The expansion of everyday life 1860–1876.* New York: Harper & Row.

Tateishi, C. A. (2007–2008). Taking a chance with words. *Rethinking Schools, 22*(2), 20–23.

Tharp, R. (1989a). Culturally compatible education: A formula for designing effective classrooms. In H. Trueba, G. Spindler, & L. Spindler (Eds.), *What do anthropologists have to say about dropouts?* (pp. 51–66). New York: Falmer Press.

Tileston, D. W., & Darling, S. K. (2008). Why culture matters. *Teachers of Color, 3*(1), 58, 60.

Toohey, K., & Norton, B. (2003). Learner autonomy as agency in sociocultural settings. In D. Palfreyman and R. C. Smith (Eds.), *Learner autonomy across cultures: Language education perspectives* (pp. 58–74). London: Palgrave Macmillan.

Tran, M-T (2008, December 1). Keeping their Vietnamese heritage alive. *Los Angeles Times,* B3.

Triandis, H. C. (1995). *Individualism & collectivism.* Boulder, CO: Westview Press.

Ukpokodu, N. (2002). Multiculturalism vs. globalism. In F. Schultz (Ed.), *Annual editions: Multicultural education 2002–2003* (pp. 7–10). Guilford, CT: McGraw-Hill/Dushkin.

Villegas, A. M., & Lucas, T. (2002). Preparing culturally responsive teachers: Rethinking the curriculum. *Journal of Teacher Education, 53*(1), 20–32.

Villegas, A. M., & Lucas, T. (2007). The culturally responsive teacher. *Educational Leadership, 64*(6), 28–33.

Willet, J. (1995). Becoming first graders in an L2: An ethnographic study of L2 socialization. *TESOL Quarterly, 29*(3), 473–503.

Woolfolk, A., & Brooks, D. (1985). The influence of teachers' nonverbal behaviors on students' perceptions and performance. *Elementary School Journal, 85,* 514–528.

Wray, M., & Newitz, A. (1997). *White trash: Race and class in America.* New York: Routledge.

PHOTO CREDITS

Adapted Instruction icons, ZouZou/Shutterstock, Iofoto/Fotolia, Goodluz/Fotolia; Example of Concept icon, Piai/Fotolia; Point Counterpoint icon, Iosif Szasz-Fabian/Fotolia; Find Out More About icon, HaywireMedia/Fotolia.

Learning about the Language Learner

Learning about the Language Learner

English learners comprise a growing proportion of school children in the United States.

© Zurijeta/Shutterstock

In sixth grade, I had one of the first in a lucky line of English teachers who began to nurture in me a love of language, a love that had been there since my childhood of listening closely to words. Sister Maria Generosa did not make our class interminably diagram sentences from a workbook or learn [a] catechism of grammar rules. Instead she asked us to write little stories imagining we were snowflakes, birds, pianos, a stone in the pavement, a star in the sky. What would it feel like to be a flower with roots in the ground? Sister Maria filled the board with snowy print . . . until English . . . became a charged, fluid mass that carried me in its great fluent waves, rolling and moving onward, to deposit me on the shores of my new homeland, I was no longer a foreigner with no ground to stand on. I had landed in the English language.

Julia Alvarez (2007, p. 34)

Because of her English-language development teachers, Julia Alvarez is a writer. She can communicate her memories, her joys, her terrors—those ideas and feelings that make her human. Learning a second language connects people across cultures, making it possible for immigrants to achieve their dreams and aspirations. This cross-cultural process enriches everyone.

Teachers in the United States are increasingly expected to educate students whose native languages are not English and whose cultural backgrounds vary considerably from that of the American mainstream culture. Although the teaching profession includes educators from minority cultures in the United States as well as from other countries, the core of the profession remains the white, middle-class, usually monolingual teacher who can benefit from teacher education that includes specialized methods and strategies for the effective education of culturally and linguistically diverse (CLD) students.

Moreover, research has documented the effectiveness of long-term primary-language education. However, numerous classrooms contain students speaking various home languages. Thus English-language development (ELD) classrooms that require modified instruction in English become increasingly important. Teachers with a strong interest in language acquisition and a sense of compassion for the difficulties faced by CLD students are often the most successful in promoting their academic success.

Common Beliefs about Teaching English Learners

Before beginning to explore the multiple factors that create complexity in teaching English learners, it is important to address four key misconceptions (see Harper and de Jong, 2004).

Misconception 1: Exposure and Immersion Are the Answer

Many teachers believe that the mind of a child, left to its own resources, will automatically learn a second language given enough time. This may stem from the parallel misconception that the first language is learned easily. However, before reaching kindergarten a five–year-old child has had more than 25,000 hours of family life in which to learn the primary language—but attending school for 180 days amounts to about 1,000 hours of English per year. Even if a second language were learned like the first, this would be nowhere near an equivalent exposure to language. Krashen's insight is that exposure must be comprehensible; school, on the other hand, often features abstract and decontextualized language.

Misconception 2: One Size Fits All

Learners do not all progress at the same rate in acquiring English. Differing levels of literacy in the first language as well as differing success in prior education, learning-style diversity, and differing social skills are just a few of the ways in which learners vary.

Misconception 3: Specially Adapted Instruction in English Is "Just Good Teaching"

Teachers may resist acquiring pedagogy designed to incorporate second-language-acquisition techniques because they think they can simply use techniques that are tried-and-true for native speakers of English—or they use remediation techniques designed for low-achieving students. In fact, neither approach is justified. For example, English learners may need modified instruction just to gain the confidence necessary for a minimal level of oral participation; silence does not indicate a lack of understanding. Teaching English learners requires a specific set of skills that are addressed in this text.

Misconception 4: Effective Instruction Means Nonverbal Teaching

Making instruction comprehensible by providing pictures and teaching using gestures are techniques designed to enhance understanding when language must be augmented—but this does not replace the need to teach language. Conceptual understanding and language are intertwined—one supports the other. The expert teacher takes responsibility for both.

Teaching in a second-language-acquisition context does not become simpler by reducing its complexity, but rather by acquiring the teaching skills required to operate effectively. Misconceptions undermine the motivation to learn how to succeed in a difficult teaching domain.

Schools, as institutions within a society, perform an important role in socializing students and helping them gain the knowledge, skills, roles, and identities they need for success. Students who enter school must develop a high level of English proficiency, and teachers are challenged to develop students' English skills during the K–12 period of schooling. The first part of this chapter presents current demographic trends. The chapter then introduces the English learner and offers ways for teachers to inform themselves about these learners' needs.

English Learners: Demographic Trends

The profession of teaching has changed dramatically in the early twenty-first century; many more classrooms contain English learners, students whose home language is not English and who are not classified as "fluent English proficient" based on test scores and other criteria. By 2025, one in every four students will initially be classified as an English learner. A quick overview of the demographics of English learners in the United States can help teachers to visualize the numbers of these learners and their distribution in the schools.

In 2010, 25.2 million (9 percent) of the U.S. population over 5 years of age was limited-English proficient (LEP) (Pandya, McHugh, & Batalova, 2011); six states

(California, Texas, New York, Florida, Illinois, and New Jersey, in order of LEP population) had more than 1,000,000 each. In 2008–2009, 49,487,174 students were enrolled in K–12 schools in the United States. Of these children, 21 percent spoke a language other than English in the home; 4.3 million are reported to speak English with difficulty (NCES, 2011). In all, 5,346,673 were English learners (NCELA, 2009). This represents a 51 percent increase since 1997–1998.

In nine states (California, Oregon, Nevada, Colorado, Arizona, New Mexico, Texas, Illinois, and Florida) more than 10 percent of students are English learners. The greatest growth in percent of population, however, has taken place in ten states, mostly clustered in the South: Alabama, Georgia, Arkansas, North Carolina, South Carolina, Virginia, Tennessee, and Kentucky, as well as Indians and Colorado (NCELA, 2009). Five states—California, Texas, New York, Florida, and Illinois—are home to almost 70 percent of all English learners in elementary schools (Cosentino de Cohen & Clewell, 2007).

California had the largest population percentage of non-English-language speakers; 37 percent of students enrolled in school speak a language other than English at home. Following California in percent of non-English speakers are New Mexico, Texas, New York, Hawaii, Arizona, and New Jersey. Other states—Florida, Illinois, and Massachusetts—also have large populations of non-English-language speakers. The majority of English learners in the United States are Spanish speaking (28.1 million); Asian and Pacific Islanders constitute the second-largest demographic group of English learners.

The National Clearinghouse for English Language Acquisition and Language Instruction Educational Programs (NCELA) put the number of children of school age with a home language other than English at 9,779,766—one of every six children of school age—and 31 percent of all American-Indian/Alaska Native, Asian/Pacific Islander, and Hispanic students enrolled in public schools (National Center for Education Statistics, 2005). Of these language-minority students, in 2005–2006, 5,074,572 do not yet have sufficient proficiency in English to be able to succeed academically in traditional all-English-medium classrooms (NCELA, 2007). Los Angeles Unified School District leads all other school districts in the nation both in the number (220,703) of English learners, number of languages (92), and percent of total enrollment (33 percent), followed by New York City at 154,466 students (2011), or 41 percent of total students, with 168 home languages represented. Following Los Angeles and New York City are Dade County, Florida; Chicago; Houston; Dallas; San Diego; and Long Beach. In 2011, California, with a school enrollment of approximately 1.4 million English learners, led the states in need for English-learner services at the K–12 level. In California, English learners constitute 23.2 percent of the total enrollment in California public schools. Almost 1 million more students speak a language other than English in their homes. This number represents about 37.4 percent of the state's public school enrollment. Although English learner data are collected for 59 language groups, 82.7 percent of the state's English learners speak Spanish (www.cde.ca.gov/ds/sd/cb/cefelfacts.asp).

Taking a closer look at the largest source of English learners, according to the latest U.S. Census data, there are 50.5 million Hispanics in the United States, comprising

16 percent of the total population. Adding the nearly 4 million residents of Puerto Rico, the total number of Latinos surpasses 54 million. Of those speaking a language other than English in the home, 62 percent (35,468,501) are Spanish-speaking (Shin & Ortman, 2011). Between 2000 and 2010, the Latino population increased by 43 percent (15.2 million), accounting for more than half of the 27.3 million increase in the total population of the United States. In the coming decades, Latinos will account for 60 percent of the nation's population growth between 2005 and 2050 (U.S. Department of Education, 2011).

In today's American public education system, Latinos are by far the largest minority group, numbering more than 12.4 million in the country's elementary, middle, and high schools. Currently, nearly 22 percent, or slightly more than one in five, of all preK–12 students enrolled in America's public schools are Latino. There are 17.1 million Latinos ages 17 and younger in the United States; therefore as they mature, their children will comprise a large group of students in the schools for many years to come.

The national distribution of English learners by grade levels is as follows: Grades PreK–3, 44 percent; grades 4–8, 35 percent; grades 9–12, 19 percent; and alternative schools, 2 percent (Rahilly & Weinmann, 2007). Of children who speak a language other than English at home, 81 percent are U.S.-born or naturalized U.S. citizens (Lapkoff & Li, 2007).

These population demographics indicate that all states need to provide services for English learners, with the need greatest in California, New Mexico, New York, Florida, Illinois, and Texas, serving Hispanics or Asian/Pacific Islanders. The linguistic and cultural variety of English learners suggests that more and more teachers serve as intercultural and interlinguistic educators—those who can reach out to learners from a variety of backgrounds and offer effective learning experiences.

Psychological Factors That Influence Instruction

Learners do not learn language in a vacuum. They learn it by interacting with others. Psychological and sociocultural factors play important roles in a learner's acquiring and using a second language. Teachers who are aware of these individual (psychological) and group (sociocultural) factors are able to adapt instruction to meet the individual needs of the learners so that each student can achieve academic success. Figure 1 offers an outline that can help teachers organize the factors they know about a given learner.

Psychological factors are traits specific to individuals that enable them to acquire a second language (L2). Learners use the assets of their personalities to absorb the ambiance of the culture, to process the language they hear, and to create meaningful responses. Psychological factors can be divided into three categories: *background* factors, *social–emotional* factors, and *cognitive* factors. Teachers can help students be aware of those psychological factors that further their language learning and can work with students to ensure that these factors promote rather than impede their learning.

Figure 1   English-Learner Profile

Psychological Factors

The Learner's Background

Learner's name _____ Age _____ Gender (M / F)

Grade _____ L1 proficiency _____

Type of bilingualism _____

Previous L2 experience _____

Assessed L2 level: Reading _____ Writing _____ Listening _____ Speaking _____

Prior academic success _____

Likes/dislikes _____

Social–Emotional Factors

Self-esteem _____

Motivation _____

Anxiety level _____

Attitudes toward L1/L2 _____

Attitudes toward the teacher and the class _____

Cognitive Factors

Stage of L2 acquisition _____

Cognitive style/Learning style _____

Learning strategies _____

Sociocultural Factors

Family acculturation and use of L1 and L2 _____

Family values _____

Institutional support for language-minority students _____

Sociocultural support for L1 in the classroom environment _____

The Learner's Background

Naming Practices and Forms of Address. A learner's name represents the learner's individuality as well as a family connection. People feel validated if their names are treated with respect. Teachers who make the effort to pronounce students' names accurately communicate a sense of caring. Students may be asked to speak their names into a tape recorder so the teacher can practice privately. Expecting students to say their names again and again so the teacher can rehearse may be embarrassing for both parties.

Naming practices differ across cultures. The custom in the United States is to have a first (or given), middle, and last (or family) name. On lists, the first and last names are often reversed in order to alphabetize the names. In other parts of the world, naming practices differ. In Vietnam, for example, names also consist of three parts, in the following order: family name, middle name, and given name. The names are always given in this order and cannot be reversed because doing so would denote a different person—Nguyên Van Hai is different from Hai Van Nguyên. In Taiwan the family name also goes first, followed by given names. Puerto Ricans, as well as other Hispanics, generally use three names: a given name, followed by the father's surname and then the mother's surname. If one last name must be used, it is generally the father's surname. Thus, Esther Reyes Mimosa can be listed as Esther Reyes. If the first name is composed of two given names (Hector Luis), both are used. This person may have a brother who is Hector José; for either to be called simply Hector would represent a loss of identity.

In many cultures, adults are referred to by their function rather than their name. In Hmong, *xib fwb* means "teacher," and Hmong children may use the English term *teacher* in the classroom rather than a title plus surname, as in "Mrs. Jasko." Middle-class European-American teachers may consider this to be rude rather than realizing this is a cultural difference.

Osgood (2002) suggests ways to enlist native-English-speaking students to make friends with newcomers: Challenge them to teach a new student their names and to learn the new student's first and last names, using recess, lunchtime, or free time to accomplish this task.

Adapted Instruction

Students' Names

- Understand the use and order of names and pronounce them correctly.
- Don't change a student's name, apply a nickname, or use an "English" version of a student's name (even at the student's request) without first checking with a member of the student's family.

Age. Second-language acquisition (SLA) is a complex process that occurs over a long period of time. Although many people believe that children acquire a second language more rapidly than adults, recent research counters this notion. While it is true that the kind of instruction varies greatly according to the age of the learner, there is little evidence to indicate that biology closes the door to learning a second language at certain ages (see Singleton & Ryan [2004] and Han [2004] for further discussion of age-related issues in SLA, as well as the Point/Counterpoint box on pages 9–10).

First-Language Proficiency. Research has shown that proficiency in the first language (L1) helps students to achieve in school. In order to learn a student's strengths in the first language, a teacher, primary-language-speaking aide, or parent who is fluent in the language of the student may observe a student working or playing in the primary language and take notes on the child's language behavior, or schools may rely on formal testing.

Acceptance of the first language and use of the first language to support instruction promotes a low-anxiety environment for students. A lower anxiety level in turn promotes increased learning.

Adapted Instruction

First-Language Proficiency

- Monitor students' fluency in their primary languages and share concerns with parents if students appear to be dysfluent in their home languages.

- In cooperative groups, allow use of the first language so that students can discuss concepts.

Types of Bilingualism. Cummins (1979) analyzed the language characteristics of the children he studied and suggested that the level of bilingualism attained is an important factor in educational development. *Limited bilingualism*, or subtractive bilingualism, can occur when children's first language is gradually replaced by a more

POINT COUNTERPOINT

What Is the Best Age for Second-Language Acquisition?

For adults, learning a second language can be a frustrating and difficult experience. In contrast, it seems so easy for children. Is there a best age for learning a second language?

POINT: Children Learn Second Languages Easily Those who argue that a child can learn a second language more rapidly than an adult generally ascribe this ability to the *critical period hypothesis*—that the brain has a language-acquisition processor that functions best before puberty (Lenneberg, 1967)—despite the fact that the critical period hypothesis has not been proved.

Evidence from child second-language studies indicates that the language children speak is relatively simple compared to that of adults; it has shorter constructions with fewer vocabulary words and thus appears more fluent. Moreover, adults are often unaware that a child's silence indicates lack of understanding or shyness, and they underestimate the limitations of a child's second-language

acquisition skills. One area that seems to be a clear advantage for children is phonology: The earlier a person begins to learn a second language, the closer the accent will become to that of a native speaker (Oyama, 1976); age of L2 learning appears to be the most important predictor of degree of foreign accent (Piske, Mackay, & Fiege, 2001).

COUNTERPOINT: Adults Learn Languages More Skillfully Than Children Research comparing adults to children has consistently demonstrated that adolescents and adults outperform children in controlled language-learning studies (e.g., Snow & Hoefnagel-Hoehle, 1978). Adults have access to more memory strategies; are, as a rule, more socially comfortable; and have greater experience with language in general. The self-discipline, strategy use, prior knowledge, and metalinguistic ability of the older learner create a distinct advantage for the adult over the child in second-language acquisition.

Marinova-Todd, Marshall, and Snow (2000) analyzed misconceptions about age and second-language learning and reached the following conclusions: "[O]lder learners have the potential to learn second languages to a very high level and introducing foreign languages to very young learners cannot be justified on grounds of biological readiness to learn languages" (p. 10). "Age does influence language learning, but primarily because it is associated with social, psychological, educational, and other factors that can affect L2 proficiency, not because of any critical period that limits the possibility of language learning by adults" (p. 28).

Implications for Teaching

Teachers need to be aware that learning a second language is difficult for children as well as for adults. Helping children to feel socially comfortable reduces their anxiety and assists acquisition.

dominant and prestigious language. In this case, children may develop relatively low levels of academic proficiency in both languages. The most positive cognitive effects are experienced in *proficient bilingualism*, when students attain high levels of proficiency in both languages. This is also called *additive bilingualism*.

Adapted Instruction

Promoting Additive Bilingualism

- Seek out or prepare handouts that encourage families to preserve the home language.
- Make sure classroom or community libraries feature books in the home language and encourage students to check out books in both languages.
- Welcome classroom visitors and volunteers who speak the home language, and ask them to speak to the class about the importance of proficiency in two languages.

Previous L2 Experience. English learners in the same grade may have had vastly different prior exposure to English, ranging from previous all-primary-language instruction to submersion in English—including students with no prior schooling at all. Moreover, no two students have been exposed to exactly the same input of English outside of class. Therefore, students' prior exposure to English and attainment of proficiency are often highly varied.

Although students at the beginner and early-intermediate levels seem to acquire English rapidly, research has shown that progress between the intermediate and advanced levels is slower (Goldenberg & Coleman, 2010). This may account for the difficulties experienced by the "long-term" English learner (Olsen, 2010).

Students who have been overcorrected when first learning English may have "shut down" and be unwilling to speak. It may take time for a more positive approach to L2 instruction to produce results, combined with a positive attitude toward L1 maintenance.

Assessed L2 Level. An important part of the knowledge about the learner that a teacher amasses as a foundation for instruction is the student's assessed level of proficiency in listening, speaking, reading, and writing in English. This can be obtained during the process of assessment for placement. In California, the California English Language Development Test (CELDT) (online at www.cde.ca.gov/ta/tg/el) is the designated placement instrument; other states have other ways to assess proficiency. The student's L2 level is the beginning point of instruction in English.

Adapted Instruction

Assessing L2 Proficiency Levels

- Be aware that a student's listening/speaking proficiency may surpass that of reading and writing, or vice versa.

- Assess each language skill independently.

- Use a measure such as the Student Oral Language Observation Matrix (SOLOM) to assess students' oral proficiency.

- Use *The English–Español Reading Inventory for the Classroom* (Flynt & Cooter, 1999) to provide a quick assessment of reading levels in two languages, or the *Cooter Flynt Cooter Comprehensive Reading Inventory* (2006) for English proficiency.

Second-language learners are individuals who vary greatly in their acquisition of a second language. However, there appear to be some generally accepted stages of development through which learners progress. These stages include *preproduction, early production, speech emergence,* and *intermediate fluency.* In preproduction—also called the silent period—the learner is absorbing the sounds and rhythms of the new language, becoming attuned to the flow of the speech stream, and beginning to isolate specific words. In this stage, the learner relies on contextual clues for understanding key words and generally communicates nonverbally.

Once a learner feels more confident, words and phrases are attempted—the early production stage. In the third stage, speech emergence, learners respond more freely. Utterances become longer and more complex, but as utterances begin to resemble sentences, syntax errors are more noticeable than in the earlier stage ("Where you going?" "The boy running."). Once in intermediate fluency, students begin to initiate and sustain conversations and are often able to recognize and correct their own errors.

Regardless of the way one labels the stages of second-language acquisition, it is important for the classroom teacher to use this level as the basis for instruction.

Adapted Instruction

Matching Instruction to Students' L2 Levels

Ideally, classroom activities match the students' second-language acquisition levels.

Beginning Level (preproduction stage)
- Provide concrete activities featuring input that is augmented by pictures, real objects, carefully modified teacher speech, and frequent repetition of new vocabulary.

Early Intermediate and Intermediate Levels (early production and speech emergence)

• Ask questions that evoke responses of single words and brief phrases.

• Provide opportunities for students to use their primary language as they acquire the second language.

Early Advanced Level

• Engage students in opportunities to speak with greater complexity, read several pages of text even though they may have limited comprehension, and write paragraphs.

• Offer a curriculum that supports and explicitly teaches learning strategies.

Prior Academic Success. A valid predictor of school success is prior academic success. By reading a student's cumulative academic record, a teacher may get a sense of the student's strengths and weaknesses. This can be augmented by observations of the student during academic activities and interviews of family members and former teachers. It is important for the current teacher to assemble as complete a record of students' prior schooling as possible to best inform instructional decisions.

Likes/Dislikes. Inquiring about students' favorite academic subjects, television shows, and extracurricular activities is one way of bridging adult–child, teacher–student, or intercultural gaps: Who/what is your favorite [native-language/culture] singer? Actor? Video game? Outdoor game? Storybook? Grocery store? Holiday? What do you like about it? Students can write about favorite subjects, and teachers can then use these culturally familiar ideas in math story problems and other content.

Psychological Factors: Social–Emotional

The affective domain, the emotional side of human behavior, is the means through which individuals become aware of their environment, respond to it with feeling, and act as though their feelings make a difference. This emotional dimension helps determine how language acquisition and communication take place. The affective factors discussed here are self-esteem, motivation, anxiety, and learner attitudes.

Self-Esteem. A large part of one's feelings revolve around how one feels about oneself, one's self-esteem. High self-esteem may *cause* language success or *result from* language success. Self-esteem enhancement, such as efforts to empower students with positive images of self, family, and culture, may facilitate language learning.

Self-esteem is particularly at risk when learning a second language, because so much identity and pride are associated with language competence. Schools that honor the primary languages and cultures of students and help students to develop additive bilingualism foster strong identities; schools in which students face disrespect and discrimination hinder students' social and emotional development (Cummins, 2001).

Children who do poorly in school face daily degradation to their sense of self-esteem as they often receive low grades, and experience disapproval from their teachers and even social ostracism from peers (McKay, 2000). A healthy sense of success is necessary not only to master academics, but also to feel valuable to society.

Example of Concept   *Building Self-Esteem*

Anita Alvarez was a Spanish-speaking first-grade student at the beginning stages of English-language acquisition. She was shy and retiring, and Mrs. Figueroa noticed that she seldom took advantage of opportunities to chat with her peers. Anita seemed to have good sensorimotor abilities and to be particularly adept at building three-dimensional models following printed diagrams. When Mrs. Figueroa observed that Mary, another student in the class, had a lot of difficulty in constructing objects, she teamed Anita with Mary; and, with Anita's help, Mary completed her project successfully. Noting this success, Mrs. Figueroa publicly praised her to the class and referred students to her for help. Mrs. Figueroa was pleased to see that, subsequently, Anita talked more with other students and seemed to acquire English at a faster rate.

Many classroom activities can be used to enhance students' self-esteem. In the Name Game, students introduce themselves by first name, adding a word that describes how they are feeling that day—using a word that begins with the same letter as their first name (the teacher may provide English learners with an alphabetized list of adjectives). Each subsequent person repeats what the others have said in sequence. Another activity, Name Interviews, lets students work in pairs to use a teacher-provided questionnaire. This includes questions such as, "What do you like about your name? Who named you? Were you named for someone? Are there members of your family who have the same name?" and more (Siccone, 1995).

Example of Concept   *Motivation for Acquiring a Second Language*

I began learning Spanish in middle school, just because it was part of the curriculum. But when I entered college, I began to develop a real interest in Spanish and learning more about Chile, about my mom's culture. I knew that I needed some sort of challenge in order for me to become more proficient in Spanish, so I decided to study abroad in Chile, to learn more about the Chilean culture and be able to understand it first-hand. I was motivated also because I believed that learning Spanish would help me advance in my career of international education.

—*Darlene Peceimer (2013)*

Motivation. "The impulse, emotion, or desire that causes one to act in a certain way" is one way to define motivation. Gardner and Lambert (1972) postulated two types of motivation in learning a second language: *instrumental*, the need to acquire a language for a specific purpose, and *integrative*, the desire to become a member of the culture of the second-language group. Most situations involve a mixture of both types.

Generally, in classrooms, teachers may believe that motivation is a trait or a state. As a *trait*, motivation is seen as being relatively consistent and persistent and is attributed to various groups: parents, communities, or cultures. Students are motivated to learn

English by such incentives as the desire to please—or not to shame—their families or by the drive to bring honor to their communities. As a *state*, motivation is viewed as a more temporary condition that can be influenced by the use of highly interesting materials or activities, or by contingencies of reward or punishment. Pittaway (2004) describes ways that teachers can increase students' motivation by investing in their success.

Adapted Instruction

Motivating Students

- Give pep talks to remind students that anything worth doing may seem difficult at first.
- Provide students with a list of encouraging phrases to repeat to themselves as self-talk.

Anxiety Level. Anxiety when learning a second language can be seen as similar to general feelings of tension that students experience in the classroom. Almost everyone feels some anxiety when learning a new language—that is, they have feelings of self-consciousness, a desire to be perfect when speaking, and a fear of making mistakes. Using a foreign language can threaten a person's sense of self if speakers fear they cannot represent themselves fully in a new language or understand others readily. Anxiety can be debilitating. As one student recalled,

> During these several months after my arrival in the U.S.A., every day I came back exhausted so I had to take a rest for a while, stretching myself on the bed. For all the time, I strained every nerve in order to understand what the people were saying and make myself understood in my broken English. I sometimes have to pretend to understand by smiling, even though I feel alienated, uneasy, and tense. (Barna, 2007, p. 71)

Because anxiety can cause learners to feel defensive and can block effective learning, language educators strive to make the classroom a place of warmth and friendliness and where peer work, small-group work, games, and simulations are featured. Highly anxious learners must divide their attentional resources into both learning and worrying about learning. Accepting English learners' use of both languages during instruction may help reduce their anxiety about speaking English (Pappamihiel, 2002).

Adapted Instruction

Ways to Deal with Excessive Student Anxiety

- Monitor activities to ensure that students are receiving no undue pressure.
- Avoid having anxious students perform in front of large groups.
- When using a novel format or starting a new type of task, provide students with examples or models of how the task is done.
- Teach test-taking skills explicitly and provide study guides to help students who may need extra academic preparation.

Source: Woolfolk (2007).

Attitudes of the Learner. Attitudes play a critical role in learning English. Attitudes toward self, toward language (one's own and English), toward English-speaking people (particularly peers), and toward the teacher and the classroom environment affect students (Richard-Amato, 2003). One's attitude toward the self involves cognition about one's ability in general, ability to learn language, and self-esteem and its related emotions. These cognitions and feelings are seldom explicit and may be slow to change.

Attitudes toward language and those who speak it are largely a result of experience and the influence of people in the immediate environment, such as peers and parents. Negative reactions are often the result of negative stereotypes or the experience of discrimination or racism. If English learners are made to feel inferior because of accent or language status, they may have a defensive reaction against English and English speakers.

Students' attitudes toward the primary language vary; some students may have a defensive reaction or ambivalent feelings toward their own primary language as a result of internalized shame if they have been made to feel inferior. Peers may incite attitudes against the L1 or may try to tease or bully those who speak the same primary language with a different dialect.

Attitudes toward the teacher and the classroom environment play an important role in school success in general and English acquisition in particular. One way to create a sense of belonging is to assign a new student to a home group that remains unchanged for a long time. If such groups are an ongoing aspect of classroom social organization, with rules of caring, respect, and concern already in place, then the home group provides an ideal social group to receive newcomers and help them develop interdependence, support, and identity (Peregoy & Boyle, 2013).

Teachers can do much to model positive attitudes toward the students' primary language. A teacher–family conference may be advisable if a student continues to show poor attitudes toward the first or second language or the school.

Psychological Factors: Cognitive

The cognitive perspective helps educators understand language learners as people who are active processors of information. Language is used in school in expanded ways: to create meaning from print, to encode ideas into print, to analyze and compare information, and to respond to classroom discussion. All of these activities involve cognitive factors. Students learn in many different ways using a variety of strategies and styles. This section addresses students' cognitive and learning styles.

Cognitive Style. A cognitive style refers to "consistent and rather enduring tendencies or preferences within an individual" (Brown, 2007, p. 119). Tharp (1989b) suggested two cognitive styles that have relevance for classrooms: visual/verbal and holistic/analytic. For students who learn by observing and doing rather than through verbal instructions, schools may be mystifying until they catch on to a different cognitive style. Similarly, students with more holistic thought processes learn by seeing the "big picture."

Adapted Instruction

Teaching to Diverse Learning Styles

Although in the typical classroom it is not possible to tailor instruction precisely to meet individuals' needs, some modifications can be made that take learning styles into account.

- Students who are dependent may benefit from encouragement to become more independent learners; the teacher may offer a choice between two learning activities, for example, or reduce the number of times a student has to ask the teacher for help.
- Students who are highly competitive may be provided activities and assignments that encourage collaboration and interdependent learning.
- Students who show little tolerance for frustration can be given a range of tasks on the same skill or concept that slowly increases in complexity, with the student gradually gaining skill and confidence.

Learning Styles. Many researchers have documented differences in the manner in which learners approach the learning task. These preferences help instructors anticipate the different needs and perspectives of students. Once learning styles have been identified, instructors can use the information to plan and to modify certain aspects of courses and assignments. Hruska-Riechmann and Grasha (1982) offer six learning styles: competitive versus cooperative, dependent versus independent, and participant versus avoidant. For Sonbuchner (1991), learning styles refer to information-processing styles and work environment preferences. Table 1 lists learning style variables that have been divided into four categories—cognitive, affective, incentive, and physiological—according to Keefe (1987).

Table 2 provides several learning style websites that feature learning style information, diagnostic checklists, and ideas for adapted instruction. The teacher who builds variety into instruction and helps learners to understand their own styles can enhance students' achievement.

Adapted Instruction

Accommodating Students' Psychological Factors

To adjust for individual psychological factors, teachers can provide verbal reassurances to timid students, alternative learning activities to address multiple intelligences, explicit opportunities to help students express their strong abilities, and additional mediation for students who need to achieve despite a possible weak ability in a specific area.

Table 1   Variables That Constitute Learning Style Differences

Cognitive	Affective	Incentive	Physiological
• Field independent/field dependent • Scanning (broad attention) v. focusing (narrow) • Conceptual/analytical v. perceptual/concrete • Task constricted (easily distracted) v. task flexible (capable of controlled concentration) • Reflective v. impulsive • Leveling (tendency to lump new experiences with previous ones) v. sharpening (ability to distinguish small differences) • High cognitive complexity (multidimensional discrimination, accepting of diversity and conflict) v. low cognitive complexity (tendency to reduce conflicting information to a minimum)	• Need for structure • Curiosity • Persistence • Level of anxiety • Frustration tolerance	• Locus of control (internal: seeing oneself as responsible for own behavior; or external: attributing circumstances to luck, chance, or other people) • Risk taking v. caution • Competition v. cooperation • Level of achievement motivation (high or low) • Reaction to external reinforcement (does or does not need rewards and punishment) • Social motivation arising from family, school, and ethnic background (high or low) • Personal interests (hobbies, academic preferences)	• Gender-related differences (typically, males are more visual–spatial and aggressive, females more verbal and tuned to fine-motor control) • Personal nutrition (healthy v. poor eating habits) • Health • Time-of-day preferences (morning, afternoon, evening, night) • Sleeping and waking habits • Need for mobility • Need for and response to varying levels of light, sound, and temperature

Source: Based on Keefe (1987).

Table 2   Websites That Feature Learning Style Information and Diagnostic Inventories

Website	Source	Content
www.engr.ncsu.edu/learningstyles/ilsweb.html	North Carolina State University	Users can take a learning styles questionnaire with 44 items to self-assess.
www.usd.edu/trio/tut/ts/style.html	University of San Diego	Learn about learning styles (auditory, visual, and kinesthetic); identify your own learning style.
http://ttc.coe.uga.edu/surveys/LearningStyleInv.html	University of Georgia	Are you visual, tactile, or auditory? Find out!

Sociocultural Factors That Influence Instruction

Language learning occurs within social and cultural contexts. A part of the sense of mastery and enjoyment in a language is acting appropriately and understanding cultural norms. Learners adapt patterns of behavior in a new language and culture based on experiences from their own culture. Thus, sociocultural factors—how people interact with one another and how they carry out their daily business—play a large role in second-language acquisition.

If, as many believe, prolonged exposure to English is sufficient for mastery, then why do so many students fail to achieve the proficiency in English necessary for academic success? Some clues to this perplexity can be found beyond the language itself, in the sociocultural context. Do the students feel that their language and culture are accepted and validated by the school? A well-meaning teacher, with the most up-to-date pedagogy, may still fail to foster achievement if students are socially and culturally uncomfortable with, resistant to, or alienated from schooling.

As students learn a second language, their success is dependent on sociocultural factors. These factors are explored here with a view toward helping teachers facilitate student learning by bridging the culture and language gaps.

Family Acculturation and the Use of First and Second Languages

Acculturation is the process of adapting to a new culture. English learners in the United States, by the mere fact of living in this country and participating in schools, learn a second culture as well as a second language. How the acculturation proceeds depends on factors beyond language itself and beyond the individual learner's motivation, capabilities, and style—it usually is a familywide phenomenon.

In studying students' differential school performance, Ogbu (1978) drew a distinction between various types of immigrant groups. Castelike minorities are those minority groups that were originally incorporated into society against their will and have been systematically exploited and depreciated over generations through slavery or colonization. Castelike minorities traditionally work at the lowest paying and most undesirable jobs, and they suffer from a job ceiling they cannot rise above regardless of talent, motivation, or achievement. Thus, academic success is not always seen as helpful or even desirable for members of these groups.

On the other hand, *immigrant minorities* who are relatively free of a history of depreciation, such as immigrants to the United States from El Salvador, Guatemala, and Nicaragua, believe that the United States is a land of opportunity. These immigrants do not view education as irrelevant or exploitative but rather as an important investment. Therefore, the internalized attitudes about the value of school success for family members may influence the individual student.

Adapted Instruction

Learning about the Family

- If possible, visit the student's home to observe the family's degree of acculturation.
- Note the family's media consumption:
  What television shows does the family watch, in which language?
  Do family members read books, magazines, or newspapers, and in which languages?

A family's use of L1 and L2 is also influenced by the relative status of the primary language in the eyes of the dominant culture. In modern U.S. culture, the social value and prestige of speaking a second language varies with socioeconomic position; it also varies as to the second language that is spoken.

Many middle-class parents believe that learning a second language benefits their children personally and socially and will later benefit them professionally. In fact, it is characteristic of the elite group in the United States who are involved in scholarly work, diplomacy, foreign trade, or travel to desire to be fully competent in two languages. However, the languages that parents wish their children to study are often not those spoken by recently arrived immigrants (Dicker, 1992). This suggests that a certain bias exists in being bilingual—that being competent in a "foreign language" is valuable, whereas knowing an immigrant language is a hurdle to be overcome.

There are many ways in which a second-class status is communicated to speakers of other languages, and because language attitudes usually operate at an inconspicuous level, school personnel and teachers are not always aware of the attitudes they hold. For example, the interlanguage of English learners—the language they use as they learn English—may be considered a dialect of English. Students learning English express themselves in many different dialects, depending on the language they hear in their homes and communities. These forms of English vary in the pronunciation of words, the selection of vocabulary that is used, and the way that words are arranged in sentences.

Some teachers only accept Standard English, the English found in textbooks. They may view nonstandard forms as less logical, less precise, or less elegant; sometimes they may even stigmatized these forms as corrupt or debased. Worse, they may view those who speak nonstandard English as less intelligent or less gifted linguistically. Research has shown that incorporating nonstandard language use in the classroom is often a helpful bridge to the learning of Standard English. When students feel that they are accepted and are confident of their language skills, they are more likely to want to acquire a second language (Siegel, 1999).

If teachers devalue the accent, syntax, or other speech characteristics of students as they learn English, English learners receive the message that their dialect is not accepted. If teachers use dialect to evaluate students' potential or use proficiency in Standard English to predict school achievement, it is possible that the teacher's own attitude toward the students' dialects—either positive or negative—has more to do with students' cognitive and academic achievement than does the dialect.

Adapted Instruction

Recognizing Biases towards Non-Standard English

- Recognize areas in which there may be differences in language use and in which those differences might create friction because the minority group's use may be deemed "inferior" by the majority.

- Be honest about your own biases, recognizing that you communicate these biases whether or not you are aware of them.

- Model correct usage without overt correction, and the student in time will self-correct—if the student chooses Standard English as the appropriate sociolinguistic choice for that context.

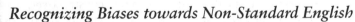

Family Values and School Values

As student populations in U.S. schools become increasingly diversified both linguistically and culturally, teachers and students have come to recognize the important role that attitudes and values play in school success. Not only the individual's attitudes as described above, but also the family's values and attitudes toward schooling, influence a child's school success.

Example of Concept   *Family Values*

Amol is a third-grade student whose parents were born in India. As the only son in a male-dominant culture, he has internalized a strong sense of commitment to becoming a heart surgeon. His approach to classwork is painstaking. Often he is the last to finish an assignment during class. The teacher's main frustration with Amol is that he cannot quickly complete his work. However, when talking with Amol's family, the teacher notes that his parents seem pleased with his perfectionism and not at all concerned with his speed at tasks. In this respect, home and school values differ.

In this example, the teacher epitomizes a mainstream U.S. value: speed and efficiency in learning. Teachers may describe students of other cultures as being lackadaisical and uncaring about learning, when in fact they may be operating within a different time frame and value system.

Other values held by teachers and embodied in classroom procedures have to do with task orientation. The typical U.S. classroom is a place of work in which students are expected to conform to a schedule, keep busy, maintain order, avoid wasting time, conform to authority, and achieve academically in order to attain personal worth. Working alone is also valued in school, and children may spend a great deal of time in activities that do not allow them to interact verbally with other people or to move physically around the room.

Children need to find within the structure and content of their schooling those behaviors and perspectives that permit them to switch between home and school cultural behaviors and values without inner conflict or crises of identity (Pérez & Torres-Guzmán, 2002). Teachers need to feel comfortable with the values and behaviors of their students' cultures in order to develop a flexible cultural repertoire within the context of teaching. The implementation of a rich and flexible cultural repertoire is the strategy that can allow cultures to mix constructively and promote achievement.

The danger of excluding the students' culture(s) from the classroom is that cultural identity, if not included, may become oppositional. Ogbu and Matute-Bianchi (1986) described how oppositional identity in a distinctly Mexican American frame of reference influenced the performance of Mexican American children. They attributed achievement difficulties on the part of some Mexican American children to a distrust of academic effort. When schools were segregated and offered inferior education to this community, a general mistrust of schools caused a difficulty in accepting, internalizing, and following school rules of behavior for achievement. This element of resistance or opposition is not always overt but often takes the form of mental withdrawal, high absenteeism, or reluctance to do classwork.

Adapted Instruction

Accommodating Students' Cultures

Dalle and Young (2003) suggest that teachers check with families to see if family cultures have any "taboos" that would make students uncomfortable performing certain activities; discuss with family members the support available for homework, and arrange for after-class supervision if needed; and explain key concepts using ideas that are familiar from the students' perspective.

Institutional Support for Language-Minority Students

Educators may view a student's ability to speak a home language other than English as an advantage or as a liability toward school success. Those who blame bilingual students for failing in school often operate from the mistaken beliefs that students and/or their parents are uninterested in education; that students who are raised as native speakers of another language are handicapped in learning because they have not acquired sufficient English; or that cultural differences between the ways children learn at home or among their peers and the ways they are expected to learn at school interfere with school learning.

In fact, schools often operate in ways that advantage certain children and disadvantage others, causing distinct outcomes that align with social and political forces in the larger cultural context. Institutional support for the primary language and students who speak it is a prime factor in school success for these students.

Some social theorists see the culture of the school as maintaining the poor in a permanent underclass and as legitimizing inequality (Giroux, 1983). In other words, schooling is used to reaffirm class boundaries. This creates an educational class system in which minority students—or any students who are not successful in the classroom—emerge from their schooling to occupy the same social status as their parents.

Example of Concept *The Way Schools Use Language to Perpetuate Social Class Inequality*

Consider this account from Erickson of a fourth-grade class that was electing student council representatives.

> Mrs. Lark called for nominations. Mary, a monolingual English-speaking European American student, nominated herself. Mrs. Lark accepted Mary's self-nomination and wrote her name on the board. Rogelio, a Spanish-speaking Mexican American child with limited English proficiency, nominated Pedro. Mrs. Lark reminded the class that the representative must be "outspoken." Rogelio again said "Pedro." Mrs. Lark announced to the class again that the representative must be "a good outspoken citizen." Pedro turned red and stared at the floor. Mrs. Lark embarrassed Rogelio into withdrawing the nomination. No other Mexican American child was nominated, and Mary won the election. Pedro and Rogelio were unusually quiet for the rest of the school day.

Source: Adapted from Erickson (1977, p. 59).

Incidents like the one in Mrs. Lark's classroom are generally unintentional on the teacher's part. A beginning step in helping all students feel fully integrated into the class and the learning environment is for teachers to become sensitive to their own cultural and linguistic predispositions.

Nieto and Bode (2008) identified numerous structures within schools that affect English learners: tracking, testing, the curriculum, pedagogy, the school's physical structure and disciplinary policies, the limited roles of both students and teachers, and limited parent and community involvement.

Tracking. The practice of placing students in groups of matched abilities, despite its superficial advantages, in reality often labels and groups children for years and allows them little or no opportunity to change groups. Secondary school personnel who place English learners in low tracks or in nonacademic ELD classes preclude those students from any opportunity for higher-track, precollege work. In contrast, a supportive school environment offers equal education opportunity to all students, regardless of their language background.

Testing. Students who respond poorly on standardized tests are often given "basic skills" in a remedial curriculum that is essentially the same as the one in which they were not experiencing success. A supportive school is one that offers testing adaptations for English learners as permitted by law; for example, academic testing in the primary language, extended time for test taking, and fully trained testing administrators.

Curriculum Design. Only a small fraction of knowledge is codified into textbooks and teachers' guides, and this is rarely the knowledge that English learners bring from their communities (see Loewen, 1995). In addition, the curriculum may be systematically watered down for the "benefit" of children in language-minority communities through the mistaken idea that such students cannot absorb the core curriculum. A supportive environment is one that maintains high standards while offering a curriculum that is challenging and meaningful.

Pedagogy. The way students are taught is often tedious and uninteresting, particularly for students who have been given a basic skills curriculum in a lower-track classroom. The pressure to "cover" a curriculum may exclude learning in depth and frustrate teachers and students alike. Pedagogy that is supportive fully involves students—teachers make every effort to present understandable instruction that engages students at high levels of cognitive stimulation.

The Physical Structure of the School. Architecture also affects the educational environment. Many inner-city schools are built like fortresses to forestall vandalism and theft. Rich suburban school districts, by contrast, may provide more space, more supplies, and campuslike schools for their educationally advantaged students. Supportive schooling is observable—facilities are humane, well cared for, and materially advantaged.

Example of Concept

A School Culture That Disconnects, Bores, and Controls—for Teachers and Students Alike

Order predominated at the traditional high school that Wells (1996) studied. Control trumped creativity. Teachers were not encouraged to voice their educational philosophies or innovate. Instruction was driven by textbooks, with few opportunities for students to write. Reading became an exercise in searching for answers to chapter questions or worksheet blanks. Little inquiry, exploration, or reflection was asked of students. Pope (2002) came to a similar conclusion. Students, for the most part, experienced little genuine engagement. They did schoolwork because they had to—there was little evidence of curiosity or interest. If this is the case for the average middle-class high school, conditions can only be worse in inner-city schools, where the majority of immigrant students are educated.

Disciplinary Policies. Certain students may be punished more often than others, particularly those who wear high-profile clothing, have high physical activity levels, or tend to hold an attitude of resistance toward schooling. Rather than defining students' predilections as deviant or disruptive, teachers can channel these interactions into cooperative groups that allow children to express themselves and learn at the same time, thus supporting rich cultural and linguistic expression.

The School Culture. The most powerful regularities about school are not found in the formalities such as course offerings and schedules. They are found in the school culture—such unspoken elements as the respect shown by students for academic endeavor, the openness that the teachers show when the principal drops in to observe instruction, and the welcome parents feel when they take an active role in the school. In its 1996 report *What Matters Most: Teaching and America's Future*, the National Commission on Teaching and America's Future argued that without a formal overhaul of school culture in America, students cannot learn well. This is a warning that applies especially to the aspects of school culture that promote success for English learners.

The Limited Role of Students. Students may be excluded from taking an active part in their own schooling, and alienation and passive frustration may result. However, in addition to language barriers, cultural differences may preclude some students from participating in ways that the mainstream culture rewards. The accompanying Example of Concept illustrates the ways in which the limited role of students is disempowering.

The Limited Role of Teachers. Teachers of CLD students may be excluded from decision making just as students are disenfranchised. This may lead teachers to have negative feelings toward their students. A supportive environment for CLD students is supportive of their teachers as well.

Example of Concept

The Limited Role of Students

Natisha has not said a word to any of her teachers since the beginning of school. It's not that she was a "bad" student; she turned in assignments and made Bs. She certainly didn't cause her teachers trouble. Therefore Mr. Williams, her high-school counselor, was somewhat surprised to hear she was dropping out of school.

Natisha described her school experiences as coming to school, listening to teachers, and going home. School was boring and not connected to her real life. Nothing she was learning in school could help her get a job. She knew from more than ten years of listening to teachers and reading textbooks that her chances of becoming a news anchorwoman or even a teacher were about the same as winning the lottery.

School had helped silence Natisha. Classes provided no meaningful experience for her. The content may have been important to the teachers, but she could find no relationship to her own world.

Source: Adapted from Gollnick & Chinn (2006, p. 355).

Limited Family and Community Involvement. Inner-city schools with large populations of English learners may exclude families from participation. Parents may find it difficult to attend meetings, may be only symbolically involved in the governance of the school, or may feel a sense of mismatch with the culture of the school just as their children do. In circumstances like these, school personnel, in consultation with community and parent representatives, can begin to ameliorate such perceptions by talking with one another and developing means of communication and interaction appropriate for both parent and school communities.

Academic Risk Factors. Stressful events and conditions during school years create risk factors for academic success. Major obstacles that students face include attending a poorly funded inner-city school or coming from a low-income home in which English is not the primary language. Many students report having their academic capabilities questioned by school personnel: teachers who have low expectations or guidance counselors who advise against attending college or scheduling Advanced Placement (AP) courses. Even when students are placed in AP or honors courses, they are often made to feel as outsiders (Pérez, 2012).

Resilience in the Face of Risk Factors. Personal characteristics can provide protective factors that mitigate risk. Being socially competent plays an important role, as do problem-solving skills, a sense of personal autonomy, and a vision of purpose and positive future (Bernard, 1995). Good communication skills, a sense of responsibility, positive self-concept, optimism, achievement orientation, and a belief in self-help are factors that can be resources in times of stress. Resilient children have more internal and external resources to draw upon when times get tough (Luthar & Zelazo, 2003). These resources are strengthened by still other academically useful traits: forging an academic identity, being competitive, showing tenacity and determination, feeling an obligation to be a role model, and feeling obligated toward one's family (Pérez, 2012).

Coupled with parental support, these internal factors help children to overcome an environment that puts them at risk for school failure.

Academic Engagement. Several distinct school contextual factors encourage students to succeed academically. Being identified early in school as gifted is a huge "plus" toward a student's success, because this designation opens doors to academic enrichment and acceleration opportunities. Academic awards such as prizes for spelling bee competitions, "student of the month" certificates, character awards, achievement awards, and perfect attendance certificates serve as concrete evidence of recognition—especially in elementary and middle schools when students are solidifying their academic identities. Later, in high school, scholarships, sports recognitions, and leadership awards recognized merit and helped students to sustain high academic goals (Pérez, 2012).

Long-Term English Learners. Large numbers of English learners in California (and in other states) are close to the age at which they should be able to graduate from high school but still have not been redesignated. They are not yet considered English proficient—they are the so-called long-term English learners, those who have been in United States schools for more than six years without reaching sufficient English proficiency to be reclassified (Olsen, 2010). They are in the majority (59 percent) of secondary school English learners.

Olsen (2010) describes their history as characterized by their

> receiving no language development program at all; being given elementary school curricula and materials that weren't designed to meet English learner needs; enrollment in weak language development program models and poorly implemented English Learner programs; histories of inconsistent programs; provision of narrowed curricula and only partial access to the full curriculum; social segregation and linguistic isolation; and, cycles of transnational moves. (p. 2)

Often these "long-term" learners have high-functioning social language yet show grave weaknesses in academic language, reading, and writing skills. Worse, many have developed "habits of non-engagement, learned passivity and invisibility in school" (Olsen, 2010, p. 3). Because of their lack of progress, they may be placed into mainstream classes for which they are underprepared, be placed with beginning English learners, be taught by largely unprepared teachers, be precluded from participation in electives, be over-referred and inadequately served in intervention and support classes, and suffer limited access to core or college preparatory curricula.

Recommendations for modifying instruction to address these concerns include providing a specialized English Language Development program that is combined with explicit language and literacy development across the curriculum and taught by teachers skilled in adapting instruction to sustain high-support instructional techniques; placing these students in heterogeneous and rigorous grade-level content classes (including honors, A–G) mixed with English-proficient students; providing heritage language classes (in an articulated sequence through Advanced Placement levels); using a master schedule designed for flexibility and movement as students progress; using systems for monitoring progress and triggering support; and instituting a school wide focus on study skills, among other components.

A supportive classroom environment for CLD students is less effective if the environment or practices of the school are discriminatory.

Sociocultural Support for L1 in the Classroom Environment

Various sociocultural factors influence the support that is offered for the primary language and its speakers in the classroom. Teaching and learning in mainstream classrooms are often organized with social structures that deny the ways in which students are most likely to learn. Many students may benefit from the opportunity to interact with peers as they learn, speaking their primary language if necessary to exchange information.

Cooperative learning has positive results in the education of CLD students. Positive race relations among students and socialization toward pro-social values and behaviors are potential outcomes of a cooperative-learning environment. Students may gain psychological support from one another as they acquire English, and this support can help the students work as a group with the teacher to achieve a workable sociocultural compromise between the use of L1 and L2 in the classroom.

Adapted Instruction

Supporting the Primary Language

- Feature the primary language(s) of students on bulletin boards throughout the school and within the classroom.

- Showcase primary-language skills in written and oral reports.

- Involve primary-language speakers as guests, volunteers, and instructional assistants.

This chapter introduced the English learner and highlighted a variety of factors that a teacher must consider to design and deliver effective instruction. Some of these factors lie within the student, and others are factors in society at large that affect the individual, the family, and the school. The teacher as an intercultural, interlinguistic educator learns everything possible about the background of the students and marshals every available kind of support to advance the education of English learners.

LEARNING MORE

Further Reading

Carolyn Nelson (2004), in the article "Reclaiming Teacher Preparation for Success in High-Needs Schools," describes her first year of teaching in an inner-city school in Rochester, New York. This article offers a memorable glimpse at her daily challenges in a school comprised largely of Puerto Rican and African-American students. She details the strengths of the elementary teacher education curriculum at San José State in the context of preparing teachers as problem-solving intellectuals, a point of view that imparts a balance to the "prescriptive, curriculum-in-a-box" approaches to teaching.

Web Search

The U.S. Census Bureau's website "Minority Links" (online at http://www.census.gov /newsroom/minority_links/minority_links.html) features demographic information on special populations (Hispanic/Latino, Asian, Native Hawaiian and other Pacific Islander, and American Indian/Alaska Native) that includes demographics by regional, state, and local areas.

Exploration

Find out about the number of English learners in your local school district by visiting a local school district office, or look it up in the demographics section of the State Department of Education website in your state. Visit a school in a neighborhood that serves CLD students, or visit your neighborhood school and ask if there are English learners being served. If there are local teachers who specialize in the education of English learners, ask them about professional development opportunities in that field.

Experiment

Give a fifteen-word list in a foreign language to three different individuals: a primary school student (age 6–11), a middle school student (age 12–14), and an adult (age 18 or older). Let them study the words for five minutes and then ask them to recall the list. Compare the success of these learners. Ask them what strategy they used to complete the memory task. Which learner had more success? Which learner had more strategies?

MyEducationLab™

Culture and Self-Esteem

This video discusses that it is important for English-language learners to retain their self-esteem. Often they are made to feel inferior to students from different cultures. Teaching culture should go both ways.

To access the video, go to MyEducationLab (www.myeducationlab.com), choose the Díaz-Rico text, and log in to MyEducationLab for English Language Learners. Select the topic Diversity, and watch the video entitled "Culture and Self-Esteem."

Answer the following questions:

1. How would you define "self-efficacy"? What role does the teacher play in fostering this?

2. What are the possible consequences of teaching without concern for an individual's native culture?

3. What specific teaching strategies should a teacher include to ensure that all students are made to feel valued?

REFERENCES

Alvarez, J. (2007). My English. In R. Spack (Ed.), *Guidelines: A cross-cultural reading/writing text* (pp. 30–35). New York: Cambridge University Press.

Barna, L. M. (2007). Intercultural communication stumbling blocks. In R. Spack (Ed.), *Guidelines: A cross-cultural reading/writing text* (pp. 66–74). New York: Cambridge University Press.

Bernard, B. (1995). *Fostering resiliency in kids: Protective factors in the family school and community.* San Francisco: West Ed Regional Educational Laboratory.

Brown, D. (2007). *Principles of language learning and teaching* (5th ed.). Englewood Cliffs, NJ: Prentice Hall.

Cosentino De Cohen, C., &Clewell, B. C. (2007). *Putting English language learners on the educational map: The No Child Left Behind Act implemented.* Washington, DC: Urban Institute.

Cummins, J. (1979). Cognitive/academic language proficiency, linguistic interdependence, the optimum age question and some other matters. *Working Papers on Bilingualism, 19,* 121–129.

Cummins, J. (2001). *Negotiating identities: Education for empowerment in a diverse society.* Los Angeles: California Association for Bilingual Education.

Dalle, T. S., & Young, L. J. (2003). *PACE yourself: A handbook for ESL tutors.* Alexandria, VA: Teachers of English to Speakers of Other Languages.

Dicker, S. (1992). Societal views of bilingualism and language learning. *TESOL: Applied Linguistics Interest Section Newsletter, 14*(1), 1, 4.

Erickson, F. (1977). Some approaches to inquiry in school-community ethnography. *Anthropology and Education Quarterly, 8*(2), 58–69.

Flynt, E. S., & Cooter, R. B. (1999). *The English–Español reading inventory for the classroom.* Upper Saddle River, NJ: Merrill Prentice Hall.

Gardner, R., & Lambert, W. (1972). *Attitudes and motivation in second language learning.* Rowley, MA: Newbury House.

Giroux, H. (1983). Theories of reproduction and resistance in the new sociology of education: A critical appraisal. *Harvard Educational Review, 53,* 257–293.

Goldenberg, C., & Coleman, R. (2010). *Promoting academic achievement among English learners: A guide to the research.* Thousand Oaks, CA: Corwin.

Gollnick, D. M., & Chinn, P. C. (2006). *Multicultural education in a pluralistic society* (7th ed.). Upper Saddle River, NJ: Merrill Prentice Hall.

Han, Z. (2004). *Fossilization in adult second language acquisition.* Clevedon, Eng.: Multilingual Matters.

Harper, C., & De Jong, E. (2004). Misconceptions about teaching English-language learners. *Journal of Adolescent & Adult Literacy, 48*(2), 162–182.

Hruska-Riechmann, S., & Grasha, A. F. (1982). The Grasha-Riechmann Student Learning Scales: Research findings and applications. In J. Keefe (Ed.), *Student learning styles and brain behavior* (pp. 81–86). Reston, VA: National Association of Secondary School Principals.

Keefe, M. W. (1987). *Learning style theory and practice.* Reston, VA: National Association of Secondary School Principals.

Lapkoff, S., & Li, R. M. (2007). Five trends for schools. *Educational Leadership, 64*(6), 8–15.

Lenneberg, E. (1967). *Biological foundations of language.* New York: Wiley.

Loewen, J. (1995). *Lies my teacher told me.* New York: Touchstone.

Luthar, S. S., & Zelazo, L. B. (2003). Research on resilience: An integrative view. In S. S. Luthar (Ed.), *Resilience and vulnerability: Adaptation in the context of childhood adversities* (pp. 510–549). New York: Cambridge University Press.

Marinova-Todd, S., Marshall, D., & Snow, C. (2000). Three misconceptions about age and L2 learning. *TESOL Quarterly, 34*(1), 9–34.

McKay, J. (2000). Building self-esteem in children. In M. McKay & P. Fanning, *Self-esteem* (3rd ed., pp. 279–313). New York: Barnes and Noble Books.

National Center for Educational Statistics (2011). *State education reforms, Table 2.10. State high school exit exams, by exam characteristics and state: 2010–11.* Online at http://nces.ed.gov/programs/statereform/tab2_10.asp.

National Clearinghouse for English Language Acquisition and Language Instruction Educational Programs (2007). *2005–2008 Poster.* Retrieved July 3, 2008, from http://www.ncela.gwu/stats/2_nation .htm.

National Clearinghouse for English Language Acquisition (NCELA). (2009). The growing numbers of English learner students. Online at www.ncela.gwu.edu/files/uploads/9/growing LEP_0708.pdf.

Nieto, S., & Bode, P. (2008). *Affirming diversity* (5th ed.). Boston: Allyn & Bacon.

Ogbu, J. (1978). *Minority education and caste: The American system in crosscultural perspective.* New York: Academic Press.

Ogbu, J., & Matute-Bianchi, M. (1986). Understanding sociocultural factors: Knowledge, identity, and school adjustment. In *Beyond language: Social and cultural factors in schooling language minority students* (pp. 73–142). Los Angeles: Evaluation, Dissemination and Assessment Center, California State University, Los Angeles.

Olsen, L. (2010). *Reparable harm: Fulfilling the unkept promise of educational opportunity for California's long-term English learners.* Long Beach, CA: Californians Together.

Osgood, K. W. (2002). It takes a class to teach a child: The challenge program. In E. P. Cochran, *Mainstreaming* (pp. 43–51). Alexandria, VA: Teachers of English to Speakers of Other Languages.

Oyama, S. (1976). A sensitive period for the acquisition of nonnative phonological system. *Journal of Psycholinguistic Research, 5,* 261–284.

Pandya, C., McHugh, M., & Batalova, J. (2011). *LEP data brief.* Washington, DC: Migration Policy Institute.

Pappamihiel, N. E. (2002). English as a second language students and English language anxiety: Issues in the mainstream classroom. *Research in the Teaching of English, 36,* 327–355.

Peregoy, S., & Boyle, O. (2013). *Reading, writing, and learning in ESL* (6th ed.). Boston: Pearson.

Pérez, B., & Torres-Guzmán, M. (2002). *Learning in two worlds* (3rd ed.). New York: Longman.

Pérez, W. (2012). *Americans by heart: Undocumented Latino students and the promise of higher education.* New York: Teachers College Press.

Piske, T., Mackay, I. R. A., & Fiege, J. E. (2001). Factors affecting degree of foreign accent in an L2: A Review. *Journal of Phonetics, 29*(2), 191-215.

Pittaway, D. S. (2004). Investment and second language acquisition. *Critical Inquiry in Language Studies: An International Journal, 1*(4), 203–218.

Pope, D. (2002). *Doing school: How we are creating a generation of stressed-out, materialistic, and miseducated students.* New Haven, CT: Yale University Press.

Public Schools of North Carolina. (2004). *The North Carolina competency tests: A handbook for students in the ninth grade for the first time in 2001–2002 and beyond.* Raleigh: Author. Online at www.ncpublicschools.org/accountability/testing/competency.

Rahilly, M. K., & Weinmann, A. (2007). *An overview of Title III programs.* Presentation at the annual conference of the Teachers of English to Speakers of Other Languages, Seattle.

Richard-Amato, P. (2003). *Making it happen* (3rd ed.). White Plains, NY: Longman.

Shin, H. B., & Ortman, J. M. (2011, April). *Language projections: 2010–2020.* Washington, DC: Presentation, Federal Forecasters Conference.

Siccone, F. (1995). *Celebrating diversity: Building self-esteem in today's multicultural classrooms.* Boston: Allyn & Bacon.

Siegel, J. (1999). Stigmatized and standardized varieties in the classroom: Interference or separation? *TESOL Quarterly, 33*(4), 701–728.

Singleton, D., & Ryan, L. (2004). *Language acquisition: The age factor* (2nd ed.). Clevedon, UK: Multilingual Matters.

Snow, C., & Hoefnagel-Hoehle, M. (1978). The critical period for language acquisition: Evidence from second language learning. *Child Development, 49,* 1114–1118.

Sonbuchner, G. M. (1991). *How to take advantage of your learning styles.* Syracuse, NY: New Readers Press.

Tharp, R. (1989b, February). Psychocultural variables and constants: Effects on teaching and learning in schools. *American Psychologist, 44*(2), 349–359.

U.S. Department of Education (2011). *Winning the future: Improving education for the Latino community.* Washington, DC: Author.

Wells, M. C. (1996). *Literacies lost: When students move from a progressive middle school to a traditional high school.* New York: Teachers College Press.

Woolfolk, A. (2007). *Educational psychology* (10th ed.). Boston: Allyn & Bacon.

PHOTO CREDITS

CHAPTER 5

Learning Strategies

- *Sergio* was unable to use his native Spanish to search for clues and links to English vocabulary. What type of learning strategy might help him?

- *Habiba* constantly confused the steps for solving math word problems. What kind of instruction could the teacher choose?

- *Thongsy* seemed lost when reading and writing tasks were assigned in history. What learning strategies might improve his performance?

Sheltered instruction is a process by which subject matter instruction is made more meaningful and accessible to English learners (ELs). As Chapter 3 indicates, effective sheltered lessons include many features, and while every content lesson may not include all features, teachers need to incorporate each feature into weekly planning and instruction. For example, use of higher-order thinking skills is an important feature of sheltered instruction that should be a part of lessons each week. In addition, learning strategy instruction may be a part of the daily planning and instruction cycle depending on the needs of the learners.

Teachers must be sensitive to the fact that ELs have extraordinary cognitive burdens when learning new information in English. Students with learning and behavioral challenges also experience cognitive overload when learning new information. Hence,

Bob Daemmrich/PhotoEdit

From Chapter 5 of *Sheltered Content Instruction: Teaching English Learners with Diverse Abilities*, 4/e.
Jana Echevarría. Anne Graves. Copyright © 2011 by Pearson Education. All rights reserved.

English learners with learning and behavioral difficulties can have exceedingly taxing cognitive burdens when learning in English. Students can be so overwhelmed by the process of deriving meaning from a second language that they do not spontaneously generate the strategies needed for efficient and effective learning (Lee, 1986; Ortiz & Graves, 2001; Yang, 1999). Teachers can facilitate learning by directly teaching strategies. Explicit instruction of learning strategies increases the comfort and learning potential of students needing support and has a long history of research supporting its efficacy in the fields of educational psychology, special education, and general education, including English learners (August & Shanahan, 2006; Dutro & Kinsella, in press: Vaughn, Wanzek, Murray, Scammacca, Linan-Thompson, & Woodruff, 2009; Fitzgerald & Graves, 2004; Gersten, Taylor, & Graves, 1999; Graham & Harris, 2005; Graves, Gersten, & Haager, 2004). Those students needing learning-strategies instruction often have content-area, academic, and English-language development issues. They present learning challenges and require language-sensitive instruction (Baca & Cervantes, 2004; Jiménez & Gersten, 1999; McIntosh, Graves, & Gersten, 2007). Language-sensitive instruction focuses simultaneously on developing content-area knowledge, academic proficiency, and English-language proficiency (Gersten, Baker, Haager, & Graves, 2005; Jiménez, 2003).

The goals of this chapter are to (1) define learning strategy and delineate types of learning strategies, (2) present examples of specific strategies for reading, writing, and content areas, (3) provide guidelines for selecting learning strategies, (4) describe lesson formats for teaching learning strategies, and (5) identify presentation methods to use in teaching learning strategies. Each section contains specific lesson and classroom descriptions.

Types of Learning Strategies

A learning strategy is a series of steps that can be repeated over and over to solve a problem or to complete a task. Some students develop learning strategies on their own. Obviously, the teacher would not teach these students strategies explicitly. Instead, the teacher should simply encourage them to use effective strategies.

There is a long history of the use of learning strategies instruction in the field of learning disabilities (Gersten & Baker, 2000). These same and similar strategies have been found to be effective with anyone who is struggling in school including English learners. The issues around whether a student has a true disability are very complex (Figueroa & Newsome, 2006; Rueda & Windmueller, 2006). In any case, the use of learning strategies instruction can serve as a prevention for unnecessary labeling and is critical for teachers to consider whenever students may be struggling to keep up in school or to learn content taught in English.

A teacher can formulate and explicitly teach strategies when students do not develop them on their own. To use learning strategies in thinking, reading, and writing in content area work, teachers can provide a minilesson (about 15 minutes daily) on the strategy (Ellis & Graves, 1990). Using a minilesson allows students to learn the strategy in a controlled practice situation during a designated period of time. Teachers can provide opportunities to memorize and use the strategy during a practice session before requiring strategy use in a content area application. Learning strategies can be developed not only for academics but for language acquisition and many other areas, such as social skills and vocational skills. Learning strategies are not a curriculum. Instead, strategies are used as a part of the curriculum to enhance access to content, academic, or life skills proficiency. Strategies

FIGURE 5.1 Science Strategy: Steps for an Experiment

Step 1: Write or state the purpose of the experiment and the expected outcome.

Step 2: Gather materials.

Step 3: Write a summary of the procedures.

Step 4: Carry out the experiment (observe and take notes).

Step 5: Write exact results.

Step 6: Discuss and summarize expectations versus actual results and what the results mean.

enhancing access to content are used in literature, science, social studies, and math classes and facilitate gaining knowledge. For example, the steps for writing about an experiment is a science strategy taught at the beginning of the school year. It should increase the knowledge a student gains from science lessons (see Figure 5.1). The science strategy can be reused for future science work and can be used as a general problem-solving method by studying information systematically.

Strategies can enhance language acquisition and second-language listening and thinking skills. Such learning strategies provide a series of steps to integrate language knowledge and content knowledge (Brown & Doolittle, 2008; Cloud, Genessee, & Hamayan, 2009; Fitzgerald & Graves, 2004; Gersten, Taylor, & Graves, 1999; Herrell, 2000; Jiménez, 2003; Jiménez, García, & Pearson, 1996). For example, the use-of-cognates strategy has five steps (see Figure 5.2). Other language-acquisition strategies can be used to think back and forth between languages and to help focus thinking while listening (Fitzgerald, 2003; Klinger, Artilles, & Barletta, 2006).

Strategies enhancing academic proficiency can improve the reading, writing, language, or math work of students (Vaughn et al., 2009; August & Shanahan, 2006). For example, finding main ideas is a reading strategy important to academic proficiency and useful in many different learning situations (see Figure 5.3). Think about Thongsy who was referred to at the beginning of this chapter. For him and other students like him, reading comprehension strategies can be very helpful for developing academic proficiency. A learning strategy such as one to assist students in "finding main ideas" can benefit a student in all pursuits involving reading.

In addition, for students who are struggling with behavior problems or other issues related to conduct in school, to assist students in learning to get along with peers and teachers, social skills strategies and interpersonal strategies can be taught as early as preschool. For example, in social situations, students may need to learn how to solve a problem (see Figure 5.4). Students can be taught the series of steps necessary to solve a social problem. As they mature, the life skills strategies could relate more to community or work-related situations. Teaching social skills is very important as students progress through school and pursue adult activities. Life skills strategies enhance

FIGURE 5.2 Use-of-Cognates Strategy

Step 1: Read the unfamiliar word in English.

Step 2: Note the spelling of the word.

Step 3: Think of a word that looks or sounds like the English word, a *cognate,* in your primary language.

Step 4: Think of what that cognate means in your primary language.

Step 5: Guess at the meaning of the unfamiliar word in English.

FIGURE 5.3 Finding Main Ideas

Step 1:	Read the paragraph.
Step 2:	Decide what the whole paragraph is about.
Step 3:	Note a few details as well.
Step 4:	Test to make sure you have the best answer (the answer that tells what the whole paragraph is about).
Step 5:	Reread and start over if you are not sure.
Step 6:	If you are sure, write the main idea down.

proficiency in social, vocational, and transition skills. Enhanced proficiency in these areas improves the interpersonal skills and job-related abilities of students and prepares them for the future.

Examples of Specific Strategies in Teaching Reading and Writing in Content Areas

In a study in the San Diego schools, nine multiple-language, first-grade classroom teachers were observed and rated (Gersten et al., 2005). Their students were assessed on oral reading fluency as part of a small battery of assessments (Graves, Gersten, & Haager, 2004; Graves, Plasencia-Peinado, Deno, & Johnson, 2005). The classrooms were very diverse; for example, in one room, there were five Spanish speakers, seven Somali speakers, three Cambodian speakers, two Hmong speakers, and three Vietnamese speakers. Teachers in these classrooms were compelled to teach in English because it provided common ground for all of the students. Native-language instruction was a logistical impossibility. Results of this study indicated extremely positive ratings for two teachers, and predictably, those teachers' students earned the highest outcome scores on oral reading fluency. Moderately strong correlations ($r = .65$) were found between student outcomes in oral reading fluency at the end of first grade and teacher ratings. Similar patterns were found between English learners and non-English learners in rate and mastery of English reading. These results are similar to those found by others (Chiappe, Siegel, & Wade-Wolley, 2002; Geva, Yaghoub-Zadeh, & Schuster, 2000; Haager & Windmueller, 2001).

Both teachers demonstrated a skill for maximizing time on task, amount of work produced, time spent reading, appropriate length for teaching segments, specialized small-group instruction, structured daily routines, consistent homework assignments, daily writing tasks, assessment of reading and writing progress, and English-as-a-second language development. Written work was corrected on a daily basis, and students were often required to self-correct errors. Both teachers had amassed multiple sets of decodable

FIGURE 5.4 Social Skills Strategy: Solving a Problem

Step 1:	Say the problem.
Step 2:	Keep a calm body (count to 10).
Step 3:	Think of three possible solutions.
Step 4:	Decide which is the best solution and do it.
Step 5:	Use positive self-talk afterward, telling yourself you did the best you could.

texts and used them regularly to enhance student reading. Students had their own boxes of books at their desks, including books of different genres and reading levels, but at least 50 percent of the books in each student's box were at his or her own level of decoding.

Mara, the teacher who received the highest score (3.75), used a structured reading instruction program that included a comprehensive curriculum with special emphasis on phonological awareness and phonics. She appeared to enjoy the challenge of following the linear scope and sequence that the reading series provided along with structured lesson plans. She tended to be quite systematic in her approach to teaching language arts, including consistent assessment and remediation for low performers. Dana, who also received a very high score (3.5), tended to teach reading by pulling materials from many sources of many eclectic origins. She used leveled readers and assigned students to homogeneous small groups that met on a regular basis, and she was diligent about assessment of reading and writing progress. The scope and sequence she used was part of an oral tradition that she can talk about when interviewed but for which she does not have an exact written source. Because she does not use a specific reading series, her activities and segments of instruction are often unique and draw from a range of sources. She was observed delivering instruction in critical domains for reading instruction, such as phonological awareness, phonics, concepts about print, spelling, writing, comprehension, and critical thinking. She is particularly skilled at comprehension questions related to reading material and critical thinking. Videotaped interviews and observations of the two teachers indicated that both teachers use sheltered techniques and considered affective issues, as outlined in Chapters 3 and 4 of this book.

Teaching Reading Strategies in Content-Area Classes

This section contains a series of classroom observations of teachers teaching English as a second language (Graves, 1998). To illustrate good reading strategy instruction, three classroom observations are presented. First, in the context of teaching a unit on coastal Native American tribes, a sixth-grade EL teacher taught the concept of finding main ideas. Similarly, a seventh-grade science teacher taught the compare-and-contrast technique as part of a unit on ecosystems. Finally, an eighth-grade history teacher taught about using a timeline for notetaking while beginning a unit on the colonial period.

The sixth-grade teacher started the Native American tribes unit by showing pictures of coastal tribes and recovered artifacts. The teacher also read some information about various tribes. As part of the effort to teach reading explicitly while covering content, the teacher established a lesson plan based on informal student assessment. The teacher used about 15 minutes a day to develop reading skills specifically during the history unit. Typically, at the beginning of the period, the teacher put a simple paragraph about a Native American tribe with a definite main idea on the overhead projector and gave each student a copy of the paragraph (see Figure 5.5). The overhead transparency and handouts provided visual reinforcement for the students. On the first day, the teacher taught main ideas explicitly. He said, "A main idea tells what the whole paragraph is about. It does not tell what part of the paragraph is about, but it tells what the whole paragraph is about. Watch me as I read this paragraph and decide what the whole paragraph is about." He continued, "Ask yourself if you know the main idea. If you do, make a check at the bottom. If not, go back and reread."

The series of steps used by the teacher was based on research demonstrating the effectiveness of the explicit strategy instruction when teaching reading and writing (Graves, 1986; Graves & Levin, 1989). On subsequent days, the teacher and the students found

FIGURE 5.5 Finding the Main Idea

The Chumash once flourished on the southern coast of California. They traveled back and forth between the mainland and the Channel Islands, which are just off the coast. They fished and grew crops for food. The artifacts that they left behind let us know that the most important animal to the Chumash was the dolphin. They made many picture stories in caves and on rocks that include dolphins. War with the Spanish con-questadors and others caused the decline of this great people.

---

main ideas together. The students then worked alone and started to develop confidence and competence. Each day, the students looked pleased with their success. The teacher learned that students taught explicitly and then given a range of practice opportunities learned faster and were able to use the skills mastered longer. Later in the year, the students used their strategy for finding the main idea to write reports about what they were reading.

A seventh-grade science teacher had students construct freshwater and saltwater aquariums for a unit on ecosystems. The students wrote reports about the aquariums before constructing them and were integrally involved in the planning and building of each aquarium. After the aquariums were completed, the students wrote about their observations and formulated hypotheses about observed changes in the aquariums.

The teacher combined the activities with daily minilessons in reading to provide strategies for increasing reading comprehension. For example, she developed a series of 15- to 20-minute segments of instruction on appropriate strategies to use when students were asked to compare. On the first day of the series of lessons, the teacher said, "Watch while I show you a way to compare two items." She drew a Venn diagram (two overlapping circles) on the board. The students were then asked to compare a seahorse to an octopus. The teacher held up a picture of each animal and taped one picture in the outside portion of each circle. She asked the students to describe each animal and made notes under the pictures in each circle. One student said a seahorse is a fish and has a head like a horse. The teacher then asked, "How are they alike?" and wrote the students' comments in the overlapping part of the circles. Students said that both animals live in the ocean, and the teacher added that females in both animals lay eggs. After this initial example, the teacher said, "Now, in your groups, compare the freshwater ecosystem to the saltwater ecosystem." Each student group was given a large Venn diagram drawn on posterboard. Each diagram had a picture of the saltwater ecosystem taped above the left circle and a picture of the freshwater ecosystem taped above the right circle. The students appeared to transfer the knowledge rapidly and learned a strategy for comparing.

An eleventh-grade history teacher used many demonstrations and visual images, such as maps, globes, graphs, charts, and timelines. To teach the students how to maximize comprehensible input while reading, the teacher demonstrated making a timeline. To provide students explicit instruction, the teacher started the unit by making a timeline of his own life from birth to that day. A personal timeline was drawn on the board with major life events entered in order. The teacher then assisted the students in constructing their own personal timelines and posted the timelines on the bulletin board. In the last 20 minutes of class, the teacher had the students read through the assigned chapter. The teacher made a historical timeline beginning with discussions of early settlements in Africa followed by northern migration of people in concert with climate changes. Students filled in a blank timeline along with the teacher as the discussion ensued. With each new chapter, the students were asked to fill in a blank timeline with the information from the chapter and keep all the timelines together in one section of their notebooks.

Teaching Writing Strategies in Content-Area Classes

Research has yielded valuable information about teaching writing to students who are struggling in school (Englert, 2009; Graham & Harris, 2005; Graves & Montague, 1991; Graham & Harris, 2009; Ruiz, 1995a, 1995b). Good writers often use a recursive or circular process during composing (Graves, Semmel, & Gerber, 1994). Students should learn five basic writing steps:

1. Prewriting or planning
2. Composing
3. Revising
4. Editing
5. Final draft or publishing

The circle in Figure 5.6 represents writing-as-a-process, and the arrows pointing each way indicate that a writer can take any number of paths in composing. The writer could start with planning or composing, go back to revising, start composing again, and then go back to revising and editing before completing the final draft.

Writer's Workshop, developed largely by Donald Graves (1983), consists of journal writing, prewriting activities for narrative or expository compositions, the five stages described as writing-as-a-process, and sharing and publishing final drafts. Writer's Workshop is a viable approach up through sixth grade for students learning English (Graves & Rueda, 2008; Graham & Harris, 2009; Graves, Valles, & Rueda, 2000; Ruiz, 1995a, 1995b), although it can also be effective with older students who have had uneven school experience and are poor writers. Writer's Workshop has been used extensively for students in general education as well as for students who are having problems in school (Englert, 2009; Graham & Harris, 2009; Graves, Valles, & Rueda, 2000; Ruiz, 1995a, 1995b).

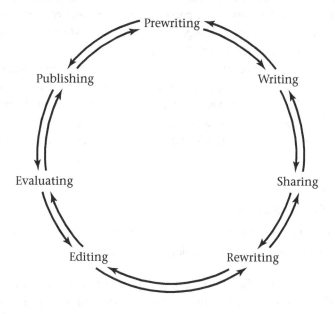

FIGURE 5.6 Writing-as-a-Process

Based on observations in upper elementary and secondary school, two descriptions of classroom practices for teaching writing are presented here. A fourth and a ninth-grade classroom are described. In each classroom teachers used Writer's Workshop while teaching writing to students learning English. In each of these classrooms, teachers often taught strategies and skills explicitly as a supplement to adapted versions of Writer's Workshop.

In a fourth-grade class, the teacher used explicit strategy instruction in writing. After teaching the students each step of the writing process overtly, the teacher used different colors of paper to represent the stages of writing (Englert, 2009). Planning was completed on yellow paper, the first draft on orange paper, and the final draft was completed on the computer or on white paper. Revising was accomplished on the orange paper by marking through and correcting spelling and punctuation. Students engaged in the process at least once a week. The students learned to start the writing process by expressing ideas. The writing process occurred in predictable stages.

The teacher consistently used about one-third of the time for writing; one-third for sharing, presenting, revising, or editing; and one-third for minilessons or teacher-directed learning (see Figure 5.11 on page 93). The teacher did not accomplish all three aspects each day but spent more than 1 hour each week on writing; this amount of time spent writing is supported by research (Lewis, Graves, Ashton, & Kieley, 1997). The teacher asked the students to pretend they lived at the time of the California gold rush and to write stories about their adventures. The students had 20 minutes each day during the week to complete the assignment. The teacher chose the narrative genre because students are usually comfortable with story structure. When writing in a new language, students must be comfortable with the genre. Story writing often makes history come alive for students. The teacher led a student brainstorming activity to help them get started. The students created their own story webs or outlines, drew illustrations, and wrote first drafts.

For students floundering on the narrative story structure, the teacher used the story grammar cueing system (Graves, Montague, & Wong, 1990). The cueing system is a list of the story grammar parts (setting, characters, problem, resolution, and ending). The students were instructed to think about the parts as they wrote and revised their stories (Graham & Harris, 2009; Graves & Hauge, 1993; Graves & Montague, 1991). The cueing system required the students to reflect on the steps.

During the next lesson, the students formed peer pairs and made corrections and changes to their stories. The peer revision provided each student with abundant feedback. The teacher provided a revision format during several minilessons. This process could be expanded to include more formal sessions using peer tutoring (see Greenwood et al., 2001). The revision strategy included four questions for students to ask themselves about their stories:

1. Does the story make sense?
2. What do I like about the story?
3. Does the story have characters, a setting, a problem, a resolution, and an ending?
4. Is the capitalization, overall appearance, punctuation, and spelling correct?

The students needed a significant amount of time to complete the assignment. Teacher intervention was necessary to ensure accomplishment. At the end of the week, the students wrote final drafts on the computer and created a class book. The book was shared with the other fourth-grade classes and was given to the school library as a gift.

Introduction:
• Theme
• Three Ideas

Idea and Three Details

Idea and Three Details

Idea and Three Details

Conclusion:
• Restate Theme
• Summary of Three Ideas

FIGURE 5.7 Five-Paragraph Essay Format

A ninth-grade English teacher noted that her students were struggling with writing expository material. The teacher decided to use a think-aloud modeling procedure to teach report writing. As the teacher read to the students about the colonial tradition of Thanksgiving, the notetaking process was modeled on the overhead projector. After the reading and notetaking lesson, the teacher taught the five-paragraph essay strategy and gave the students a handout with the format of that strategy specified (see Figure 5.7). The format called for an introductory paragraph, three supporting paragraphs, and a concluding paragraph. The teacher then modeled essay writing by using the format to think aloud about a topic. The students were encouraged to make comments and suggestions as the outline was constructed on the overhead projector. If students were each assigned a role, this could be set up as cooperative learning (Chambers, Cheung, Madden, Stavin, & Gifford, 2006). Finally, the teacher talked with students about the accuracy and logic of the outline.

After the outlining process on the topic of Thanksgiving, the teacher used the overhead projector again and wrote a report on it in concert with student participation. At another time, the students worked together in table groups and wrote reports about famous people in colonial history, such as Pocahontas, John Smith, and Miles Standish. For 20 minutes each day over the course of a week, each group completed five tasks: reading together while taking notes on orange paper, preparing an outline on pink paper, preparing a first draft on yellow paper, editing the first draft, and entering a final draft into the computer at the end of the week. During the next week, the groups shared their reports with the rest of the class. The students' writing quality was good compared to work done before they had been exposed to the essay strategy and the writing-as-a-process strategy.

Guidelines for Selecting a Learning Strategy

Students can learn strategies that provide maximum benefits and that can be used in a multiplicity of settings. The following guidelines can assist teachers in determining the strategies most beneficial to students. First, determine the exact knowledge or proficiency level of the student. Second, determine the strategies the student would use the most. Consider teaching the simplest and most useful strategies first, and introduce them in an order that reflects the content curriculum and proficiency goals for the year. Finally, use simple wording and the fewest number of steps when teaching each strategy.

Determine Levels of Knowledge

Teachers are concerned about students' levels of content knowledge and academic and language proficiency (Espin, Scierka, Skare, & Halverson, 1999). A teacher must determine the level of knowledge students possess in literature, math, science, or social studies and then mold instruction to fit what the students do or do not know. The teacher can use information assessment to determine the current reading, studying, and computational skills of students and teach accordingly. Based on the informal assessment phase, the teacher can construct new materials or use existing materials to test students. The tests may be traditional or nontraditional. For example, the nontraditional test might ask students to choose a book and read a few pages out loud. From the test, the teacher can gather baseline information on reading skills, reading level, and reading comprehension. Examples of tests that provide valuable performance information on basic skills include the Diagnostic Indicators of Basic Early Literacy Skills (Good & Kaminski, 1996) and Curriculum-Based Measurement (Deno, 1985; Espin et al., 1999; Graves, Plasencia-Peinado, Deno, & Johnson, 2005). The tests allow the teacher to determine what students know and what to teach. Strategies may be part of the curriculum. For example, if at the beginning of the year the teacher finds that history students do not know the steps needed for making an outline, the teacher might teach everyone a strategy for outlining. If the teacher determines that students have difficulty writing an expository paragraph, the teacher might teach the steps for writing a paragraph and provide a useful strategy for improved academic proficiency. For example, the teacher might teach students to use an introductory sentence describing the intended content, three detail sentences elaborating on the content, and a conclusion sentence summarizing the content.

Determine Which Strategies Will Be Most Useful

A teacher teaching the paragraph-writing strategy fulfills the second guideline for choosing a strategy, because the learning strategy is useful in other subjects and other life tasks. Grade, performance level, and life goals are important considerations when determining the strategies most useful to students. For example, in middle school math, for students struggling with English and who have very weak math skills, a teacher would be more likely to teach a check-writing strategy than a scientific notation strategy. Teachers should teach strategies that students can use over and over again. For example, strategies for finding the main idea in reading or regrouping in math obviously have significant applications. On the other hand, teachers may need to teach scientific notation as part of math instruction, but they would be wise not to create a formal strategy for this because it may not have broad enough application. If teachers create strategies for everything students are learning, students will be less likely to remember the key strategies and their long-term applications.

Decide Order of Instruction

Once the most beneficial strategies are determined, the teacher must decide the teaching order. He or she should analyze the strategies and decide if they are embedded in one another or if one strategy is a prerequisite of another. For example, when students need to learn notetaking from chapters in a book, finding main ideas is a prerequisite. The teacher can focus on the steps for finding main ideas until the skill is mastered by the students. The notetaking strategy will be easier to teach once students can successfully find the main ideas in a section or chapter and then write notes about them.

Use Simple Wording and the Fewest Number of Steps

For students to understand a strategy, each step must be as simple as possible. Students are more likely to remember a strategy if it is stated in clear, concise words. Teachers should highlight or underline keywords within steps and encourage the students to memorize the keywords. Unnecessary words and steps should be eliminated to simplify the strategy. The teacher must think: Is the strategy as simple as possible? Are all the words clear and necessary? Many times, students will start to memorize strategy steps and reword what teachers have specified. The teacher can facilitate learning by changing the strategy to conform to the student-created version if it improves the efficiency of the strategy or the economy of words. Some teachers use acronyms when teaching strategies by taking the first letter of each of the steps to form a new word. This mnemonic device often facilitates the memorization of a strategy. For example, for the editing strategy capitalization, overall appearance, punctuation, spelling, COPS is a great acronym (see Figure 5.8). The teacher can reinforce the strategy with the visual image of a "cop" looking over the paper to make sure everything is correct. However, an acronym should not be used as a mnemonic device if it must be forced in place. Teachers should not try to create an acronym by using sophisticated wording or stretching the strategy to accommodate it. Students focus on memorizing the keywords of a simple strategy quickly and often do not need an acronym to remember the strategy. If a strategy becomes more complex in order to create an acronym that works, the teacher can defeat the purpose of the learning strategy (that is, to enhance the academic and language proficiency of the learner).

FIGURE 5.8 The COPS Strategy

- Capitalization
- Overall appearance of paper
- Punctuation
- Spelling

Teaching Learning Strategies

Research indicates explicit instruction in learning strategies facilitates and improves proficiency for students with learning and behavioral challenges and for language (Abedi & Lord, 2001; Graham & Harris, 2005; Graves & Rueda, 2008; Linan-Thompson, Cirino, & Vaughn, 2007). Explicit instruction requires sound lesson structure, lesson preparation, and extensive teacher–student interaction to enhance learning.

Optimal learning strategy instruction requires a teacher to (1) determine the necessary preskills students need to learn the strategy and to teach them, (2) arrange lessons with an opening, a body (including modeling and guided practice), and a closing, (3) plan a series of lessons over time to allow the mastery and generalized use of the strategy, and (4) add a self-monitoring component requiring students to check-off steps when they use the strategy.

Determine Preskills and Preteach Them

The teacher can analyze the strategy and list all of the preskills a student must know before the strategy will be easy for the student to learn. A strategy involves a multiplicity of actions. Students will learn the strategy more easily if the difficult steps are taught before the complete strategy is introduced. If students are unable to perform the difficult steps, the entire strategy will be more difficult to accomplish.

Embedded in the steps of a strategy are preskills, concepts, and rules. For example, if a teacher decides to teach an editing strategy to students, such as the COPS strategy (see Figure 5.8), necessary preskills are the ability to write a paragraph, the ability to use correct sentence structure, and handwriting proficiency. Some concepts for the successful use of this strategy are capitalization, neatness, punctuation, and spelling. Some rules for the successful use of this strategy are:

1. Capitalize the first word in each sentence.
2. Capitalize proper nouns.
3. Write on the line.
4. Use the one-finger rule between words.
5. Use the two-finger rule between sentences.
6. Indent paragraphs.
7. Use an end punctuation mark.
8. Try to spell words correctly but check to determine correctness.

Students may need significant instruction in these underlying concepts and rules before they can successfully learn the editing strategy. Rules are taught by focusing on critical attributes, which are the defining elements of each rule. Defining elements are used to create examples to illustrate a rule. Defining elements are also used to create nonexamples to sharpen understanding of the application of the rule. The nonexamples serve as distracters in an example set and hone the discrimination skills necessary for correct rule applications. For example, in teaching students to indent paragraphs, the teacher will show what a proper indentation is and what it is not in order to clarify exactly how to follow the rule. Lessons that focus on the rules are important precursors to strategy instruction. Once the identified concepts and rules are mastered, students are better prepared to learn a strategy. Learning a strategy requires automatic knowledge of all preskills. This allows the student to focus on the application of the strategy and helps the student avoid a struggle with the semantic or procedural knowledge that is inevitably embedded in the strategy.

Include an Opening, a Body, and a Closing

Opening.   At the beginning of each strategy instruction minilesson, the teacher should review relevant preskills. For example, in the COPS strategy lesson, the teacher might review rules for capitalization, neatness, and punctuation before introducing the strategy. The teacher should also describe the strategy and explain how the strategy can be used. For example, to introduce a strategy on good listening, the teacher tells the students about the importance of listening and talks to them about when not listening could adversely affect them (for example, if the teacher tells them to raise their hands if they like ice cream, because Juan's mother is bringing ice cream for everyone who raises a hand). The teacher might also ask students to think of times when good listening is important. After the students understand why the strategy is important, the teacher should state the goal of the lesson. The teacher might tell them that for the next few weeks, they are going to work very hard on becoming good listeners and that today they are to learn some steps to follow to become good listeners. Teachers must use language the students understand to emphasize what is being taught and to explain why the students will benefit from learning the strategy.

Body.   The body of the strategy instruction minilesson contains three basic steps.

1. The teacher demonstrates or models.
2. The teacher and students practice together.
3. Students practice using the strategy independently.

The demonstration and modeling by the teacher is the most critical part of the lesson. A strategy should be taught using a two-stage model. The first stage is verbal rehearsal. The steps of the strategy are explicitly stated, and the students practice the words of the steps over and over. If the students are readers, the students should be given a list of the steps, and the steps should be written on a wall chart or shown on the overhead projector. The teachers can underline or highlight the key words for each step and illustrate any action involved in the step. For example, if students are learning a good-listening strategy, the teacher might draw a set of eyes beside the step "Look at the person" (see Figure 5.9). In a more elaborate strategy, such as COPS, for the step "Capitalization,"

Step 1:   Look at the person

Step 2:   Keep your hands and body still

Step 3:   Keep a pleasant face

FIGURE 5.9 Good Listener Strategy (including use of visuals)

FIGURE 5.10 Capitalization in the COPS Strategy*

Step 1:   Check for Capitalization
           (Capitalization Rules)
  • Each sentence must begin with a capital letter.
  • Each proper noun must begin with a capital letter.

*See Figure 5.8 for the complete COPS strategy.

the teacher might write capital letters beside the step and write the two rules for capitalization in smaller print underneath or beside it (see Figure 5.10).

The second stage of modeling is the physical model. During this stage, the teacher actually demonstrates the strategy step-by-step for students. As part of the demonstration, the teacher might think-aloud through each step. In teaching the COPS strategy, the teacher might say, "Step 1: Check for capitalization. Hmmm, I'd better think about each rule for capitalization. The first one is: Each sentence must begin with a capital letter. Hmmm, does each sentence begin with a capital letter? Yes, but here's one that doesn't; I'd better fix it." The teacher can continue to demonstrate each step by correcting a writing sample shown on an overhead transparency. After the teacher has demonstrated the steps of the strategy sufficiently, students can be asked to practice the process with the teacher. The teacher uses new examples of sentences that need to be corrected and continues to apply the steps of the strategy, working together with the students. For the COPS strategy, the teacher and the students go through each step talking about it and answering together. Students are encouraged to ask questions and to continue practicing the steps of the strategy until no errors occur. If errors do occur, the teacher can repeat the demonstration, modeling in a similar manner to the original. Hearing the same words from the teacher and seeing the same behaviors reinforces the steps for the students and helps clear up any misunderstandings. In the final part of the body of the lesson, teachers give feedback while the students practice the strategy on their own. The students may work in small groups, in pairs, or on their own when practicing the steps and completing the strategy. The first practice examples should be short and simple. The following samples should progress to grade-appropriate and perhaps to more difficult examples. After enough varied practice, students should be able to apply the strategy to different situations. The examples show how the strategy is applied to other subjects and to real-life situations such as letter writing.

Closing.   At the end of each lesson, the teacher may focus the students on homework or on the lessons to follow. During the closing, the teacher typically assigns independent practice for a later time during class or as homework. The teacher can also preview the next lesson or review the strategy by repeating the steps or by asking the students to reflect on uses for the strategy.

Plan a Series of Lessons

A lesson plan for most days should include work on the strategy preskills, concepts, or rules. Over time, given enough instruction and practice, students can master the strategy. A 10- to 15-minute minilesson on the strategy works best as part of the instructional period (see Figure 5.11). For example, in elementary school typically an hour-and-a-half is designated for language arts. During that time, the students may engage in various 15- to 20-minute activities. Focusing on an important learning strategy could be just one

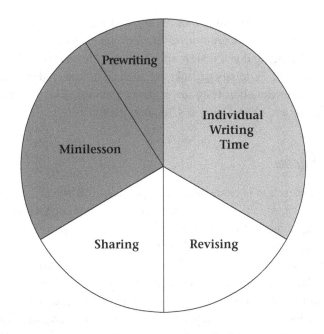

FIGURE 5.11 Writing Instruction Time Management

of the segments of the language arts or content area instructional period. If the strategy is taught, be sure to post it on the wall or on the student's desk or in the notebook to enhance memory and use. Strategy instruction is not intended to be a one-time lesson; instead, the instruction becomes a strand, stretching across several weeks. A series of lessons provides the students ample time to practice, apply, and master the strategy.

Presentation Methods Used to Teach Learning Strategies

The type of interaction a teacher chooses to maximize student learning is based on many of the aspects of sheltered instruction. For strategy instruction, teachers can focus on (1) active student involvement with maximum student participation, (2) the appropriate pace that helps students to move neither too rapidly nor too slowly through the material, (3) careful monitoring so error correction occurs immediately, or (4) independent practice, controlled practice, and grade-appropriate practice.

Active Student Involvement with Maximum Student Participation

Active student involvement is a recurrent theme throughout this book, as it is in the literature on instruction for English learners. In the context of learning-strategy instruction, teachers may ask students to tell them about why a strategy will be useful. Teachers can ask students to talk more about when a strategy could be used and what has happened when they have used the strategy. They can ask what made the strategy work and what could be done to make it work better the next time. The teacher can also ask students to engage in verbal rehearsal of the steps of the strategy. During practice the teacher can ask, "Did we use the strategy properly? How do you know?" When the teacher poses questions like this often throughout demonstration and practice sessions, accuracy can be monitored to ensure maximum learner involvement. The teacher can require the students to think about the strategy and can determine whether each student is absolutely sure of the correct application of a strategy or lacks confidence or knowledge. The more active involvement the teacher can elicit from the students, the more likely the students are to learn (Baca & Cervantes, 2004; Harry & Klingner, 2006).

Appropriate Pacing

Effective teacher interaction is characterized by precise, slow speech, gestures, and controlled vocabulary. Controlled vocabulary involves the use of cognates and the limited use of idiomatic expressions. Consistent wording without the use of synonyms is critical for efficient language development. Teachers are most successful when they avoid references to reading materials and cultural information that are not familiar to the learners (Jiménez, 2003). Pacing is also important. Teachers need to know when to move through lessons quickly and when to move through them slowly. A teacher should quicken the pace when the confidence and accuracy level of the students increases. The opposite is true when students make errors or struggle with the strategy application. When students are learning information for the first time, a teacher must pace the lesson carefully so the students capture the content. It is better for a teacher to proceed slowly during the modeling and prompting than to go back and correct errors or to repeat lessons. Of course, at times the latter is necessary and can be the appropriate choice.

Monitor and Correct Errors

The teacher can monitor each phase of a lesson to decide how to pace the lesson, which lesson parts to repeat, and which examples will maximize learning. This monitoring provides teachers with information on when to mediate learning and when to provide student feedback. During strategy instruction, error correction is determined by the type of response the student gives. If the error is careless, the teacher may ask the student to repeat the answer. If the error is due to a lack of knowledge, the teacher should return to the model, repeat the steps, and involve the student in additional practice. The teacher should work with the student to practice the strategy. One point of contention between researchers and practitioners is when to provide corrective feedback. Whole language and writing-as-a-process approaches often prohibit error correction, particularly at the beginning of reading and writing development. It is commonly believed that as students progress, they will begin to notice correct forms and begin to use them spontaneously. Reyes (1992) claims that this practice is not always best for learners. Her research indicated that students who were not corrected did not progress and were often left further and further behind. These conclusions lend support to the "perfect final copy" requirement of the Writer's Workshop approach. Many teachers insist that students continually rewrite their work until everything is perfect, hence insisting on self-correction.

To minimize anxiety, teachers can approach error correction cautiously when students are learning content material (Graves & Rueda, 2008). Students who have experienced school failure or who are learning to speak English as a second language often need to be praised when they have responded correctly. Teachers can approach error correction indirectly (Baca & Cervantes, 2004). For example, in a sixth-grade sheltered instruction class, a student described a close-up picture by saying, "It looks more big." The teacher responded indirectly and said, "Yes, it looks bigger." The student understood the correction and repeated, "Yes, it looks bigger." The student seemed to appreciate the information. Reyes (1992) and Short (1994) report positive results from explicit teaching of vocabulary, academic language, academic strategies, and English language, followed by teacher monitoring and nonthreatening error correction. The direct feedback approach requires the teacher to model the correct response and ask the student to repeat or copy it. The teacher then asks a related question that requires the student to use the correct information. If an EL writes "bruder" in his journal instead of the word "brother," the teacher can write the correct word above the misspelling and ask the student to spell the word correctly the next time. At the same time, the teacher should compliment the student's work, respond in writing to its content, and point out correctly spelled words.

Controlled, Grade-Appropriate Practice and Independent Practice

Practice is necessary when students are learning strategies. Once they have memorized the steps of a strategy, they must practice with clear examples. Suggestions on how to design learning strategies have been very clearly articulated in the work of Deshler and colleagues at the University of Kansas (Deshler & Schumaker, 1994); this work is an extension of a long tradition in educational research related to generalization and transfer (Woolfolk, 2010).

The first practice phase for learning a strategy is controlled practice. For example, a student has learned to sound out a word by looking at the word, saying all the letter sounds without stopping between sounds, and saying the word the "fast way." The controlled practice examples are words that are absolutely decodable, such as on, cat, or mast. The examples provide practice of the sounds the student knows.

After students master controlled practice, grade-appropriate practice should follow (Ellis & Graves, 1990). This will include grade-level reading words that might be found in content-area reading assignments. Grade-appropriate practice shows students the range of a strategy's application and how to generalize and transfer the knowledge they have gained. In this process, students learn that the strategy works better with some words than with others. They learn the limitations and the value of the strategy as it applies to their own life experiences.

Independent practice is appropriate only after students have mastered a strategy. A student can practice a strategy without supervision when it can be performed without frustration and error. If students practice applying the strategy to grade-appropriate words for homework too soon, errors may go uncorrected and cause confusion. The strategy is likely to be more valuable to students when the teacher avoids assigning homework or independent practice before students are quite familiar and comfortable with a strategy. An alternate homework assignment when students are learning a strategy is practicing one of the early example sets that have already been mastered. The assignment would then be relevant but would not require the student to perform the strategy prematurely in a frustrating situation.

Summary

Explicit teaching of learning strategies can assist students in overcoming challenges they face in school. If a student has difficulty understanding a concept or rule or has been unable to devise a strategy, the teacher should provide explicit instruction to help the student succeed.

This chapter includes examples of how strategies can be embedded in sheltered content lessons. It offers specific lesson descriptions and classroom examples to demonstrate various types of learning strategies. It includes guidelines for selecting learning strategies and planning lessons to teach learning strategies. Various methods for teaching specific learning strategies to promote learning skill are also explained. Strategies are essential for developing academic proficiency but are only a part of a quality instruction program for English learners. Chapter 6 will present another important approach to working with English learners: differentiated instruction.

ACTIVITIES

1. Sergio and six other students in your tenth-grade history class are struggling with reading and writing tasks. What type of information needs to be gathered about these students (see Chapter 1)? If the teacher is currently involving students in role-plays and utilizing video and other concrete examples of historical events, what other options does the teacher have to improve reading and writing performances?

2. If you are teaching a learning strategy to students with intermediate fluency in English, what specific guidelines are critical for you to consider when you are planning your minilesson?

3. Outline the parts of a minilesson intended to teach the COPS strategy explicitly. What preskills must be mastered before the strategy is taught? When you teach the strategy what parts will you include in your minilessons?

English-Language Literacy Development, Lesson Planning, and Specially Designed Content Instruction in English

The greatest challenge in teaching today is to communicate content in English to students whose English is under development. Research has shown that students learn best in their primary language, but in most schools, primary-language instruction is not an option. Students today are expected to learn not only English but also science, mathematics, social studies, and other subjects in English. How is this possible? Instruction must be systematically modified so that teachers can make academic content more accessible to learners.

Specially designed academic instruction in English (SDAIE) comprises a set of techniques for adapting instruction for English learners. For English learners, ELD instruction is guided by a careful progression through the ELD standards, and SDAIE is used to make academic instruction comprehensible. Without ELD and SDAIE, students are mainstreamed without access to the curriculum—the sink-or-swim approach.

According to Gersten and Baker (2000), a high-quality ELD program should include three components:

- Development of proficiency and fluency in social and academic English
- Explicit instruction in grammar, including such formal aspects as tense agreement, use of plurals, and word order in sentences
- Content learning merged with English acquisition

Ideally, English-language development is not confined to one period of the school day but is instead a part of content area instruction. Each content area has a specialized knowledge base, vocabulary (consider, for example, the different meanings of *foot* in mathematics, biology, geography, furniture construction, poetry, and theater), and particular graphic and verbal means for organizing information. Each content area has standards guiding curriculum development that must be addressed along with ELD standards. Table 5.1 offers suggestions for implementing ELD in a variety of ways across the curriculum.

TABLE 5.1   Examples of English-Language Development in Content Areas

Facet of Literacy Development	Examples
Creating a language-rich environment	Teachers can provide new experiences that arouse interest in and attention to a topic: field trips, guest speakers, fiction and nonfiction films, experiments, classroom discovery centers, music and songs, poetry and other literature, computer simulations, and so on.
Meaningful and purposeful activities	After students have had the opportunity to learn new literacy material in a meaningful way, they can transform that knowledge through other means, such as illustrating, dramatizing, creating songs, dancing, rewriting stories. Students can share their learning in a variety of ways—in learning centers; through dramatic, visual, or oral presentations; by staging a reader's theater; by developing slide, video, or computer-based audiovisual shows; or through maps and graphs.
Using standards-based thematic unit organization	After demonstrating the basic tools associated with mathematics (rulers, protractors, calculators, computers, etc.), the teacher provides students with a real-life opportunity to use them. Students are told that the classroom needs to be recarpeted. They first have to estimate the area, then check their estimates with the actual tools (using both standard and metric measuring instruments), and then use calculators to find the percentage of error in their estimates. This fits with ELD standards relating to negotiating/initiating oral activities.
Selecting appropriate reading materials	Teachers can choose to have one primary content source or a package of content-related materials (chapters from various texts, video- and audiotapes, magazine and newspaper articles, encyclopedia entries, literary selections, Internet sources, software programs, etc.). Regardless of what is chosen, the teacher must consider two main criteria: Are the content objectives for the lesson adequately presented by the material? Is the material comprehensible to English learners?
Providing organized, systematic, explicit instruction in key skills	Students identify key words in mathematics problem solving and determine how other words are linked to the key words. For example, in the problem "The sum of two numbers is 77. If the first number is ten times the other, find the number," students need to know they are dealing with two different numbers (Dale & Cuevas, 1992).
Adapting instruction and materials for English learners	Some learners may need special textual material, such as excerpts taken from textbooks, advance organizers for the text that highlight the key topics and concepts in outline form, focus questions, concept maps, or tape-recorded text passages.
Integrating listening, speaking, reading, and writing	During the first week of the solar system unit, the names of the planets were tossed into a hat. Each of nine pairs of native-English-speaking and English-learning students selected one planet and developed a poster session about their planet based on resources in the school library. After each pair presented their planet, the teacher combined pairs into small groups. Each group was to create a tenth planet based on what they had learned and present that planet to the class.

Using content area standards as the basis for content instruction combined with level-specific ELD standards ensures organized, systematic, explicit progress in language proficiency. A language-rich environment adds literacy to meaningful and purposeful instruction in key content knowledge and skills, integrating listening, speaking, reading, and writing with content objectives.

Instructional Planning and Organization for ELD and SDAIE

When instruction is delivered in English and the student has not achieved advanced proficiency in English, a fundamental chasm undermines learning. This gulf between instruction and comprehension cannot be bridged by reducing the standards of expectation for the student—it must be overcome by adapting instruction to the student's second-language-acquisition level by using specially designed academic instruction in English (SDAIE). This chapter addresses pedagogy for English learners by focusing on SDAIE-enhanced curriculum design and lesson delivery, cognitive academic language proficiency, and use of learning strategies as core elements in teaching English-language development and content area knowledge.

SDAIE is an approach used in multilinguistic content classrooms to provide language support to students while they are learning academic subjects. This can take place either in mainstream classes made up of native English speakers mixed with non-native English speakers of intermediate proficiency or in classes consisting solely of non-native speakers who operate at similar English proficiency levels (Echevarría, Vogt, & Short, 2004).

Planning affords teachers the opportunity to adapt lessons for English learners so instruction is understandable and interactive. An SDAIE lesson plan follows a fairly predictable format. Box 5.1 describes the five main parts of the SDAIE lesson.

SDAIE combines second-language-acquisition principles with elements of quality teaching so students can improve listening, speaking, reading, and writing as they study an academic subject. SDAIE is the preferred method used by both middle and high schools when primary-language instruction is not available or is offered in only one primary language.

Instead of organizing this chapter by content area—treating only mathematics in its own section, for example—I have organized this material by the main parts of the SDAIE lesson. By viewing the same SDAIE principle across several content domains, it is easier to grasp the concept.

Careful planning and a well-organized classroom, combined with effective teaching, are keys to success for English learners. The cycle of instruction consists of the following five phases: (1) The teacher becomes familiar with the characteristics of the students (age, grade level, language-acquisition level); (2) the teacher plans instruction using state and local curriculum standards and textbooks as guides; (3) the teacher delivers instruction using formative assessment to monitor progress; (4) the teacher employs summative assessment to give grades and make information available about student progress; and (5) the teacher reflects.

This cycle is repeated throughout the school year. Based on assessment data, the teacher modifies instruction for the class as a whole or for individual students, groups and regroups students, and acquires additional resources as needed. Over this entire classroom-based cycle is the spector of standardized testing, which reports to the community at large, including federal,

Box 5.1   Fundamental Elements of the SDAIE Lesson Plan

I. Setting objectives
   Content: Activity goals linked to grade-level standards
   English-language development:
      Speaking
      Listening
      Reading
      Writing
   Learning strategy: Augmenting long-term cognitive, metacognitive, or social-affective abilities
II. Preparing modified materials
III. Differentiated instruction
   Bridging: Accessing and building prior knowledge
   Appealing to diverse learning modalities
   Access to cognitive academic language
   SDAIE techniques
   Scaffolding: Temporary support for learning
   Guided and independent practice that promotes students' active language use
   Formative assessment and reteaching
IV. Summative assessment of objectives
V. Reflective pedagogy

state, and local authorities, sometimes with the threat of dire consequences to the school if expectations are not met. This is the contemporary context for planning and instructional delivery.

Planning for Standards-Based ELD and Content Instruction

Lesson planning involves the careful design of content, language, and learning-strategy objectives and the selection, modification, and organization of materials and text that support those objectives. Objectives are necessary to guide teaching. A lesson with a clear objective focuses instruction by concentrating on a particular goal and guides the teacher to select those learning activities that accomplish the goal. Once objectives are clearly stated, the teacher selects materials that will help students achieve those objectives. Finally, assessment provides evidence that learning has, or has not, taken place.

Considerations When Planning   Instructional planning takes the following factors into consideration:

Knowledge about Students
- Cultures and home languages
- Prior knowledge of the content
- Interests
- Reading, writing, and oral skills

Knowledge about the Content Area
- Standards that must be addressed
- What objectives will be set

Knowledge about Language Development
- Literacy requirements of the content area
- Language objectives needed

Knowledge about Students' Cognitive Development
- The learning strategies that students already have
- The learning strategies that will be useful in the lesson
- Ways to integrate the learning strategies (particularly critical thinking tasks) with students' cultural perspectives (Adapted from Quiocho & Ulanoff, 2009, p. 12)

Objectives What is a lesson objective? The objective states, in behavioral terms, what the student will be capable of doing at the close of the lesson. Such verbs as *contrast, identify, list, summarize, compare, predict, survey,* and *outline* are specific, describing a behavior that can be measured or has a tangible product. In contrast, such verbs as *learn, look at, evaluate, think about, know, review,* and *become aware* are not specific or measurable. Moreover, some verbs do not specify a goal but merely a process or activity. Such terms as *listen to, reflect, practice,* and *work in groups* describe activities, not goals. Hence it is difficult to measure what is accomplished. In contrast, *draw, map, record data, plan,* or *punctuate* are terms that result in a product that can be assessed.

Knowledge and language cannot be separated—language is the brain's input device, whether verbal or figural (pictures, numbers, graphs). Content instruction (mathematics, social studies, literature, science, physical education, visual arts, music, and performance arts) takes place using language as the medium, so language objectives are an integral part of content instruction. To maintain grade-level content objectives and sustain academic expectations for achievement, both language and content objectives are included in SDAIE lessons. Moreover, the current emphasis on cognitive teaching mandates that learning-strategy objectives be included as well. This gives every SDAIE lesson a three-part focus.

- *Content objective.* Knowledge, skill, or disposition in a subject area or domain of communicative competence
- *Language-development objective.* Knowledge or skill in some facet of English
- *Learning-strategy objective.* Knowledge, skill, or learning strategy that teaches the student how to acquire or process information

Objectives can include more than one content area. Middle school as well as elementary school instruction increasingly features thematic units that integrate content areas. The teacher considers the various tasks that language users must be able to perform in the unit (listening, speaking, reading, writing) and makes provisions for students to learn the vocabulary and concepts needed in the discourse of the content areas involved.

Objectives and Standards   How are objectives chosen? Schools, school districts, or state agencies publish standards documents that spell out what students should know and be able to do. These furnish goals for each grade. A classroom teacher plans instruction using curriculum guides at the specific grade level. Units may be organized based on a theme or, if the course is text-driven, based on chapters in the text (instructional planning is presented in greater detail later in this chapter). Units or chapters are further divided into specific lessons containing the essential content area objectives. The classroom teacher is responsible for presenting the material in an understandable way, arranging for students to participate in learning activities, and then measuring the extent of the students' mastery of the material. Thus, instruction and assessment are linked.

The chosen objectives must be matched to specific performance that students will demonstrate. This is central to the contemporary focus on accountability because the specific performance expected of the student as a learning outcome can be directly linked to some standard for the performance. Together, these constitute *standards-based learning*.

A standard becomes useful to teachers only when they can identify when the standard has been met or progress is being made toward meeting it. Moreover, when schools communicate performance standards to students, students know what is considered important for them to accomplish, and they can judge where they stand in relation to the standard. Students must be prepared to receive targeted feedback in a way that encourages them to compare their work to specific standards. Assessment should provide information on what students already do well and pinpoint what they still need to learn; this provides information about aspects of instruction that need to be redesigned (Jametz, 1994).

Content Standards   Each content domain has standards suggested by the professional organization that represents expertise in the field, such as the National Council for the Social Studies, National Council of Teachers of Mathematics (NCTM), and National Association for Sport and Physical Education (NASPE). In turn, the state departments of education (such as the California Department of Education) incorporate these standards into state content standards, designed to define the knowledge, concepts, and skills that students should acquire at each grade level. These are in turn incorporated into curriculum frameworks (blueprints for implementing the content standards) that are then used by individual school districts to determine what instructors in each grade level should teach. When these goals are met, standardized testing should provide evidence that students are learning.

Standards-Based Content Objectives   The teacher first specifies learning goals using standards documents, usually in the form of school district curriculum programs. The teacher divides the overall goals for the year into units, then into specific lessons, and then into the content area objectives for each lesson.

Table 5.2 displays content domains, typical content standards topics, and matching objectives. The idea is to accomplish one content objective in one lesson.

In developing their sequence of content objectives, teachers want to keep two important questions in mind: (1) Have I reviewed the objectives for the year and organized them for thematic flow? (2) Have I considered the sequence of objectives and rearranged them, if necessary, putting more concrete concepts before more abstract ones (i.e., those that can be taught with hands-on materials, visuals, and demonstrations before those that are difficult to demonstrate or that require more oral or written skills)?

TABLE 5.2 Content Domains, Content Standards, Typical Topics, and Matching Objectives (Sources for standards are in parentheses)

Content Domains	Content Standard	Typical Topic	Matching Objective
Mathematics	(Gr. 7) (Algebra and Functions). Students express quantitative relationships by using algebraic expressions, equations, inequalities, and graphs. (1)	Finding the unknown	Identify orally or in writing the pre-algebra concept of finding the unknown.
Social Studies	(Gr. 6) (World History and Geography: Ancient Civilizations). 6.2. Students analyze the geographic, political, economic, religious, and social structures of the early civilizations of Mesopotamia, Egypt, and Kush. (2)	Religion of Egypt	Identify Egyptian gods from tomb paintings.
Literature	(Gr. 11 & 12) (Literary Response and Analysis). 3.4. Analyze ways in which poets use imagery, personification, figures of speech, and sounds to evoke readers' emotions. (3)	Analyze poem	Analyze "We Real Cool" by Gwendolyn Brooks (Brooks, 1944) for plot, language, and theme.
Science	(Gr. 1) (Life Sciences). 2b. Students know both plants and animals need water, animals need food, and plants need light. (4)	Plants need light	Expose plants to different conditions of light to observe consequences.
Physical Education	(High school course 1, Standard 2). 2.7. Develop and implement a one-month personal physical fitness plan. (5)	Personal physical fitness	Compare two kinds of exercise that could become part of a one-month personal physical fitness plan.
Visual Arts	(Gr. 4) (Aesthetic Valuing). 4.3. Describe how using the language of the visual arts helps to clarify personal responses to works of art. (6)	Interpreting a painting	Compare personal responses to Picasso's *Las Meninas* with Renoir's *The Luncheon of the Boating Party at Bougival.*
Music	(Gr. 5) (Historical and Cultural Context). 3.2. Identify different or similar uses of musical elements in music from diverse cultures. (7)	Comparing music from different cultures	Contrast the use of drums in three cultural contexts: Brazil, Nigeria, and the United States.
Performance Arts	(Gr. 3) (Creative Expression). 2.2. Create for classmates simple scripts that demonstrate knowledge of basic blocking and stage areas. (8)	Staging a play	In groups, students will act out a scene from the Chinese fable *The Magic Sieve.*

Sources: (1) California Department of Education (1997); (2) www.cde.ca.gov/be/st/ss/hstgrade6.asp; (3) www .cde.ca.gov/be/st/ss/enggrades11-12.asp (English Language Arts Content Standards); (4) www.cde.ca.gov/be/st/ss/ scgrade1.asp; (5) California Department of Education (2004a); (6) www.cde.ca.gov/be/st/ss/vagrade8.asp; (7) www .cde.ca.gov/be/st/ss/mugrade5.asp; (8) www.cde.ca.gov/be/st/ss/thgrade3.asp.

Classroom Glimpse

MATCHING AN OBJECTIVE TO A STANDARD

Emil Chantal's fourth-grade class read *Amelia's Road* (Altman, 1993) as a focal point for studying the regions of the state of California where certain crops grow. He based this lesson on History Social Science Content Standard 4.1: "Students demonstrate an understanding of the physical and human geographic features that define places and regions in California," specifically, 4.1.3: "Identify . . . and describe the various regions of California, including how their characteristics and physical environments (e.g., water, landforms, vegetation, climate) affect human activity," and 4.1.5: "Use maps, charts, and pictures to describe how communities in California vary in land use, vegetation, wildlife, climate, population density, architecture, services, and transportation."

The content objective for this lesson was "Using a map of California, link regions and crops to the plot of *Amelia's Road*."

Using a map of California's farm regions (http://score.rims.k12.ca.us/score_lessons/amelia_road/map.html), students located where Amelia was born, as well as the locations described in the book. On a study sheet, they also answered questions such as "What grew in the area in which Amelia went to school?"

Language Standards   The California English Language Development (ELD) Standards (California Department of Education, 1999) require that English learners develop proficiency in both the English language and the concepts and skills contained in the English language arts (ELA) content standards (California Department of Education, 1997). Like the ELA standards, the California ELD standards are organized in areas of reading, writing, and listening/speaking. The California English Language Development Test is aligned with the standards as a placement and achievement test. Using the ELD and ELA standards, teachers can work with students through a developmental framework that stipulates the requirements of each proficiency level.

Classroom Glimpse

LANGUAGE STANDARDS

In a content-based intermediate/advanced ELD high school social studies class, standards-based instruction was incorporated into the unit Exploring World Religions. Students created a word web journal to define religion; used reading passages and journals combined with discussions about religion; and read library and Internet research to identify important religious figures. Final portfolios were used to archive students' essays and other writings. Through the unit, note-taking skills, outlines, timelines, maps, games, and other knowledge technologies were incorporated into group research, oral presentations, paragraph writing, and grammar work. (Riles & Lenarcic, 2000)

Content-Related Language-Development Objectives   The language-development objectives of an SDAIE lesson are drawn from the ELD standards. Because students in a class are usually at various CELDT levels—even a single student usually scores at different CELDT levels on listening/

speaking, reading, and writing—the teacher plans for differentiated instruction by incorporating more than one level of language skill in each lesson. The language objective must also address the language needed to accomplish the content objective. In other words, if the lesson features a science laboratory objective, the language objective is integrated with laboratory activity—for example, making observations orally and recording data by writing in a lab manual.

The CALLA Handbook (Chamot, 2009) is a valuable resource for helping teachers understand the language demands of various disciplines. Each of the chief subjects—science, mathematics, social studies, and literature and composition—is the focus of a chapter in which the authors specifically address its language demands.

Table 5.3 illustrates the alignment of content and language-development objectives for two ELD levels. This demonstrates differentiated instruction.

In reviewing language objectives, teachers should keep the following questions in mind:

- What is the concept load of the unit and what are the key concepts to demonstrate and illustrate?
- What are the structures and discourse of the discipline and are these included in the language objectives?
- Are all four language modes included in the planning (listening, speaking, reading, writing)?

 Classroom Glimpse

PLANNING FOR SDAIE SCIENCE

In a sheltered (SDAIE) seventh-grade science class, students improve their English language skills while studying about the universe. The teacher's primary goal is for students to understand the content materials (in this case, about the origin of the universe). But she also spends some time helping students with language-related issues (e.g., academic vocabulary, reading skills) that pertain to the science unit they are studying. The exposure to higher-level language (through the content materials) and the explicit focus on language issues by the teacher set the stage for successful language acquisition. (Brinton, 2003, p. 203)

Strategic Learning   The cognitive revolution in learning turned the spotlight on how people transform, elaborate, store, and recover information. According to the cognitive view, people are active learners who initiate experiences, seek out information, and reorganize what they already know in order to achieve new insights, pursue goals, solve personally relevant problems, and attempt to make sense of the world (Bruner, 1986).

Cognitive training includes the use of learning strategies, study skills, memory enhancement, text-processing competencies, note taking, research techniques, test-taking abilities, problem solving, transfer, graphic organizers, and information processing tips, as well as learning the characteristics of the brain. A cognitivist view of learning means teaching students *how* to learn.

Teachers motivate students best when they provide course activities and projects that tap students' natural abilities and interests and develop their confidence in their ability to think. Teachers who ask thought-provoking questions and use concrete examples, activities, and demonstrations stimulate students' imaginations and develop their critical thinking skills.

TABLE 5.3 Content and Language Objectives for Two ELD Levels in Two Content Areas (Sources for standards are in parentheses)

Content Standard	Content Objective	Language Standards	Language- Development Objectives
Life Sciences (Grade 1)			
2b. Students know both plants and animals need water, animals need food, and plants need light. (1)	Expose plants to different conditions of light to observe consequences.	(Beginning). Responds to simple directions and questions using physical actions. (Intermediate). Participates in instructional conversations using expanded vocabulary.	(Beginning). Working in a group, students will follow verbal directions to set up a plant light exposure experiment. (Intermediate). Students will discuss in a group how to set up an observation sheet for plant light exposure experiment.
Physical Education (High School Course 1, Standard 2)			
2.7. Develop and implement a one-month personal physical fitness plan. (2)	Compare two kinds of exercise that could become part of a one-month personal physical fitness plan.	(Early Intermediate). Uses writing to convey meaning. (Early Advanced). Produces independent writing using consistent grammatical forms, mechanics, and word order.	(Early Intermediate). Students will list three reasons for and three reasons against two types of exercise for their personal fitness plan. (Early Advanced). Students will write a comparison paragraph giving three reasons for and three reasons against two types of exercise for their personal fitness plan.

Sources: (1) California Department of Education (1997); (2) California Department of Education (2004a).

This includes metacognition in the form of cognitive self-knowledge (multiple intelligences, learning styles), goal setting, planning, self-monitoring, and self-evaluating.

Learning-Strategy Objectives   A cognitive lesson needs one or more learning-strategy objectives, which can be defined as the achievement or practice of direct or indirect strategies that facilitate acquiring new skills or information (Díaz-Rico, 2008). Learning strategies can be distinguished from content objectives by a simple test: Can the objective be applied outside the specific lesson? Is it a skill that can be used again and again as part of a learner's "mental toolkit"?

Cognitive Academic Language Learning Approach (CALLA)   Learning strategies are being recognized more and more as an integral part of teaching, an idea made explicit in Chamot's Cognitive Academic Language Learning Approach (CALLA) (2009). CALLA, designed for

---

Best Practice   HELPING STUDENTS DEVELOP A PERSONAL SET
OF LEARNING STRATEGIES

Teachers can help students become aware of, and acquire, learning strategies in the following ways:

- Modeling multiple ways to solve a problem
- Asking students to describe how they came up with an answer, solution, or process
- Being flexible and changing strategies if one approach does not achieve the desired result
- Praising the use of diverse strategies
- Offering systematic instruction in strategy use

(Adapted from Gregory & Kuzmich, 2005, p. 105)

English learners at the early intermediate to advanced levels of English-language proficiency, incorporates explicit teaching of learning strategies within academic subject areas. The CALLA model includes three components: topics from the major content subjects, the development of academic language skills, and explicit instruction in learning strategies for both content and language acquisition (Chamot, 2009).

The content topics, aligned with the all-English curriculum, are introduced gradually, emphasizing those that have extensive contextual supports or reduced language demands. The second component, academic language skills, includes all four language modes in daily content lessons. Students learn not just vocabulary and grammar but also important concepts and skills using academic language. In addition, they learn language functions important for specific curricular areas, such as analyzing, evaluating, justifying, and persuading.

The third—and central—component is instruction in learning strategies, which are divided into three major categories: *metacognitive, cognitive,* and *social-affective.* The metacognitive strategies help students to plan, monitor, and evaluate their learning processes. Teachers help students learn to preview the main concepts in material to be learned, plan the key ideas that must be expressed orally or in writing, decide in advance what specific information must be attended to, check comprehension during listening or reading, and judge how well learning has been accomplished when the lesson is completed.

 Classroom Glimpse

THINK-ALOUDS AS METACOGNITION

Mrs. Barr, a first-grade teacher, verbalizes her thoughts aloud to show students how she experiences reading comprehension. "I always model a think-aloud before asking anything from students," she says. Then students try it with a partner before sharing their thoughts with the whole group. Finally she asks students to write down what they are thinking, so she can assess how they use this metacognitive strategy.

(Adapted from Herrera, Pérez, & Escamilla, 2010, p. 142)

Cognitive strategies include using reference materials resourcefully; taking effective notes; summarizing material adequately; applying rules of induction or inference; remembering information using visual images, auditory representation, or elaboration of associations to new knowledge; transferring prior skills to assist comprehension; and grouping new concepts, words, or terms understandably. Social-affective strategies teach how to elicit needed clarification, how to work cooperatively with peers in problem solving, and how to use mental techniques or self-talk to reduce anxiety and increase a sense of personal competency.

 Classroom Glimpse

LEARNING-STRATEGY OBJECTIVES

The high school ELD classroom just got three new computers. Mrs. O'Dale knew that several students had computers at home, but nevertheless she wanted to make sure that all the students had basic word-processing skills. Before beginning a unit on autobiography, she identified a set of skills that are useful in word processing. In addition to such content objectives as identifying a topic, including descriptive details, and using time sequence connectors, each lesson in the writing unit would have an objective relating to word processing, beginning with saving and retrieving files, moving text within a file, and spellchecking. Thus, the acquisition of computer skills became learning-strategy objectives.

Skillful lesson planning includes integrating content, learning-strategy, and language-development objectives. A unit on bacteria would include a learning-strategy objective on the use of microscopes and a language objective relating to writing a brief summary (of laboratory observations). In contrast, a social studies lesson would use the reading selection as content but a comprehension-enhancing technique such as "using a cause-and-effect organizer" as a learning strategy.

 Classroom Glimpse

INTEGRATING THREE TYPES OF OBJECTIVES

The Most Beautiful Place in the World is an instructional unit based on the book by the same title (Cameron, 1988) about a young boy in Guatemala who longs to attend school and learn to read (Levine, 2000). Levine found that the Spanish words, foods, and other cultural aspects incorporated in the novel were particularly appropriate for her students, who were all from Spanish-speaking families. The unit also integrated social studies curricular goals as students studied map locations, compass directions, and cultural comparisons.

Teaching with SDAIE Strategies

English learners need support to enable them to successfully complete tasks that require academic language proficiency. SDAIE means a curriculum that teaches content first and English second. Bell (2002) explained the rationale for such classes at the high school level:

Students, parents, teacher, and counselors were concerned when we proposed [SDAIE] classes because they felt they might not match the curriculum, and they might affect acceptance into four-year colleges and universities. We explained that our English language development classes would focus on English language acquisition at the student's proficiency level. The SDAIE classes would focus on teaching the same curriculum as the regular courses, with added support materials.

My students were so relieved to be in these classes. They have struggled with lowered self-esteem from lowered grades in previous years. In English 10, they learn the themes, symbols, and plot of important literature. In history they learn the key events, the important political concepts, and key people from the time period. They can understand and keep up with the materials, getting grades that reflect their knowledge in the SDAIE classroom. (p. 15)

SDAIE strategies include increasing the use of cooperative learning, activating connections to students' previous knowledge, differentiating instruction to meet the needs of students with varying learning styles, promoting cognitive academic language proficiency, modifying instructional delivery without simplification, furnishing scaffolding (temporary support for instruction), providing graphic organizers, and providing assessment to promote learning and reflection. These strategies are addressed in the following pages, followed by examples in such content areas as language arts, social studies, math, science, music, and visual and performing arts.

Lesson plans in science using the Sheltered Instruction Observation Protocol (SIOP) model for SDAIE can be found in Short, Vogt, and Echevarría (2011). SIOP plans for mathematics are found in Echevarría, Vogt, and Short (2010).

Cooperative Learning

Many teachers include opportunities for discussion about key concepts, ensuring that students have numerous conversational partners and occasions to interact with the content of lessons. A noncompetitive environment can be established through cooperative learning activities, both formally and informally structured. Heterogeneous groups encourage language development as students talk about learning experiences with one another.

Material presented in a mainstream class may be difficult for English learners if the topics are cognitively complex and highly language dependent. Using cooperative learning, English learners have increased opportunities to verify their comprehension by receiving explanations from their peers and sharing prior knowledge. This helps them clarify and familiarize themselves with the lesson content.

Probably more was written on cooperative and collaborative learning in the last twenty years of the twentieth century than in all the previous history of education. David and Robert Johnson (c.f. Johnson, Johnson, & Holubec, 1993), Robert Slavin (1991), and others advocated the use of cooperative learning for elementary students. Others documented the success of cooperative learning with elementary school English learners (c.f. Cohen, 1994; Johns, 1992; Johnson & Johnson, 1994; Kessler, Quinn, & Fathman, 1992) as well as with secondary school ELD students (Faltis, 1993).

Benefits to English Learners Small-group learning provides English learners with a rich discourse environment and multiple opportunities for face-to-face interaction. This is particularly necessary when students must exchange information about academic content and procedures. When students are collaborating in small groups, they have substantially more chances to practice language—without worrying about whether their production is exactly right. This lowers their anxiety and lets them concentrate on the content of learning. They can hear and say key words and phrases and repeat them in a variety of ways until they feel comfortable with their language mastery (Faltis, 2001). Cooperative grouping also increases the possibility that English learners will feel a part of the culture of the classroom as a whole.

Guidelines for Cooperative Learning Developing cooperative skills requires a focus in the classroom on communication and teamwork. Kluge (1999) emphasized the following elements:

- *Positive interdependence:* Members of a group depend on one another, and no one is exploited or left out.
- *Face-to-face interaction:* Students work in proximity to one another.
- *Individual accountability:* Each group member bears full responsibility for the work performed by the group.
- *Social skills training:* The teacher explicitly explains and models the kind of communication and cooperation that is desired.
- *Group processing:* The teacher makes time for reflection on how the group is working together and helps the group set goals for improvement. (n.p.)

Table 5.4 summarizes the instructional use of cooperative learning with English learners. This information represents a synthesis of tips and guidelines from Bassano and Christison (1995), Cantlon (1991), and Kagan (1998, 1999). (Sources are identified with number keys.)

Even under the best of circumstances, cooperative learning has its challenges. Even though many educators seize on the advantages of having English learners help one another in class, this should not become the default strategy for classroom cooperative learning. Cohen

Cooperative learning helps to build a sense of community in the classroom.

Myrleen Ferguson Cate/PhotoEdit

TABLE 5.4 Instructional Use of Cooperative Learning

Component of Cooperative Learning	Explanation or Example
Definition	"An approach to education and a repertoire of teaching strategies based on the philosophy that students can learn effectively in small groups. Cooperative learning restructures the traditional classroom into small, carefully planned learning groups to provide opportunities for all students to work together and to learn from one another." (Source: 5, p. 3)
Rationales for using cooperative learning	Practice speaking and listening. Share information. Create things together. Learn democratic processes. Practice negotiating and compromising. (Source: 1, p. 29) Develop leadership, communication, decision-making, and conflict management skills. (Source: 2) Promote real-world team skills. **T**ogether **E**veryone **A**chieves **M**ore (TEAM)! Builds positive interpersonal relations. Transcends differences (cliques). (Source: 4)
Roles in teams	Language Monitor, Task Monitor, Timekeeper, Secretary, Clarifier, Encourager, Reporter. (Source: 1, page 29) Materials Monitor, Quiet Captain. (Source: 3)
Optimal team size	For initial start-up, dyads (teams of two) are most successful. (Source: 2) If teams of three are necessary, have them sit side by side. (Source: 2) Teams of four are ideal, small enough for active participation and split evenly for pair work. (Source: 3)
Frequency of use of cooperative structures	Minimum of three times a week; but simple structures (pair/share) can be used more often. (Source: 2)
Room and seating arrangements	Partners should sit side by side. If students are in fours, provide two sets of materials. No student's back should be to the teacher. (Source: 2)
Role of the teacher	Source of task; arranger of materials; accountable authority; partner in learning. (Source: 1)
Team composition	Heterogeneous (mixed gender, ethnicity, ability); teacher-assigned, long term; this is preferable. (Source: 3) To form heterogeneous ability groups, list students in ability from high to low (1–28), divide into quartiles, then form one group from 1, 8, 15, 22; next group 2, 9, 16, 23, etc. (Avoids highest grouped with lowest.) Random (randomly mixed ability, etc.); breaks up the monotony; short term. (Source: 3) Random teams may be a problem if all high achieving are in one group, or two students create mutual discipline problems. (Source: 2) Random grouping: Use colored marbles or slips with group numbers in a jar; group students by month of birth; count off around class. (Source: 1)

(continued)

TABLE 5.4 Continued

Component of Cooperative Learning	Explanation or Example
Team management	Inform students how much time is allotted to task; have an agreed signal to stop working (clap pattern, ringing a bell, countdown, etc.). (Source: 2)
Rationale statement	Teacher explains why work is done in a team, what the benefits are, and what behavior is expected. (Source: 2)
Necessary group skills	Forming into groups quickly. Participating with muted voices. Establishing turn-taking routines. Involving more hesitant members in group processes. (Source: 1)
Trust building/bonding	Rapport building; discuss favorite foods, hobbies, likes, dislikes. Nonacademic fun activities: games, puzzles. Academic tasks: partner reading, checking homework together (staple papers together, teachers correct top paper). (Source: 2)
Teaching social skills	Teacher models behavior: quiet voices, taking turns, everyone participating, encouraging partner, signal to stop. (Source: 2)
Appreciation statements by peers at debriefing	"(*Name*), you helped the team by ____." "(____), you did a great job of ____." "(____), I appreciated it when you ____." "(____), you are very good at ____." (Source: 2)
Clarification statements by peers	"I don't understand." "Excuse me?" "Speak more slowly, please." "Okay?" (Source: 1, p. 29)
Procedural statements by peers	"It's my/your/his/her turn." "Quickly! We have four minutes." "You first, then me." (Source: 1, p. 29)
Peers asking for/offering help	"Are you finished?" "I need help." "Do you need help?" (Source: 1, p. 29)
Individual accountability	Students have progress conferences with instructor. Groups are rated by teacher using monitoring chart. Groups monitor themselves periodically using rating charts. (Source: 1)
Rewards (nonmaterial); avoid message that reward involves escape from work (extra recess)	Elementary: Happygrams, applause, display group work, AV treat, play a special game. Middle/high school: library passes, computer time, daily announcements recognition, newsletter recognition, display work, special privileges, team picture displayed. (Source: 2)
Feedback	At the close of activity, teammates write on 3" × 5" card: "Which question/problem gave you difficulty?" "Give examples of what you might do differently next time." "List ways in which your partners helped the team to reach its goal." (Source: 2)

Sources: (1) Bassano & Christison (1995); (2) Cantlon (1991); (3) Kagan (1998); (4) Kagan (1999); (5) Coehlo, Winer, & Olsen (1989).

(1994) found barriers to successful group work, including "undesirable domination on the part of some students, and nonparticipation and withdrawal on the part of others" (p. 26). As Beaumont (1999) noted, the quality of collaborative learning varies with the maturity of students, and "often peer assistance did not provide sufficient support for students whose academic success depended on additional instructional interventions" (p. 235). Table 5.5 offers tactics for teachers to address barriers to successful cooperative learning.

Many types of tasks have been designed that feature cooperative structures. These range from simply pairing students for discussion to more elaborate setups requiring extensive time for preparation and monitoring. Table 5.6 presents a few cooperative structures and tasks. (Sources are identified with number keys.)

The jigsaw model of cooperative learning is particularly useful in that students are individually accountable for learning their own material and for sharing their information effectively with other group members. In the jigsaw method, each member (A, B, C, or D) of each base team (I, II, III, or IV) attends an expert group session (all the As huddle together) to study one aspect or section of the topic and thus has one piece of the knowledge puzzle (hence the name "Jigsaw"). Then the individuals return to their base team to share what they have learned.

TABLE 5.5 Challenges to Cooperative Learning and Tactics to Meet Them

Challenge	Tactics for Teachers
Students cannot get along.	Keep activities short and simple while students are learning how to work together. Group students wisely; place a socially immature student with two who are more mature. Teach social skills and review regularly.
Student prefers to work alone.	Provide encouragement by emphasizing importance of working in a group, giving examples from teacher's work. Give bonus points to class for working well together. Provide individual work occasionally as "safety valve."
Student is unmotivated.	Use interest inventory to discover student's likes and dislikes. Ask previous teachers what works for the student. Give student a role in the group in which he or she will succeed.
Student cannot keep up with others.	Let student prepare some part of task prior to group work. Provide a modified worksheet for slow student. Provide an alternate way for student to perform.
Group finishes before others.	Provide an extension or enrichment task that extends the activity. Two groups who finish first can compare their products.
Group finishes last.	See if task can be modified so all groups will finish together. Teacher or member of early-finishing group can spend some time to help slow group. Let individuals take home tasks.
Too much noise.	Monitor groups and commend those who are quiet and on task. Use a standard signal for noise such as blinking room lights. Assign a member of each group as noise control.

Source: Ellis & Whalen, 1992.

TABLE 5.6 Sample Cooperative Learning Activities

Name of Activity	Description of Activity
Relay	Four students learn a skill; they teach it to four others; eight teach it to eight more, until everyone knows it. (Source: 1)
Group Memory	In groups of six, give each group a line to memorize. Group members receive extra credit if everyone can say it when time is up. (Source: 1)
Listen Please (also called Information Gap)	In this paired activity, student A has words on various cards and student B has a matching set of picture cards. Listening to the description on a card, student B must pick out the matching card. (Source: 1)
Sequencing Task	Students put a cut-up sequence in correct order. Example: scrambled dialogue from a phone call to a friend. (Source: 1)
Scavenger Hunt	With a stack of newspapers, group finds one of each: some good news, some bad news, weather map, letter to editor, overseas news, etc. (Source: 1)
Round Robin	Each person does a problem (using one color ink) and then passes paper to next team member, who does the next problem. Teacher corrects one sheet. (Source: 2)
Jigsaw	Students receive number and letter (Ex.: I–IV, A–D). Base teams: I, II, III, IVs. Students exit base team; all As group to study one aspect, etc., then return to base team to share expertise. (Source: 2)
Numbered Heads Together	Each student in the group has a number (1–4); students huddle to make sure all can respond, then a number is called and that student responds. (Source: 3)
Rotating Review	Students visit wall charts; each chart has different review question; they write answers, then rotate to next chart. (Source: 3) If they agree with what is already written, they mark with asterisk.
Send-a-Problem	Groups create problems that are sent around the class for other teams to solve. (Source: 3)
Pairs Compare	Pairs come up with ideas to solve a problem. When pairs are through, two pairs make a team of four and compare ideas, generating more ideas. (Source: 4)
4S Brainstorming	While brainstorming solutions to an open-ended prompt, team members take one of four roles: Speed Sergeant: Encourages many responses quickly; Sultan of Silly: Tries to come up with silly ideas; Synergy Guru: Helps members build on one another's ideas; and Sergeant Support: Encourages all ideas, suspends judgment. (Source: 4)
Group Memory	Students write everything they know about a topic they plan to study, including unanswered questions that come to them. In groups of three, they read the paper to the group, and everybody adds ideas to their list. The group compiles unanswered questions and turns in a Group Memory Sheet. (Source: 5)
Partner Prediction	Teacher preidentifies places in a literature story where the students can stop and predict what happens next. They share predictions with a partner. They must then share aloud what the partner predicts.

TABLE 5.6 Continued

Name of Activity	Description of Activity
2/4 Question Some More	Teacher identifies key points in a read-aloud story. Partners talk about the story so far, then discuss what questions occur to them. They share these in a team of four, then with the class. (Source: 5)
Panel of Experts	Students read selected passages, taking notes of possible comprehension questions. In a group, students agree on four questions. One group in the room forms a panel, and others question them. Play continues until panel gets two right or one wrong; then questioning group becomes panel. (Source: 5)
Picture Dialogue	Before reading, teacher displays a picture from the book or sets a mental image using words. Working in pairs, students take character A or B and write a dialogue that characters say to each other. They read them aloud. (Source: 5)

Sources: (1) Bassano & Christison (1995); (2) Cantlon (1991); (3) Kagan (1998); (4) Kagan (1999); (5) Whisler & Williams (1990).

The ultimate learning goal is for each member of the base team to have the whole set of information, so each member must communicate what has been learned in the expert group.

 Classroom Glimpse

JIGSAW COOPERATIVE LEARNING

In one use of the jigsaw model, intermediate ELD students studied the use of persuasion in advertising by looking at three different types of ads in three expert groups and completing worksheets with questions such as "How is the ad trying to persuade you? Is it using reason, an appeal to the emotions, or an appeal to a feeling of right or wrong? Is the advertisement effective? Why or why not?" Returning to their base group, group members described the ad they studied and completed a second worksheet summarizing the types and effectiveness of persuasion used in various ads. Students then worked cooperatively to write their own ads. (Weatherly, 1999, p. 79)

Activating Connections to Students' Previous Knowledge

In the teaching context, prior knowledge refers to what students bring with them that can be tapped and built on during the lesson, consisting of students' existing concepts, understandings, and relevant experiences. These ideas may include misconceptions, so some "unlearning" may have to take place. Also, some prior knowledge may be based on experiences and conceptualizations of the students' home cultures that are beyond the teacher's experience.

Brain-based theory postulates that learners are engaged when the brain is able to create meaning by blending knowledge from previous experiences with concepts from present experiences. Effective teachers thus orchestrate meaning by making connections, instead of leaving this to chance. These connections can be made by establishing links to students' lives and their previous academic knowledge and then by anchoring previous knowledge to new ideas and concepts.

Best Practice   TAPPING INTO PREVIOUS KNOWLEDGE

The following strategies elicit information from students and help the teacher understand the extent of students' understanding:

- Brainstorming
- K-W-L (What do I *know*? What do I *want* to learn? What have I *learned*?)
- Mind maps
- Pretests
- Questionnaires
- Interviews

If students have little prior knowledge about the topic at hand, teachers can help them build schema or schemata—that is, construct a framework of concepts that shows the relationships between old and new learning and how they are connected. Semantic mapping and webs are ways of presenting concepts to show their relationships. After a brainstorming session, the teacher and students could organize their ideas into a semantic map, with the main idea in the center of the chalkboard and associated or connected ideas as branches from the main idea. Alternatively, a teacher could be more directive in creating a map by writing the central topic and branching out from it with several major subtopics. Students could provide information that the teacher then writes into the appropriate category.

Classroom Glimpse

BUILDING SCHEMATA

Mrs. Figueroa read *Cloudy with a Chance of Meatballs* (Barrett, 1978) to her second-grade students. Using a concept map with the words "junk food" in the center, they brainstormed on the following questions: "What is junk food?" "What junk food can you think of?" and "What is in junk food that our bodies don't need?" Students then grouped in pairs to write an adventure story with junk food as the villain.

An anticipation guide can help to determine the extent of students' prior knowledge. As a prelearning exercise, students receive five to ten statements presented in written or oral form, which they judge as true or false. Reviewing the same statements after teaching can help students clarify any misunderstandings they might have had initially.

Classroom Glimpse

ANTICIPATION GUIDE FOR EARTHQUAKE UNIT

Ellen Wexford's sixth-grade earth science class was about to begin a unit on earthquakes. She knew from experience that despite being residents of an earthquake-prone region, her students held many misconceptions about tectonic activity. So she constructed an anticipation guide that would be useful to her and her students. She chose items that would correlate with the core knowledge they would need for the unit. Included was the statement, "California might break off from the continent because of a large earthquake." By the end of the unit, she hoped that students would be able to give a reason-based response, choosing "False!" (Adapted from Fisher & Frey, 2009, pp. 43–47)

Differentiating Instruction to Meet Students' Learning Style Diversity

Appealing to Diverse Learning Modalities   The nature of teaching requires some kind of standardization and grouping because class sizes are usually too large to treat each student in a unique manner. The reality in U.S. classrooms, however, is that students are increasingly heterogeneous in an array of ways beyond language: religion; mainstreamed students with disabilities; race/ethnicity (one-third of the U.S. school population is non-White; see Marlowe & Page [1999]); and mobility (43 million people in the United States move every year; see Hodgkinson [1998]). The challenge is clear: How can curriculum, instruction, and assessment be responsive to this learner diversity?

The use of learning styles is based on a few basic hypotheses: (1) that every learner—and teacher—has a learning style preference; (2) that all styles are equally valid, although the educational context may value some more than others; (3) that learning about one's preferences, and acquiring styles other than one's preference, may assist students in learning; and (4) that learning strategies are linked to learning styles (Reid, 1995). Teachers can reduce the complexity of the learning style typologies by surveying various systems, analyzing themselves, and settling on one or two systems that both explain individual differences and offer a relatively easy way to accommodate instruction to learner differences.

In the typical classroom, some modification may be made that takes learning styles into account. If students as a group are both competitive and dependent, for example, assignments that enhance other characteristics (such as collaborative and independent learning) might be developed. Teachers can use a variety of learning activities to accommodate distinct learning styles. Students' awareness of their learning style preferences constitutes a metacognitive strategy. Once aware of their own preferences, students can use this knowledge to support their learning.

A comprehensive source for the incorporation of learning styles into second-language acquisition instruction is Reid's (1995) *Learning Styles in the ESL/EFL Classroom,* a compendium of articles on research and practice in this area. The book features various inventories of learning styles; suggestions for learners with visual, auditory, and haptic preferences; and a look at crosscultural implications.

Teachers can incorporate learning styles into instruction in the following ways:

- Diagnose one's own learning style preferences to understand oneself as a teacher.
- Settle on one or two systems that help create awareness of students' learning style diversity.
- Find a way to add variety to instructional plans that makes a difference on this set of preferences.

Best Practice LEARNING CENTERS FOR DIFFERENTIATED INSTRUCTION

Centers can be used in any content class to provide intentional experiences that allow students to learn in diverse ways, such as the following examples of centers that can be used at the secondary level:

- *Poet's corner.* Using different types of verse as models, students can work alone or with partners to read or create poetry.
- *Technology center.* Students can write and publish their own stories, using Inspiration software that displays the sequence of events in the story.
- *Storyboards.* Students can create storyboard pictures, with text underneath to tell the story.
- *Cool stuff.* Using interesting materials such as gel pens and paper with interesting borders, students can create ads for books they write or have read. (Adapted from Gregory & Kuzmich, 2005, p. 195)

Using Realia, Manipulatives, and Hands-On Materials Student learning activities should develop students' interactive language but not disadvantage an English learner. Collaborative problem-solving teams include member roles that provide a variety of input and output modalities to balance the English skills and nonverbal talents of students. English learners can benefit from the use of media, realia, science equipment, diagrams, models, experiments, manipulatives, and other modalities that make language more comprehensible and that expand the means and modes by which they receive and express information.

Promoting Cognitive Academic Language Proficiency

Cummins (1979, 1980) has posited two different yet related language skills: basic interpersonal communication skills (BICS) and cognitive academic language proficiency (CALP). BICS involves those language skills and functions that allow students in school to communicate in everyday social contexts that are similar to those of the home: to perform classroom chores, chat with peers, or consume instructional media as they do television shows at home.

BICS is *context embedded* because participants can provide feedback to one another, the situation itself provides cues that further understanding, and factors apart from the linguistic code can furnish meaning. In contrast, CALP, as the name implies, is the language needed to perform abstract and decontextualized school tasks successfully. Students must rely primarily on language to attain meaning. For English learners, BICS has been found to approach native-like levels within two years of exposure to English, but five or more years may be required for minority students to match native speakers in CALP (Collier, 1987; Cummins, 1981a; Hakuta, Butler, & Witt, 2000). Students need skills in both kinds of language.

Because CALP provides few concrete cues to assist comprehension, Cummins (1984) calls CALP *context-reduced* communication. CALP also involves systematic thought processes, the cognitive toolbox needed to categorize, compare, analyze, and accommodate new experiences and is therefore key to acquiring the in-depth knowledge needed in a complex modern society.

CALP requires growing beyond the simple *use* of language to the more complex ability to *think and talk about* language—metalinguistic awareness (Scarcella & Rumberger, 2000). Precise differentiation of word meaning and the ability to decode complicated sentences demand from students a gradual understanding of the cultural and social uses of the language to which they are exposed. CALP is not gained solely from school or solely from the home—one reinforces the other. However, CALP is highly dependent on the assistance of teachers because, for the most part, CALP is learned in school.

Some teachers confuse CALP and BICS as correct versus incorrect usage of English. CALP is *not* just hypergrammatical BICS. Teachers can help students to acquire CALP by analyzing the conceptual and critical thinking requirements of the grade-level curriculum *and* taking the time to ensure that all students are explicitly taught such requirements. Good teachers use CALP with their students; but excellent teachers ensure that students can use CALP themselves.

Without this explicit attention to teaching CALP, one of three outcomes is all too common. First, students who come to school already having acquired CALP as a benefit of a privileged home environment may outshine English learners. Second, the curriculum for English learners may be watered down due to the assumption that those who lack CALP cannot perform academically at a high cognitive level. Third, students lacking CALP in English are not able to participate knowledgeably and are often confined to a skills-based, direct instruction approach that does not encourage a constructivist learning environment.

Academic materials that incorporate CALP teach not only content but also the cognitive skills to acquire content. *High Point* (Schifini, Short, & Tinajero, 2002) makes CALP explicit by listing CALP terminology to be covered in each unit. For example, Level C Unit 4 Theme 1 (A Fork in the Road) presents words such as *choice, decision, advantages, disadvantages, pros,* and *cons* to accomplish the academic function of "justifying" (p. 223). Level C Unit 5 Theme 2 (Moving Forward) offers CALP terms such as *responsible, avoid, accept,* and *solve a problem;*

Pictures and hands-on activities help students to gain basic interpersonal communicative skills as well as academic language.

Will Hart/PhotoEdit

129

subsequent vocabulary work teaches *denotation, connotation, thesaurus, substitute,* and *synonym.* Thus, *High Point* is an exemplar of a CALP-equipped curriculum.

The complexity of CALP can be captured by examination of the five Cs: communication, conceptualization, critical thinking, context, and culture (see Table 5.7). Many of the skills that are a part of CALP are refinements of basic interpersonal communication skills (BICS), whereas others are more exclusively school-centered.

 Classroom Glimpse

DEVELOPING CALP

Mrs. Álvarez found in her second-grade structured English immersion class that, although the students were fairly fluent in English when chatting with one another, they lacked the vocabulary to perform on academic tasks. When she gave instructions or briefly reviewed concepts, the students appeared lost. She became aware that students needed to move along the continuum from their everyday English usage to more abstract academic language.

The class was studying the ocean. Mrs. Álvarez set up learning centers with shells, dried seaweed, fish fossils, and other ocean objects. The instructions for these centers featured patterned, predictable language tied to the concrete objects, with words such as *group, shape,* and *size.* Gradually Mrs. Álvarez tape-recorded more complex and abstract instructions for use in the learning centers, such as *classify, arrange,* and *attribute.* This progression and integration of activities helped the children move along the continuum from BICS to CALP.

Modifying Instructional Delivery without Simplification

Teachers must ensure that students understand what is said in the classroom. Teachers in SDAIE classrooms devote particular attention to four communication strategies: *language contextualization, teacher's speech modification, repetition and paraphrase,* and *use of patterned language.*

Language Contextualization   Teaching should be focused on the context of the immediate task, augmenting vocabulary with gestures, pictures, realia, and so forth to convey instructions or key words and concepts. This provides a rich visual and/or kinesthetic (e.g., through drama and skits) environment. Verbal markers are used to organize the lesson, such as *note this* to denote importance, or *now, first, second,* and *last* to mark a sequence. To help with directions, teachers can determine the ten most frequently used verbal markers and teach these through mini-total physical response (TPR)-type lessons. The teacher might also learn how to say simple directions in the students' language(s).

Teacher's Speech Modification   To be understandable to those who do not speak or understand English well, the teacher must adjust speech from the customary native speech patterns. This takes place at many linguistic levels—phonological (precise articulation); syntactic (shorter sentences, with subject–verb–object word order); semantic (more concrete, basic vocabulary; fewer idioms); pragmatic (frequent and longer pauses; slower delivery; and exaggerated intonation, especially placing more stress on important new concepts); and discourse (self-repetition; main idea easily recognized and supporting information following immediately). Teachers in SDAIE classrooms also speak less in the classroom, encouraging students to talk. There is much

TABLE 5.7 Components of Cognitive Academic Language Proficiency (CALP)

Component	Explanation
Communication	Reading: Increases speed; masters a variety of genres in fiction (poetry, short story) and nonfiction (encyclopedias, magazines, Internet sources).
	Listening: Follows verbal instructions; interprets nuances of intonation (e.g., in cases of teacher disciplinary warnings); solicits, and benefits from, help of peers.
	Speaking: Gives oral presentations, answers correctly in class, and reads aloud smoothly.
	Writing: Uses conventions such as spelling, punctuation, report formats.
Conceptualization	Concepts become abstract and are expressed in longer words with more general meaning (*rain* becomes *precipitation*).
	Concepts fit into larger theories (*precipitation* cycle).
	Concepts fit into hierarchies (rain → precipitation cycle → weather systems → climate).
	Concepts are finely differentiated from similar concepts: (*sleet* from *hail*, *typhoons* from *hurricanes*).
	Conceptual relations become important (opposites, subsets, causality, correlation).
Critical thinking	Uses graphic organizers to represent the structure of thought.
	Uses textual structures (outlines, paragraphing, titles, main idea).
	Reads between the lines (inference).
	Detects bias; separates fact from opinion; tests validity of sources.
Context	Nonverbal: Uses appropriate gestures; interprets nonverbal signs accurately.
	Formality: Behaves formally when required to do so.
	Participation structures: Fits in smoothly to classroom and schoolwide groups and procedures.
Culture	Draws on background knowledge.
	Uses social-class markers, such as "manners."
	Moves smoothly between home and school.
	Marshals parental support for school achievement.
	Deploys primary-language resources when required.
	Maintains uninterrupted primary-culture profile ("fits in" to neighborhood social structures).

evidence indicating that teachers should reduce teacher talking time (TTT) while teaching and increase the amount of student talking time (STT). As Harmer (2007) pointed out,

> Overuse of TTT is inappropriate because the more a teacher talks, the less chance there is for students to practice their own speaking—and it is students who need the practice, not the teacher. If the teacher talks and talks, the students will have less time for other things, too, such as reading and writing. For these reasons, a good teacher maximizes STT and minimizes TTT. (p. 38)

As students become more proficient in English, teachers again adjust their speech, this time increasing speed and complexity. Ultimately, English learners will need to function in an all-English-medium classroom; therefore, over time, SDAIE teachers need to reduce the speech modification scaffolds they use to accommodate their students' evolving proficiency. Table 5.8 summarizes the modifications teachers can make in speech and instructional delivery to make their teaching more comprehensible.

Repetition and Paraphrase   Verbal repetition can be employed to increase comprehensibility (for example, using the same type of directions throughout various lessons), as can organizational repetition (lessons that occur at specific times, lessons with clearly marked verbal and nonverbal boundaries, such as "Now it's time to . . . ," or the use of specific locations for specific content). Concepts are presented numerous times through various means. Elaboration, in which the teacher supplies redundant information through repetition and paraphrase, may also prove effective.

Use of Patterned Language   It is helpful for teachers to signal the beginnings and endings of lessons clearly, using stock phrases (e.g., "Math time is over. Put away your books"). Procedures and classroom routines should be predictable so that English learners do not feel they have to be ever-vigilant for a change in rules. This reduces stress and gives students a feeling of security.

Although SDAIE teaching involves presentation of subject matter in English, opportunities are available throughout the lesson for students to clarify their understanding using their primary language, supplemented whenever possible by primary-language resources (print, electronic, personnel) that can help students with key concepts.

The scope of this book does not permit an exhaustive discussion of SDAIE. For an excellent in-depth treatment, refer to *Making Content Comprehensible for English Language Learners: The SIOP Model* (Echevarría, Vogt, & Short, 2004).

Explanation of Concepts in the Primary Language   In SDAIE classrooms, students are afforded opportunities to learn and clarify concepts in their own language. When possible, the teacher offers primary-language resources (print, electronic, personnel) that can help students with key concepts. Although SDAIE teaching involves presenting subject matter in English, teachers continue to provide opportunities throughout the lesson for students to clarify their understanding using the primary language.

Recourse to the primary language is still a controversial issue, and many teachers shy away from it on the mistaken belief that primary-language use detracts from developing English proficiency. However, research continues to show that when students are able to employ their first language, they make more academic gains in both content and language than if they are prohibited from using it (Collier, 1995).

Clarification Checks   Teachers monitor listening and reading comprehension at intervals to gain a sense of the students' ability to understand. The teacher might pause to ask a question requiring a simple response, such as "Show me how you are going to begin your work," or ask individual students to restate the instruction using their own words.

Questions at the literal level are designed simply to check whether students understand directions, details, or procedures. During formal presentations, teachers often use strategies such as asking students to "vote" on their understanding of what has been said by a show of hands. This helps to maintain interest and check for understanding. Depending on student

TABLE 5.8 Teachers' Language Modification in SDAIE

Type of Modification	Definition	Example
Precise articulation	Increased attention to enunciation so that consonants and vowels in words are understandable	"Trade your *homework* with the person *beside* you."
Use of gestures	Showing with hands what is to be done	Make a swapping gesture with papers to act out "trading homework."
Intonation	Increased stress on important concepts	"The number of *correct* answers goes at the top of the page."
Simplified syntax	Shorter sentences, with subject-verb-object word order	"Mark the papers. Give them back."
Semantic clarity	More concrete, basic vocabulary; fewer idioms	"Turn in your work. I mean, give me your homework."
Pragmatic distinctness	Frequent and longer pauses; slightly slower delivery	"Check the chemicals . . . Check the list . . . Be sure your team has all the chemicals for your experiment."
Use of discourse markers	Careful use of transition words, emphasis, and sequence markers	"Note this" to denote importance, or "now," "first," "second," and "last" to mark a sequence.
Use of organizational markers	Clearly indicating change of activity	"It's time for recess . . . Put away your books."
More structured discourse	Main idea easily recognized and supporting information following immediately	"Today we are learning about mole weight. . . . I will show you how to calculate mole weight to make the correct solution."
Use of clarification checks	Stopping instruction to ask students if they understand; monitoring students' comprehension	"Hold your thumb up in front of your chest if you understand how to use the formula for acceleration."
Soliciting written input	Having students write questions on index cards	"I have a card here asking for another explanation of longitude degrees and minutes. OK . . ."
Repetition	Revisiting key vocabulary terms	"*Precipitation* means overall rain or snowfall; we are going to study the precipitation cycle."
Use of mini-TPR lessons to preteach key terms	Acting out terms to increase understandability	" 'On the other hand' ": Carlos, stand over here, and Elena, stand here—you are 'on one hand,' *he is* 'on the other hand.' "
Use of primary language	Saying simple directions in the students' language(s)	"*tsai jher*, over here, *tsai nar*, over there" (Mandarin).

response, teachers may need to rephrase questions and information if the students do not initially understand.

Using Questions to Promote Reflection   Effective questioning techniques can probe for students' abilities to infer and evaluate. Teachers need to be patient when asking questions—to wait for students to understand the question before calling on individuals. Even after nominating a student to answer, wait-time is necessary to allow an English learner to compose and deliver a response. He or she may know the answer but need a little more processing time to say it in English.

Effective mediational questions—those that promote reflection—focus on the process of thought rather than on low-level details. The following questions or requests provoke thought:

- Tell me how you did that.
- What do you think the problem is?
- What's another way we might approach this?
- What do you think would happen if . . . ?
- What might you do next? (Adapted from Costa & Garmston, 2002)

Students need to be encouraged by teachers to engage in active oral participation in class. Zwiers (2008) suggested five kinds of prompts to urge students to elaborate their talk. First, teachers should *prompt further thinking* using phrases like "You're on to something important. Keep going" or "You're on the right track. Tell us more." Students can be asked to *justify their responses:* "That's a probable answer. How did you get to that answer?" or "What evidence do you have to support that claim?"

Teachers can *ask for a report* on an investigation by saying, "Describe your result," or "What do you think caused that to happen?" *To see other points of view,* students can be asked, "If you were in that person's shoes, what would you have done?" or "Would you have reacted like that? Why or why not?" Finally, to prompt students to *consider consequences,* one might say, "What if she had not done that?" or "How can we apply this in real life?" Open-ended questions like these elicit a greater balance between the amount of student talk and teacher talk.

Skilled questioning using a linguistic hierarchy of question types helps teachers ascertain students' understanding. For students in the "silent period," questions elicit a nonverbal response—a head movement, pointing, or manipulation of materials. Once students begin to speak, they can choose the correct word or phrase to demonstrate understanding of either/or questions: "Does the water expand or contract to form ice?" "Did Russians come to California from the west or the north?" Once students are more comfortable producing language, *wh-* questions are used: "What is happening to the water?" "Which countries sent explorers to California?" "What was the purpose of their exploration?" Skillful teachers can ask questions requiring critical or creative thinking even at the beginning level; students at advanced English levels are not the only ones capable of inferential thinking.

Scaffolding: Temporary Support for Learning

In education, scaffolding is used to help the learner construct knowledge (Berk & Winsler, 1995). During scaffolding, the teacher helps to focus the learner's attention on relevant parts of the task by asking key questions that help to determine the zone of proximal development for that student on the particular task. Questions and verbalizations give students the opportunity to think and talk about what they must do.

Dividing the task into smaller, manageable subcomponents and sensitively withdrawing assistance when it is no longer required furthers success (Díaz, Neal, & Vachio, 1991). The teacher who uses scaffolding skillfully does so in a form of dynamic assessment, evaluating and teaching at the same time. Table 5.9 presents scaffolding strategies in various content areas.

Providing Graphic Organizers

Another way to scaffold is to make verbal information visual. Graphic organizers are visual frames used to represent and organize information—"a diagram showing how concepts are related" (McKenna & Robinson, 1997, p. 117). Many kinds of graphic organizers can also be used to help students focus their thoughts and reactions—for example, as they read a literature selection. Because graphic organizers balance visual with verbal representation, they can help to make visible the conceptual structures that underlie content. This helps students make models for understanding ideas and outcomes.

Graphic organizers are particularly useful in content instruction. With mind maps or other information organizers, students can interact with the concepts presented in various content areas in a way that supplements verbal text (Flynn, 1995). Thus, English learners can access core content even when their reading skills are weak. This results in greater student engagement in their learning.

Graphic organizers have at least three major applications. First, *representative/explanatory* organizers are used to increase content understanding, either by building background

TABLE 5.9 Scaffolding Strategies for Use in Content Areas

Scaffolding Strategy	Description of Use in the Content Class
Previewing vocabulary	Before beginning a social studies lesson, students in pairs skim the chapter and look up definitions in the glossary.
Prereading activities	Students make collages with pictures of vegetables cut from magazines before reading in the health book about the vitamins found in common foods.
Language experience approach	After performing a laboratory experiment, students interview one another and write down a report of the experiment results.
Interactive journals	Students describe personal exercise goals and write daily results in a journal; their peer "personal trainer" reads and provides feedback and encouragement.
Shared reading	Students "buddy read" encyclopedia entries as they write a group science research report.
Learning logs	In a mathematics center, students make entries into a group log as they try to solve a weekly puzzle.
Process writing	Students working on a monthlong family history project share their rough drafts with family members to gain input before final revision.

knowledge before students read a text or synthesizing new information that is gained from a text. Second, *generative* organizers promote ideas related to content. Students can talk or write about the information presented on a chart. Third, *evaluative* organizers help explain content. Figure 5.1 shows examples of these three types.

A *sequential organizer* is an explanatory diagram that shows items in order, such as parts of a book, a letter, or an essay; events in a story plot; or steps in written directions (Kagan, 1998, 1999). Figure 5.2 shows a sequential organizer used to list the beginning, middle, and end of a story. Figure 5.3 shows the problem–solution chain in a Native-American "coyote" story. If the events repeat, a cycle graph might be used. A sequence can be a cartoon, a picture strip, or a timeline.

FIGURE 5.1   Three Types of Graphic Organizers

Representative/Explanatory	**Generative**	**Evaluative**
■ Sequential	■ Concept development	■ Grade scale
■ Compare/contrast circles	■ Mind map	■ Likert scale
■ T-chart	■ Spider map	
■ Comparison chart	■ K-W-L	
■ Embedded		
■ Whole/part		
■ Cause/effect		
■ Classification		

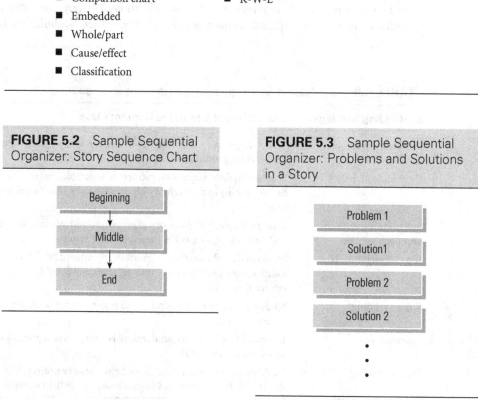

FIGURE 5.2   Sample Sequential Organizer: Story Sequence Chart

Beginning
↓
Middle
↓
End

FIGURE 5.3   Sample Sequential Organizer: Problems and Solutions in a Story

Problem 1

Solution1

Problem 2

Solution 2

⋮

FIGURE 5.4 Sample Compare/Contrast (Venn) Diagram Used for the Questions "How Are Two Things Alike? How Are They Different?"

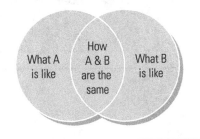

FIGURE 5.5 Sample T-Chart: Comparison of Same and Different

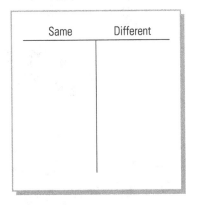

Compare/contrast organizers can be used to compare characters in the same story or in different stories, types of correspondence (business versus friendly letters), or genres of reading (fiction versus nonfiction). Visually, comparison charts can be of various types: compare/contrast circles (Venn diagram, see Figure 5.4), T-charts (see Figure 5.5), or comparison charts (see Figure 5.6).

Other *relational organizers* can show information that is embedded (see Figure 5.7), whole/part (see Figure 5.8), or cause/effect (see Figure 5.9).

Classification organizers are used to create hierarchies (Figure 5.10), matrixes (Figure 5.11), or other concept relations that show specific structures. Figure 5.12 shows a two-dimensional plot; Figure 5.13 demonstrates an alternative way to display a hierarchy.

FIGURE 5.6 Sample Comparison Chart Showing Comparison by Attributes

Comparison of Civilizations

	Egypt	*United States*
Duration	More than 4000 years	About 400 years
Political structure	Towns united by centralized government	Hierarchy: towns, counties, states, federal government
Religion	Pharaonic, later Islam	Predominantly Protestant Christian, then Catholic Christian, then Jewish, Islam, other

etc.

FIGURE 5.7 Sample Relational Organizer Showing Embedded Concepts (Teacher's Phenomenal Field of Personal Relations in the Role of Teacher)

FIGURE 5.8 Sample Relational Organizer Showing Whole/Part (Parts of the Atom)

Atom	Nucleus	Protons
		Neutrons
	Electrons	

Best Practice **A CLASSIFICATION TASK**

Students can practice a classification graphic organizer by sorting a list of recyclable items: newspapers, soda bottles, soup cans, shampoo containers, office paper, clean aluminum foil, junk mail, a shoe box, plastic water bottles, and so on. (Let them make their own categories.)

(Adapted from Bonesteel, Gargagliano, & Lambert, 2010, p. 169)

Concept development organizers are used to brainstorm. They do not display information that is already related. The K-W-L chart is used to introduce a theme, a lesson, or a reading. It can help generate interest in a topic and support students in using their prior knowledge as they read. Students can enter K (what we Know) and W (what we Want to know) in advance, reserving L (what we Learned) for the end of the unit or lesson (see Figure 5.14). The mind map is basically a circle showing the topic in the center, with lines or other connectors around it that tie students' ideas to the topic (see Figures 5.15 and 5.16).

Evaluation organizers show degree of positivity (Kagan, 1998). These can be grade scales (A to F); Likert scales (from 1 = strongly disagree to 7 = strongly agree); rubric scales (needs work→ satisfactory→ good→ excellent); or they can comprise two boxes ("I like/agree with" versus "I dislike/disagree with") or three boxes (plus/maybe/minus).

Once students and teachers become familiar with graphic organizers, they are a help to English learners in grasping basic concepts without dependence on language as the sole source of understanding. An excellent source is Parks and Black's *Organizing Thinking: Graphic Organizers* (1990).

FIGURE 5.9 Sample Relational Organizer Showing Cause/Effect (Possible Causes of Lightbulb Nonfunctioning)

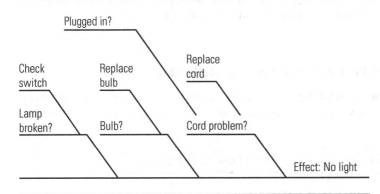

FIGURE 5.10 Sample Classification Chart Showing Main Ideas

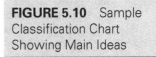
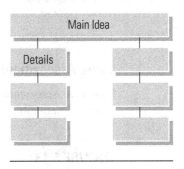

FIGURE 5.11 Sample Classification Chart Showing a Matrix

	Boys	Girls	Totals
Blue-eyed	4	7	11
Brown-eyed	13	10	23
Totals	17	17	34

FIGURE 5.12 Sample Classification Chart Showing Dimensions (Learning Styles)

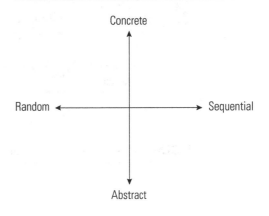

 Classroom Glimpse

TUTORING WITH GRAPHIC ORGANIZERS

Semantic mapping proved to be a successful approach for three English learners, two boys ages five and nine and their sister, age ten, whom Judy was tutoring. The children had chosen "Halloween" as an interesting topic to explore as a way to increase their vocabulary in English. Starting with words they knew in English (skeleton, witch), Judy wrote the words on chart paper, which the children copied in their notebooks. The children gave other words in Spanish, and Judy found the English equivalents and wrote them too. (Continued)

Using a fresh piece of chart paper, Judy asked the students how the list of words could be grouped into categories. The activity continued until the words had been grouped into the categories Animals, Monsters, and Trick-or-Treat. Judy followed up this activity by reading a book on Halloween, *Rotten Ralph's Trick or Treat*. When they came to a word on the chart, Judy pointed it out for reinforcement. (Brisk & Harrington, 2000, pp. 71–72)

Using Assessment to Promote Learning and Reflection

Formative Assessment and Reteaching As students are learning, the teacher can help them maintain momentum and solve ongoing problems through a process of formative assessment

FIGURE 5.13 Sample Classification Chart Showing Hierarchy

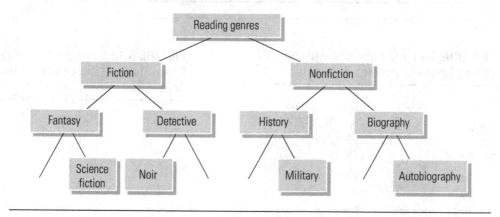

FIGURE 5.14 Sample Concept Development Chart: K-W-L

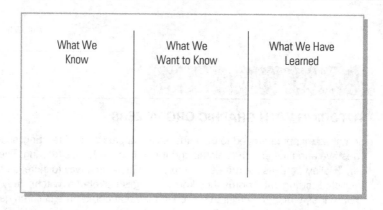

FIGURE 5.15 Sample Concept Development Chart: Mind Map or Idea Web

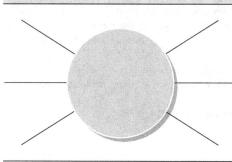

FIGURE 5.16 Sample Concept Development Chart: Character Trait Web

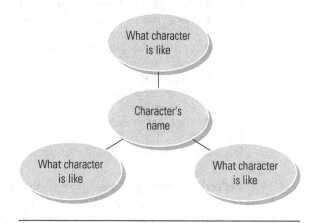

involving progress checks, which helps students to evaluate their efforts in the light of their goals and stay on track. The teacher may require formal weekly progress reports, ask for partial products at predetermined times, or set deadlines for circulation of rough drafts. Formative evaluation can permit much valuable ongoing readjustment of the learning process.

Teachers exercise patience in helping students monitor and adjust their learning to meet the desired performance standards; vanquish students' habits of sloth or procrastination, if these are a problem; conquer the students' lack of faith in themselves by providing encouragement, structure, and guidelines; overcome students' impatient desire to improve instantly, as they perhaps try and fail several times before succeeding; help students accept the disappointment of failure if there is some aspect of a complex problem that eludes solution; or make themselves available during students' basic struggle to use English as a means of expression.

Not all learning is successful. Sometimes problems that are worth addressing are beyond comprehension, and sometimes problems that are comprehensible are simply not interesting. Most teachers do everything possible to facilitate successful learning. But, in the last analysis, it is not the teacher's job to rescue students from disappointment or failure; these are a part of authentic learning. Sometimes metalearning—the wisdom about learning—comes after the learning has been attempted, in a process of reflection and hindsight.

Summative Assessment, Culminating Performance, and Metalearning   A final performance on a certain day—such as a play with other students as audience or an exhibit for parents—helps students understand the real world of promise and fulfillment. Despite the satisfaction these culminating events offer, the substance of assessment remains with the content standards that have been achieved. Peer evaluation, self-evaluation, and teacher evaluation together garner the final evidence: Was the learning successful? What was learned about the content? What was learned about the process? And most excitingly, what is still not known? What remains to be discovered?

Box 5.2   Critical Reflection in Lesson Planning

- What were the strengths in the lesson?
- Were content, learning, and language objectives clearly stated to students?
- Were students, including English learners, engaged in the lesson?
- How many opportunities were provided for English-language development?
- What evidence do I have to demonstrate that lesson adaptations for English learners were adequate?
- Which evidence demonstrated learning by English learners?
- Which opportunities allowed students to self-assess and be responsible for their own learning?
- What areas require changes for lesson improvement?

Source: Balderrama & Díaz-Rico (2006).

Reflective Pedagogy   Pausing to reflect is the final step in lesson delivery; it occurs at the end of instruction for English learners and in turn reactivates the cycle of teaching and planning. Some questions teachers may use to frame critical contemplation of their teaching are listed in Box 5.2.

Effective Resource Use in ELD and SDAIE

A key to success in the SDAIE classroom is the provision of resource-rich teaching to expand the modalities in which English learners can receive information. But which materials? And how to select them?

Selecting and Using Appropriate Materials

Choosing the right genre is one way to help English learners develop their conceptual and linguistic schemata. The literature curriculum, for example, can be a planned sequence that begins with familiar structures of folktales and myths and then uses these as a bridge to more complex works of literature. Myths and folktales from many cultures are now commonly available in high-quality editions with vibrant illustrations. Students can move from these folktales and myths to selected short stories by authors of many cultural backgrounds, then to portions of a longer work, and finally to entire works.

 Classroom Glimpse

A VARIETY OF MATERIALS

William Pruitt (2000, pp. 31–49) describes how his students move from studying different versions of a folktale to studying other kinds of tales.

 One of the goals of the story unit is for students to examine how the same story may differ as it appears in different perspectives, media, and cultures, and to compare and contrast these forms. Over the course of the two-week unit, we read and compare and contrast an original (translated) version of "Beauty and the Beast," a poem entitled "Beauty and the Beast," and three video versions of the story. Once students have gained experience with this folktale and understand the pattern of activities, we move to other texts that have film adaptations, for example, *Tuck Everlasting* (Babbitt, 1976).

Materials used in the classroom are most accessible when they match the age, language ability, and prior content knowledge of the students. Materials in the primary language can supplement content delivery in English. In fact, with a rich theme, materials from around the world can be featured in instruction.

Best Practice MATERIALS FOR A RICH THEME

A good example of an application of a rich theme is "Tool Use" (*Into English*, Level C, pp. 58–71). Students identify, graph, and discuss their use of tools; they can investigate what tools are found at home or at their parents' workplaces; they can explore tools used for everyday life such as in cooking; they can brainstorm new uses for tools and learn the names of common academic tools. This unit can incorporate crosscultural study (Chinese abacus) and total physical response (a game of charades acting out tool use). Classroom visitors can discuss the tools they use in their work. (Tinajero & Schifini, 1997)

Selecting materials involves an initial choice by the teacher whether to have one main content source or a package of content-related materials (chapters from various texts, video- and audiotapes, magazine and newspaper articles, encyclopedia entries, literary selections, Internet sources, software programs, etc.). Regardless of what is chosen, the teacher must consider two criteria: Are the content objectives for the lesson adequately presented by the material? Is the material comprehensible to English learners?

The following list enumerates items to consider when selecting materials:

- The information is accurate, up-to-date, and thorough.
- The tasks required of students are appropriate to the discipline and promote critical thinking.
- The text is clearly organized and engaging, with attractive print and layout features that assist students' comprehension.
- The text appeals to a variety of learning styles.
- Sources represented in the text include various literary genres (e.g., narrative, descriptive, analytic).
- The language of the text is straightforward, without complex syntactic patterns, idioms, or excessive jargon.
- New content vocabulary is clearly defined within the text or in a glossary.
- Diagrams, graphs, and charts are clearly labeled and complement and clarify the text.

Content area teachers must also use primary-language resources, such as dictionaries, books, software programs, Internet sites, encyclopedias, textbooks, and illustrated charts as well as people resources, such as cross-age tutors, parents, and community volunteers, in helping students to understand concepts. English learners in the content class are continually exposed to new content material and often find primary-language sources helpful.

Modifying Materials for Linguistic Accessibility

The teacher selects, modifies, and organizes text material to accommodate the needs of English learners. In modifying text, the goal is to improve comprehensibility through such means as providing study guides or defining new content vocabulary by showing definitions pictorially. Other modifications that may be necessary to help English learners comprehend connected discourse include the following approaches:

- Supply an advance organizer for the text that highlights the key topics and concepts in outline form, as focus questions, or as concept maps.
- Change the modality from written to oral. By reading aloud, the teacher can also model the process of posing questions while reading to show prediction strategies used when working with text (see the discussion of directed reading–thinking activity in Chapter 7).
- Selected passages can be tape-recorded for students to listen to as they read along in the text.
- By working in groups, students can share their notes and help one another complete missing parts or correct misunderstood concepts.

These adaptations increase readability. As students' language proficiency increases, so should the complexity of their reading material. The goal is to move students toward the ability to work with unmodified texts (Richard-Amato & Snow, 1992).

Culturally Appealing Materials

Multicultural materials are a rich source of language and content area learning, including books and other print media, visual aids, props, realia, manipulatives, materials that access other modalities, and human resources. Students may be able to bring in pictures, poems, dances, proverbs, or games; new ways to do math problems; or maps that show a different perspective than that given in the textbook. Shen's Books (www.shens.com) carries a wide selection of multicultural materials that include such themes as multicultural Cinderella stories and other fables; music around the world; foods of the world; immigrant life, adoption, and interracial families; Arabic and Islamic culture; Southeast Asia; and alphabets around the world.

The Internet is also a rich source of multicultural content. Students can search for their own primary-language materials. However, it's possible that the teacher who does not speak or read the primary language of the student may not be able to screen for inappropriate content. However, family or community members might be able to assist in finding educationally relevant content.

Sources for multicultural viewpoints and materials for various curriculum areas are presented in Table 5.10.

TABLE 5.10 Multicultural Materials: Sources for the Content Areas

Content Area	Suggested Material
Mathematics	*Multicultural Mathematics: A More Inclusive Mathematics.* Accessed May 24, 2010, from www.ericdigests.org/1996-1/more.htm.
Social Studies	Multicultural history and social studies sites. Accessed May 24, 2010, from www.edchange.org/multicultural/sites/history.html.
Literature	*Multicultural Children's Literature.* Accessed May 24, 2010, from www.multiculturalchildrenslit.com.
Science	*Multicultural Science and Math Connections: Middle School Projects and Activities.* Accessed May 24, 2010, from http://fermat.nap.edu/html/rtmss/5.72.html.

Technological Resources to Enhance Instruction

Computer-assisted instruction (CAI) has been used in classrooms since the earliest days of word processing (late 1970s), with large-scale tutoring systems available in the 1980s that enabled the individual user to attempt repeated answers and receive error feedback without public embarrassment. Computer-mediated communication (CMC) and more sophisticated computer-simulated learning environments have come into use in the twenty-first century (see Bitter, Pierson, & Burvikovs, 2004; Herring, 1996).

Tools for Instruction and Communication The digital revolution is changing the way people learn (Murray, 2000). Websites offer lesson plans, quizzes, chatrooms, and bulletin boards that allow the learner to sample English idioms, prepare for standardized tests, or connect with English learners in other parts of the world. Many teachers have access to Internet hookups in the classroom. Students can interact with others meaningfully, writing informal e-mails with "keypals" in different areas of the world or using writing-based chatrooms online in real time (Warschauer, 1995).

The instant communication available through the Internet connects students with other parts of the world, with speakers of English, and with rich sources of information. The World Wide Web delivers authentic materials, including texts, images, sound recordings, videoclips, virtual reality worlds, and dynamic, interactive presentations. Students can listen to live radio stations from around the world or hear prerecorded broadcasts of music, news, sports, and weather (LeLoup & Ponterio, 2000). Search engines (e.g., Google, Yahoo!, Bing) help the student find authentic materials on classroom, group, or individual research topics.

Today's teachers are educated to maximize the instructional and communicative use of the Internet, CD-ROM-based software, and other CMC tools, including audio and video production using computers, although in the process, older non-computer-based tools of multimedia production are falling by the wayside (see Herrell, 2000, pp. 134–138, for tips on the use of a variety of multimedia formats, including camcorder and overhead projector). Some teachers are also skilled in using computer-managed instruction (CMI) techniques such as grade book programs and database management.

Students who are literate in their native language can use the computer to access primary-language content information as they learn English.

Computers Support Learning Word processing supports the formal writing process by allowing students to electronically organize, draft, revise, edit, and publish their work. Students can develop oral skills by using presentation or authoring software to create professional-looking oral presentations, and they can apply both aural and oral skills in Web-enabled telephone conversations.

Software available for ELD includes traditional drill-and-practice programs focusing on vocabulary or grammar; tutorials; games; simulations that present students with real-life situations in the language and culture they are learning; productivity tools, such as word processing, databases, spreadsheets, graphics, and desktop publishing (DTP); and presentation or authoring programs. Material from encyclopedias and even *National Geographic* is available on CD-ROM and DVD formats.

The computer is a powerful learning tool that requires the teacher to organize, plan, teach, and monitor. Egbert and Hanson-Smith (1999) found that computer technology can provide students with the means to control their own learning, to construct meaning, and to evaluate and monitor their own performance.

Although language learning has long consisted of face-to-face interaction between teachers and students in the same physical location, new virtual learning environments have been made possible by the development of widespread, rapid Internet access. During virtual learning, students can participate when they choose (many events do not take place simultaneously) and where they choose (students can "log on" from home, from a neighborhood Internet-enabled café, or from a self-access computer lab at school). Software such as Skype enables users to see one another while learning, but even so, it is difficult to replicate the immediacy of real-life presence. Virtual learning is made possible by up-to-date software and hardware and fast, reliable Internet connections; but it is made effective in the same way that learning has always been effective—by expert teaching and motivated, receptive learners.

Best Practice   TIPS FOR ONLINE TEACHING

When designing Web-based virtual environments, some aspects are important to remember:

- Students often need mentoring in addition to academic content; in their minds, the two are intertwined to the extent that learners want to see that course assignments are part of a "bigger picture" of real-world applicability.
- Students may not be computer-savvy to the same degree. Computer-based delivery should require middle-of-the-road abilities, not expecting an extreme degree of expertise but not boring those who are accomplished "net-denizens."
- One cannot take for granted that students know their way around online educational software. They may need an orientation module before content delivery. Some students may need the instructor specifically to take them step-by-step through the software, with explicit modeling of what is required.
- Students often want "instant" turnaround and feedback on assignments. Instructors must balance these demands with a responsive yet controlled rhythm of communication in order to accustom students to regular patterns of reinforcement.
- Students often want a high degree of interactivity and communication not only with the course instructor but with other students in the class, using both synchronous (simultaneous) and asynchronous (delayed) delivery.
- There should be some mechanism for mediating communication issues that arise between students if they are engaged in peer communication online.

Examples of SDAIE in the Content Domains

When the planning for instructional objectives aligned with content standards has been completed, consideration then moves to the needs of the English learner. The following sections address the issue of making instruction meaningful to the learner using various facets of SDAIE.

Bridging: Accessing Prior Knowledge and Building Schemata

All learning builds on what has been previously learned, because the brain uses schemata to think. When exposed to new information, students access what is already known to them. If little prior knowledge exists, the teacher must supply background knowledge so that instruction can make sense.

Best Practice   WAYS "INTO" LITERATURE

Before reading a work of literature, the teacher can employ various ways to access prior knowledge:

- *Anticipation/reaction guides.* A short list of statements with which students agree or disagree
- *Pictures, art, movies.* Visual cues to build a feeling for the setting
- *Physical objects.* Items relating to the reading selection that students identify and discuss
- *Selected read-alouds.* Passages that pique students' interest in the selection

---

Assessing What Is Known   Before teaching, one must assess students' prior knowledge of the concepts and vocabulary that will be presented in the lesson in order to establish a starting point for the lesson, help students to review and stabilize their background information, and avoid spending instructional time on what is already known. Assessments can include a quick written pretest, informal survey, show of hands, pair/share (students discuss in pairs, then tell the whole class), teacher-led oral review, or a student quickwrite of some key points.

Sometimes what is already known is a mishmash of media images and hearsay that must be clarified. At other times, students may not be familiar with, or may disagree with, commonly held beliefs of the mainstream culture.

> [S]tudents bring much more background knowledge to the study of history than we sometimes credit them with. History is, after all, not confined to historians. The media also interpret historical events.... [T]here are also persistent historical myths and legends held dear by parts of the larger culture—Betsy Ross sewing the first flag, Columbus discovering a new world, and so forth. For some students, these images are comforting; others may feel excluded by the popular culture's mythologies. (Levstik & Barton, 2001, p. 25)

Best Practice   SOME QUESTIONS TO ASK BEFORE BEGINNING

Sometimes students can write down their prior knowledge. Before beginning a new topic, students can interview each other in pairs to ask the following questions:

- Have you ever read or heard anything about this topic?
- Can you tell me about a similar topic that you think will help us learn about this one?
- If you were a reporter and could talk to someone about this topic, who would you seek out? (Adapted from Fisher, Brozo, Frey, & Ivey, 2007)

Building Background Schemata   Teachers can provide new experiences that arouse interest in and draw attention to a topic, including field trips, guest speakers, fiction and nonfiction films, experiments, classroom discovery centers, music and songs, poetry and other literature, and computer simulations. To deepen these experiences, the teacher can guide the students to talk and write about them.

 Classroom Glimpse

INTEREST-GENERATING QUESTIONS

Mr. Gruen, a seventh-grade science teacher, wrote the following statement on the board: "It's only a matter of time before the earth will be hit by a large object from space." He then asked students to find a partner and think of three questions they would most like answered about this statement. Afterward, he gathered the questions and wrote them on the board, placing a star next to the ones that were similar so students could see common themes of interest. This is part of a larger sequence known as Student Questions for Purposeful Learning (SQPL) (Ediger & Pavlik, 1999; Guthrie & Wigfield, 2000). (Adapted from Fisher et al., 2007, p. 113)

 Classroom Glimpse

NEW EXPERIENCES TO BUILD BACKGROUND KNOWLEDGE

The firsthand experiences of a field trip piqued the interest of Dorothy Taylor's students in Virginia history and prepared them for the unit she had planned about colonial America.

In the fall, all of the fourth-grade classes in the school went on a field trip to Jamestown, Virginia. The children returned from their trip eager to talk about what they had learned. The field trip and students' enthusiasm were a perfect introduction to the social studies unit on the hardships faced by the Jamestown colonists. The students shared with one another what they knew about Jamestown and colonial America and added to their knowledge and vocabulary by reading and watching a video. (Taylor, 2000, pp. 53–55)

Teachers who are familiar with the background of the students can elicit beliefs, observations, and questions using students' everyday knowledge and cultural patterns.

Best Practice   THE CHECHE KONNEN SCIENCE PROJECT

Case studies in classrooms with low-income students from African-American, Haitian, and Latino backgrounds found ways that students deployed "sense-making practices—deep questions, vigorous argumentation, situated guesswork, embedded imagining, multiple perspectives, and innovative uses of everyday words" (Lee, 2005, p. 504)—to construct new meanings that were productive bridges to scientific practices. The teachers in the Cheche Konnen project tapped students' linguistic and cultural experiences to link their prior experiences to instruction, letting students draw on the forms of reasoning they employ in their daily lives as intellectual resources in science learning (Rosebery, Warren, & Conant, 1992; Warren, Ballenger, Ogonowski, Rosebery, & Hudicourt-Barnes, 2001).

Contextualization   When students are asked to learn a new concept, the use of materials, resources, and activities can provide contextualization. The verbal presentation of a lesson is supplemented by manipulatives, realia, media, and visual backup as teachers write key words and concepts on the chalkboard or butcher paper and use graphs, pictures, maps, and other physical props to communicate. By presenting concepts numerous times through various means and in a rich visual, auditory (for example, software programs and Internet sources that offer sounds and experiences), and kinesthetic (drama and skits, "gallery" walks) environment, teachers provide lessons that also appeal to students' different learning styles.

Teachers can contextualize mathematics instruction by having sports fans calculate batting average, points per game, or average speed; students who shop with their parents can help to keep purchases within budget by determining the best-priced item. Many activities in mathematics lend themselves to multicultural reference. Systems of numeration and measurements that originated in ancient civilizations (e.g., Egyptian, Inca, Aztec, Maya) can be explored and contrasted (Hatfield, Edwards, Bitter, & Morrow, 2004). Many countries around the world use the metric system, and English learners may have expertise in this system that they could share.

 Classroom Glimpse

CULTURAL CONTEXTUALIZATION

Linda Arieto, a Puerto-Rican American who grew up in a low-income community in the Bronx, shared a great deal in terms of language, culture, race, and class background with her students at Peter Towns Elementary. She was skillful using and responding to multiple varieties of language familiar to her students, such as Puerto-Rican Spanish, Puerto-Rican English, Black English vernacular, and Standard English. In the area of mathematics, she consistently found and applied lessons in the text that made sense to her students' cultural backgrounds and urban experiences. She used dominoes as math manipulatives, for example, because they correspond to a game that is popular in Caribbean culture. (Remillar & Cahnmann, 2005, pp. 178–179)

One example of contextualization is the effort to organize science instruction around common themes (e.g., nature of matter or magnetic energy) or societal issues (e.g., water pollution, drug addiction) to increase the relevance of scientific knowledge to students' lives. This makes science more approachable, allowing for more understanding and reflection, and permits key vocabulary to be used again and again.

Vocabulary Preteaching

Building vocabulary concept by concept is integral to content teaching. Not all vocabulary is learned when it is pretaught; it can be presented before a lesson, but it must also be repeated again and again during the lesson as well as afterward, for purposes of long-term memory.

Several strategies are central to vocabulary retention. To encourage *visual cueing*, teachers can post important concepts on the bulletin board throughout a unit, offer key terms in test questions to be used in short-answer responses, color or highlight new words, or try to connect concrete images with terms. Teachers cue *episodic memory* by having students role-play the meanings of key terms, demonstrate or model new ideas, or create semantic maps, posters, or collages to make key ideas more memorable. To promote *verbal rehearsal*, teachers can praise the use of key terms during student discussions, require important words to be used during oral presentations, or use a pointer to refer to central concepts during lectures (Gregory & Kuzmich, 2005).

Best Practice VOCABULARY DEVELOPMENT ACROSS PROFICIENCY LEVELS

Instructors of English learners should not assume that all vocabulary instruction must be concrete. Each particular word calls for a unique balance of concrete (real objects, meaningful movement [TPR], modeling, actual experience), symbolic (pictures, charts, icons, maps, models, graphic organizers), or abstract representation (verbal-only explanations orally or in print). Boyd-Batstone (2006) recommends a three-part checklist to judge the best way to teach or depict a new word: (1) Can a real object or experience be used? (2) Is a visual model useful? (3) Can an abstract term be "unpacked" (using word origin, related roots, cognates, primary-language translation, or metaphors)?

 Classroom Glimpse

TEACHING THE WORD *METAMORPHOSIS*

Ny Ha took considerable care to teach her third-grade students the term *metamorphosis*. She brought in a fishbowl with tadpoles and students observed and recorded the change of life cycle. She provided numerous picture books as well as computer programs that showed sequential pictures. Students created semantic maps of the concept. They made life cycle collages. They looked at models of caterpillars undergoing change. They used Kidspiration to generate mind maps using pictorial clip art. In the end, Ny thinks they "got it"! (Adapted from Boyd-Batstone, 2006)

Strategic Teaching Using Multimodalities

Students can be provided with cognitively engaging input (both oral and written) in ways that appeal to their learning styles and preferences. Many students need to see, hear, smell, touch, and feel knowledge all at the same time!

 Classroom Glimpse

SUPPLEMENTING THE VERBAL PRESENTATION

In a middle school life science class, Ms. Chen teaches about flowers by referring students to the explanation in the text (paragraph form), to a diagram of a flower in the text (graphic form), to a wall chart with a different flower (pictorial form), to a text glossary entry (dictionary form), and to actual flowers that students can examine. Through these numerous media, the concepts "petal," "stamen," "pistil," and "sepal" are understood and provide a basis for future study about life-forms. The teacher's task here is to ensure that these multiple sources are organized to communicate clearly and distinguish each concept.

Access to Cognitive Academic Language Across the Content Areas

Each academic subject makes distinct demands on the student. For example, mathematics uses discourse that is unlike natural language. Readers may find confusing the tendency to interrupt for the inclusion of formulae. Such texts require a reading rate adjustment because they must be read more slowly and require multiple readings. Charts and graphs are an integral part of the text, not a supplement, and technical language has precise meaning. Besides the key words and phrases heard in lesson presentations, there are also key direction words that students need to know, such as *analyze, compare, contrast, define, describe, discuss, explain, evaluate, illustrate, justify, state,* and *summarize.*

The Language of Mathematics   Language difficulties for English learners lie in vocabulary, syntax, semantics, and discourse. Vocabulary in mathematics includes technical words such as *numerator, divisor,* and *exponent.* Words such as *regroup, factor,* and *table* have a meaning different from everyday usage. Two or more mathematical concepts may combine to form a different concept: *line segment, cross multiply.* A variety of terms can signal the same mathematical operation: *Add, and, plus, sum, combine,* and *increased by* all represent addition (Dale & Cuevas, 1992). Sentence structures may involve complex syntax: "____ is to ____ as ____ is to ____" and "____ is percent of ____." Statements must be translated into logical symbols before problems can be completed, posing additional linguistic difficulty.

Problems with meaning (semantics) occur when natural language becomes the language of mathematics. For example, in the problem "Five times a number is two more than ten times the number," students must recognize that "a number" and "the number" refer to the same quantity.

Abbreviations and other math symbols may need to be interpreted. For example, *ft* for foot or the use of the apostrophe may be confusing for students, especially those who were previously educated in the metric system. Vocabulary charts that include the use of abbreviations and symbols can be placed around the classroom to help students remember. Teachers must be aware of these language differences and mediate the transition in learning a new language to express mathematical concepts.

 Classroom Glimpse

EMBODYING THE LANGUAGE OF RATIO

In a lesson on fractions, Mr. Goodall asked three students to come to the front of the class for a demonstration. One student measured the height and arm spread of a second student while the third student wrote the measurements on the board. The students used these numbers to express the relationships both as a ratio and as a percentage. (Adapted from Weiss & Pasley, 2004, p. 25)

The Language of Science   The four major language areas (vocabulary, syntax, semantics, discourse features) detailed in the section on mathematics are also relevant for science. Students not only have to learn scientific definitions, but they must also learn complex syntactic structures, which include passive voice, multiple embeddings, and long noun phrases (Pérez & Torres-Guzmán, 2002).

A number of types of text structures are common in science content materials. The *cause/ effect* structure links reasons with results or actions with their consequences. The *compare/ contrast* structure examines the similarities and differences between concepts. The *time-order* structure shows a sequential relationship over the passage of time (Pérez & Torres-Guzmán, 2002). To assist in their comprehension, students can receive special training in following written instructions for procedures or experiments.

English-language development must be an objective in all science instruction. Teachers should review vocabulary terms to be used in a lesson before beginning, including the names of equipment and activities that will be used; scientific definitions of some common words (e.g., *energy, speed, work*); and new content words (e.g., *acceleration, inertia*). Students need to be taught text processing techniques (how to take notes, how to reread text for answers to study questions, how to interpret charts and picture captions) and then held to a high level of recall about the information they read (Anderson & Gunderson, 2004). To assist their learning of scientific language, students can receive special training in following written instructions for procedures or experiments and in using glossaries.

Best Practice **DEVELOPING SCIENTIFIC LANGUAGE**

- Provide appropriate contexts for new vocabulary, syntactic structures, and discourse patterns. Isolated lists or exercises do not appear to facilitate language acquisition.
- Engage students in hands-on activities in which they discuss concepts in a genuine communicative context.
- Promote activities in which students actively debate with one another about the truth of a hypothesis or the meaning of data gathered.

(Adapted from Carrasquillo & Rodríguez, 2002; Kessler et al., 1992)

The Language of Social Studies   Because history itself has taken place in many languages, a strong social studies curriculum builds on dual-language skills. Students can use communication skills in two languages to gather oral histories from their families and communities. Their own family histories can teach them firsthand about complex historical issues. For more information about oral history projects, read "Junior Historians: Doing Oral History with ESL and Bilingual Students" (Olmedo, 1993).

As a discipline, social studies is concept-rich in ideas that may be difficult to depict in visuals. Student interaction is necessary for concept acquisition and subsequent application in different situations. Inquiry skills that are used first in the classroom and then in the community help students practice what they are learning in authentic situations (Sunal & Haas, 2005).

The Language of Music   Music is a universal language. All cultures make music, expressing their cultural heritage in the particular sounds they make. However, music has its own language that requires specific understanding before an individual can become a proficient performer. For example, words such as *jazz, pitch, atonality,* and *folk music* are important technical concepts specific to music; if not taught within the proper context, they may pose a challenge for many English learners.

Music can also be used to teach concepts in other content domains. A first-grade lesson teaches opposites through music. Students listen to a story about opposites, which they then discuss before seeking opposites in music, using the books *Elmo's Big Lift and Look Book* and *Pooh Popping Opposites* and the music tapes *Down on Grandpa's Farm* and *Lullaby and Goodnight.* After a warm-up in which the teacher asks students, "What are opposites?" and "How do we find them?" the teacher reads books that illustrate the concept, asking students for some more examples and stating some pairs that are not opposites. Then the teacher plays tapes of songs that show opposites: fast/slow, number of instruments or people singing, etc.). For assessment, students listen to two more tape selections and write the opposites found (Graves, 1996).

Language in the Visual Arts   Artists have specific ways of doing art, and there is a language to express those ways. Part of an effective visual arts education involves exposing students to appropriate language that describes artistic expression and creates a common language in the community of artists. Accomplished teaching, particularly with English learners, requires explicit teaching of words such as *movement, medium,* or *organic.* Art lends itself to contextualization of terms but still demands careful and skillful teaching to connect language and art.

Scaffolded Content Instruction

Each content domain has particular ways of presenting content, including differences between elementary and secondary methods. Scaffolded teaching approaches support learning in various content areas at both elementary and secondary levels.

Elementary Mathematics   Adapting math instruction for English learners takes many forms. Table 5.11 shows how math centers set up to teach multiplication in the mainstream classroom can be adapted for English learners.

Secondary Mathematics: The Three-Phase Pattern   Many mathematics teachers follow a three-phase pattern. The first phase involves the introduction, demonstration, and explanation of the concept or strategy by the teacher, followed by an interactive questioning segment, in which the teacher establishes how well students are grasping the concept. The second phase involves guided practice, in which students make the transition from "teacher regulation" to student "self-regulation" (Belmont, 1989). Supporting techniques can include coaching, prompting, cueing, and monitoring student performance. The third phase allows students to work independently. If students are having difficulty during independent practice, they can receive more guided practice.

Further research in secondary mathematics teaching suggests the importance of making short- and long-term goals clear, as well as explaining to students the usefulness of each mathematical concept. Projects are very effective, although long projects need to be used with discretion. Table 5.12 shows additional strategic approaches for teaching mathematics to English learners.

TABLE 5.11 Adapting Math Centers for English Learners: Multiplication Station Activities

Unadapted Center	Suggested Adaptations
1. In Shopping Spree, students make purchases from a list of items, spending exactly $25 for their combination of items.	Directions can be in pictorial form.
2. In Circles and Stars, students use dice to play a multiplication game. The roll of the first die determines the number of circles the student will draw. The second roll, using a different colored die, indicates the number of stars the student should draw in each circle. The student then writes a number sentence that reflects the roll of the dice and the product (the total number of stars drawn).	A peer or older tutor can be stationed at the center to explain directions in L1.
3. In Comparison Game, students use a deck of cards from which the face cards have been removed. Aces are equal to one. Students draw two cards each and use the numbers to create a multiplication number sentence and the product of the two numbers. A "more or less" spinner is used to determine which student's product wins for each round.	A pair of students can observe while another pair plays until they get the idea.

Source: Adapted from http://mathforum.org/t2t/message.taco?thread=5024&message=4.

TABLE 5.12 Mathematics Teaching Strategies for English Learners

Teaching Strategy	Description
Encourage exploration.	Plan activities that facilitate explorations and investigations of mathematical concepts, nurture students' curiosity, and stimulate creativity.
Use manipulatives.	Manipulatives help make abstract concepts concrete.
Use real-world problem-solving activities.	Using mathematics as it applies to daily life and to solve real-life problems makes it interesting and meaningful.
Encourage oral and written expression.	Mathematics requires specific language and CALP, and students should be provided opportunities to practice and express their mathematical knowledge orally and in writing.
Offer an enriched curriculum and challenging activities.	Mathematics is a discipline with its own CALP characterized by specific experiences and abilities involving inquiry, problem solving, and higher thinking.
Use a variety of problem-solving experiences.	Teachers should plan challenges that stimulate higher-order thinking and problem solving and that are nonroutine and open-ended. For example, provide math problems that may have various correct solutions and answers, problems with multiple interpretations, and answers that can be represented in multiple ways.

Source: Balderrama & Díaz-Rico (2006).

Elementary Science   The important idea in science instruction is to adopt a problem-solving approach featuring questions that are both comprehensible and interesting. Students can be assisted to solve problems in science by developing a personal set of learning strategies. Teachers can help students describe the thinking they use to come up with solutions and praise innovative techniques they apply. Students can share their processes with one another, resulting in multiple ways of approaching a problem. Teachers can also discuss with students the biographies of famous scientists, showing the perseverance it took to solve the problems they addressed.

Secondary Science   Alternative means of representing information is important in secondary science instruction. T-charts and other graphic organizers are ways to train students to translate verbal information from texts and lectures into mental structures for purposes of memorization as well as understanding. Pictures are important sources of information, whether from texts or supplementary sources. In summary, any method of noting and organizing details or creating and testing hypotheses furthers the goals of science inquiry.

Elementary Literature   Many graphic organizers are available for use in scaffolding literature instruction: character trait charts, sequence-of-events outlines, cause-and-effect diagrams, setting description maps, and so forth. One key method of scaffolding literature that can be used in other content areas is the *cognitive apprentice model*. Children learn to read from teachers, but they also learn from teachers to enjoy reading. Teachers can model why they like certain genres, why a certain turn of phrase is delightful, why a plot is compelling, and so forth. Students then become the apprentices of teachers' thinking about literature—an apprenticeship in literature appreciation.

Secondary Literature   Building on the love of reading that is the foundation of elementary instruction, students at the secondary level must balance consumption with production. It is one thing to read poetry and entirely another to write it, to struggle firsthand with the freshness of images, the discipline of meter, the lure of rhyme. To appreciate literature, one must be willing to dive in, to create and re-create in the leading genres of the day. Therefore, scaffolding literature is intrinsically bound up with creative production of language.

Integral to production of language is scaffolded creativity in the primary language. Students who create in two languages are addressing a peer audience that appreciates the effort. Even students with a primary language not understood by peers can share the poetic sound and meaning (in translation). All creativity stimulates the common underlying proficiency that makes language a human treasure.

 Classroom Glimpse

PRIMARY-LANGUAGE POETRY

Judith Casey (2004) encourages students to share native language with classmates during a poetry activity, in which students bring in and read aloud a poem in their L1. On Poetry Day, the atmosphere of the class is charged. No one knows exactly what to expect, but the students are excited. Amazingly, hearing one another read in their L1 lets the students see each other in a new light. The class is forever changed as students recognize the value, contributions, and abilities of their classmates. (pp. 51–52)

Elementary Social Studies   Scaffolded social studies starts with the timeline and the map as the basic graphic organizers. Students need a firm understanding of when and where events took place. Any mental device is useful that helps students visualize when and where. If the computer program Google Earth can be displayed from the computer screen onto a large surface at the beginning of each lesson, students can start "zoomed in" at their own school and then "zoom out" to the picture of the earth in space, move the map to the location of the day's lesson in history or geography, and then "zoom in" to locate any feature under discussion. This grounds students in their own place before making the transition to another.

Secondary History/Social Science   The reading load in secondary history often needs to be scaffolded. Bradley and Bradley (2004, n.p.) offered several useful methods to help students monitor their comprehension during reading.

- *Analyzing captions.* Look at the picture captions and ask, "How does this tie into the reading?"
- *Turning subheads into questions.* By rephrasing a subheading into a question, readers are able to predict upcoming content.
- *Making margin notes.* Using small sticky notes, students write new vocabulary words they encounter—even words not in the content glossary.

A useful scaffolding technique for secondary social studies, the question–answer relationships (QAR) model (Raphael, 1986), describes four kinds of questions: Right There (direct quote from the text), Think and Search (the answer must be inferred from several text passages), Author and You (text integrated with personal experience), and On Your Own (drawn from personal experiences). Each question requires a different set of text processing or thinking resources. This method can be taught in one lesson, and thereafter students can learn to classify questions and locate answers independently.

Best Practice   **TEACHING NOTE-TAKING SKILLS**

Better note takers produce greater academic achievement in middle and high school (Faber, Morris, & Lieberman, 2000). Here are tips on taking better notes:

- Date and title notes at the top of the page.
- Split the page: Keep lecture notes on the left side and organizational and summary notes on the right side.
- Skip lines to show change of topic.
- Apply the same organization as the lecturer to number subpoints or mark details.
- Use underlining, circling, or highlighting to indicate important ideas. (Adapted from Stahl, King, & Henk, 1991)

 Classroom Glimpse

COLLABORATION IN MIDDLE SCHOOL SOCIAL STUDIES

At Gerona Middle School (pseudonym) in a medium-sized California agricultural town, more than half of the students are English learners, some from migrant labor families. The majority of students are academically underprepared according to their scores on standardized tests.

In a recent unit about the Crusades, students wrote expository essays in which they described, justified, and persuaded. At the end of each group activity and each unit, students wrote a final essay, making connections between their group activities and the central theme of the unit. Content area and language arts teachers coordinated interdisciplinary responsibility for this writing, in what is known as sustained-content instruction. (Adapted from Bunch, Abram, Lotan, & Valdés, 2001)

Guided and Independent Practice That Promotes Students' Active Language Use

Guided Practice   Teachers working in mixed-ability classrooms can plan group activities that help students in different ways. Students can work in homogeneous groups when the goal of the activity is accuracy and in heterogeneous groups when the goal is fluency. For example, to develop accuracy, first-grade students can listen to a reading of the Chinese folktale "The Magic Sieve." A group of beginning students can retell the story using pictures and then talk about the pictures. Intermediate students can retell the story to the teacher or a cross-age tutor. The teacher writes their story for them, and then students can reread, illustrate, and rearrange the story from sentence strips. A group of more proficient students can create a new group story.

At the secondary level, as students work in class, teachers can use various strategies to guide their learning. Groups of students can work together to create visual summaries or chapter reviews of textbook content. Specific students can each take on the persona of a literary character or historic personage and provide background for other students' questions throughout the reading. Charts, graphs, pictures, and symbols can trace the development of images, ideas, and themes.

Best Practice   GUIDED PRACTICE IN READING LITERATURE

Scaffolded activities help students as they work with text. Reading aloud as students follow along can give them an opportunity to hear a proficient reader, get a sense of the format and story line, and listen to the teacher think aloud about the reading. In the think-aloud, teachers can model how they monitor a sequence of events, identify foreshadowing and flashback, visualize a setting, analyze character and motive, comprehend mood and theme, and recognize irony and symbolism. To help students develop a sense of inflection, pronunciation, rhythm, and stress, a commercial tape recording of a work of literature can be obtained for listening and review, or native-English-speaking students or adult volunteers may be willing to make a recording.

Maintaining the First Language in Guided Practice   Students can be encouraged to use and develop their native language during guided practice. Aides and tutors can help explain difficult passages and guide students in summarizing their understanding. Native-language books, magazines, films, and other materials relating to the topic or theme of the lesson can support and even augment students' learning. They can also maintain reading logs or journals in their native language.

Independent Practice   Computers and other resources can be used to extend practice in various content domains. Many English learners are unfamiliar with the basic tools associated with mathematics (rulers, protractors, calculators, computers, etc.) (Buchanan & Helman, 1997). After demonstrating each, teachers can provide students with real-life opportunities to use them. For example, students are told that the playground needs to be repaved. They first have to estimate the area, then check their estimates with the actual tools (using both standard and metric measuring instruments, as they will not know which system the parking company uses), and then use calculators to find the percentage of error in their estimates. Computer programs can also help to provide estimates and calculations.

Best Practice   INDEPENDENT REACTIONS TO WORKS OF LITERATURE

- Authentic written responses encourage students to reflect on the piece of literature and to express their interpretations to an audience beyond the classroom.
- Students write poems and share them with other classes or parents at a Poetry Night.
- Student journalists write reviews of literature works for the school or classroom newspaper or act as movie critics and review the film version of a text studied in class. They can then compare the differences and draw conclusions about the pros and cons of the different media.
- Students write letters to authors to express their reactions to the story or to pen pals recommending certain pieces of literature.
- Favorite parts of selections can be rewritten as a play and enacted for other classes as a way to encourage other students to read that piece of literature.
- Students can plan a mock television game show and devise various formats that include ideas from the literature studied.

Best Practice   INDEPENDENT QUESTIONING STRATEGIES

"Question swap" (Gregory & Kuzmich, 2005) is a useful device for helping students personalize social studies. For any given topic, students write out two questions each (with answers) and then swap one question with the first partner, each writing out answers. The questioners then do the same with the second question. This process restructures information from verbal input to mental schemata. The questions are the scaffold. The teacher should gather up the questions and answers at the end and skim quickly to clear up any misrepresentation.

Resources for Independent Practice

Across the content areas, teachers can help make resources available for students as they approach learning tasks autonomously. This helps students take responsibility for their own learning.

Classroom Glimpse

USING MULTIPLE RESOURCES FOR INDEPENDENT RESEARCH

Students studying a fifth-grade unit on settlement of the West can examine the legal issues involved in the Treaty of Guadalupe-Hidalgo, compare the various cultures that came into contact in the Southwest, delve into the history of land grant titles, and pursue many more issues of interest. Through filmstrips, films, videos, computer simulations, literature, nonfiction texts, and oral discussions, students develop conceptual knowledge. Such a unit incorporates history, geography, sociology, economics, values, information-seeking skills, group participation, and perhaps dramatic talents as students act out the signing of treaties and other cultural events.

Math Resources for Elementary English Learners   Almost all math programs at the primary level are supported by sets of manipulative materials; however, manipulatives are not a magic substitute for intensive, multimodal instruction that ensures all students acquire mathematics concepts at every stage. The World Wide Web is a vast source of problems, contests, enrichment, and teacher resources to supplement classroom instruction.

Family Math is a program that focuses on families learning mathematics together in support of the elementary math curriculum. Adults and children come to Family Math classes together once a week for several weeks, doing activities in small groups, with two or three families working together. As a follow-up, family members use inexpensive materials found in the home (bottle caps, toothpicks, coins) to practice ideas that were presented in class. The website www.techteachers.com/mathweb/familymath/index.htm offers resources for Family Math activities.

Math Resources for Secondary English Learners   The Internet provides numerous sites that are both resources for teachers and opportunities for students to practice mathematical skills. Table 5.13 features several websites recommended by some of the mathematics teachers with whom I work, including their descriptions of how these sites help them in working with English learners.

Internet Social Studies Resources for English Learners   Classroom teachers can combine the enormous range of materials from the Internet with other instructional resources and methods. Field trips via the Internet include visiting the White House (www.whitehouse.gov), exhibitions of African and pre-Columbian Native-American art (www.nmai.si.edu), or the Egyptian pyramids (www.pbs.org/wgbh/nova/pyramid). Many of the virtual field trip sites are designed specifically for education, featuring lesson plans and interactive student activities (see www

TABLE 5.13 Websites for Teaching Secondary Mathematics to English Learners

Website	Description
http://matti.usu.edu/nlvm/nav/vlibrary.html	Provides manipulatives as a visual demonstration of concepts taking place in the class. The graph is an excellent tool; one can graph several lines on the same Cartesian plane and see the variations made by changing a coefficient.
www.purplemath.com/modules/translat.htm	Translates word problems into algebraic expressions. When English learners are faced with word problems, it is rarely one word that gives them problems, but more often a phrase. That phrase is usually the key to setting up the problem. The website provides a step-by-step account of how to set up these problems.

Source: Balderrama & Díaz-Rico (2006).

.internet4classrooms.com). Students can also create their own virtual field trips of local historical sites, or even of their school. Table 5.14 offers selected websites for teaching secondary social studies to English learners.

 Classroom Glimpse

A HISTORIC WEBSITE

Ms. Rosie Beccera Davies's third-grade class at Washington Elementary School in Montebello, California, made a historical website for their community, beginning with the Gabrielino (Tongva) Indians, and including many local historical sites.

Science Resources outside of the School The school science program often extends beyond the walls of the school to the resources of the community. Teachers can work with local

TABLE 5.14 Websites for Teaching Secondary Social Studies to English Learners

Website	Description
www.DiscoverySchool.com	An excellent supplement to world history videos. The site offers vocabulary words and terms used in the video, rubrics, and a list of additional resources.
http://atozteacherstuff.com	Contains many ELD lessons specifically designed for all content areas, especially for English learners in U.S. history and government.
www/eduref.org/Virtual/Lessons	An easy to use site, containing social studies lessons for English learners.

personnel, such as those at science-rich centers (museums, industries, universities, etc.), to plan for the use of exhibits and educational programs that enhance the study of a particular topic. In addition, the physical environment in and around the school can be used as a living laboratory for the study of natural phenomena in project-based and service-learning activities.

Resources for Music   When adapting music lessons for English learners, primary-language music audiotapes are available through Shen's Books at www.shens.com, including tapes in Spanish, Hmong, Vietnamese, Cambodian, Korean, Japanese, and Mandarin, as well as tapes from cultures other than the native cultures of the students.

Technology is increasingly an important resource in music education. A powerful application for music education is the use of computers, allowing students to improvise, make arrangements, and access vast libraries of recorded music. When instruments are connected to electronic instruments and computers, they can be used to record, transcribe, and even permit practice performances.

Musical and cultural resources abound in all communities, and skillful music educators tap into these resources by working with parents, churches, and other civic organizations. Local musicians, professionals, music faculty at local universities, family members, and students at colleges and universities can conduct sessions and workshops in conjunction with the regular instructional program.

Formative Assessment and Reteaching Content

The hands-on nature of problem solving in science can naturally align with performance-based assessment. By performing actual science activities, students are actively demonstrating the skills for which assessment holds them responsible. The use of formative assessment involves teachers in the role of offering guidance and feedback so the given skills can be accomplished.

Classroom Glimpse

CHECKING EXIT COMPREHENSION IN SCIENCE

Mr. Petersen uses exit slips as a strategy just before students leave their middle school science class. He provides a preprinted prompt, such as "I'm still not clear about . . . ," to help students pinpoint what is still fuzzy for them about the day's lesson. Students can reflect on what they have just learned, show their thinking process, and prepare for continued learning on the topic. Teachers can use this information to select what to revisit, elaborate, or expand on in the next lesson. (Adapted from Fisher et al., 2007)

Summative Assessment of Content Lessons

Multiple strategies can be used to assess students' mastery of language objectives and grade-level content objectives across diverse content domains.

Assessment in Mathematics   Although traditional assessment in mathematics focuses on the mastery of algorithms, many alternative forms can be used to measure mathematical thinking and problem solving. Authentic assessment allows the teacher to evaluate mathematics understanding while students are actively engaged in such learning activities as running a school store or simulating trade on the stock market. Assessments should allow for differences in understanding, creativity, and accomplishment. Flexible expectations permit different pacing for students with basic versus advanced math skills.

Best Practice   ALTERNATIVE MEANS OF DEMONSTRATING
MATH KNOWLEDGE

Students can use various methods to show math learning:

- Produce or find three different drawings for the number x.
- Write three story problems that have the number x as an answer.
- Make up a pattern and explain it.
- Interview ten people to find out the favorite ice cream flavors and then invent a way to show this information to the class.

Source: Adapted from Rowan & Bourne (1994).

Assessment in Visual and Performing Arts   Instruction and assessment go hand in hand in the visual and performing arts. The teacher and the artist interact and collaborate in ongoing feedback, with self-monitoring and self-assessment being a part of the daily experience. Portfolios are very common assessment tools used by artists in the performing arts because they track individual growth. They can help high school students, for example, apply for college entrance to an art institute or for employment in the visual arts.

Student exhibitions are also a way that teachers can create safe opportunities for assessment, whereby peers and other adults give feedback on completed works or works-in-progress. These exhibitions can take place in the classroom, and rubrics can be developed by the class to evaluate basic elements in a work.

Best Practice   ASSESSMENT AS MUSICAL PERFORMANCE

Showcasing musical talent by means of group and individual performance is a time-honored assessment of musical involvement. The excitement of performance and the responsibility of individuals toward their peers and audience teach maturity and poise. Bridging cultural gaps by offering music in many languages helps to involve the families and community in preparing for, attending, and enjoying concerts.

Assessment in Social Studies   Assessment of all students must be equitable in a social studies program. English learners can show proficiency in multiple ways: portfolios, performance

Members of the community can share cultural activities such as music and art with students.

assessments, written reports, role-plays, and research projects. When high-stakes educational decisions for individual students are made, the decisions should be based on a variety of assessments, rather than on a single test score. Assessments of students in social studies should be designed and used to further the goal of educating students to be active citizens in a democratic society (see Chapter 3 for more on assessment).

Table 5.15 presents strategies for adapting curricula in secondary school social studies. Similar strategies may apply in other content areas. These strategies represent a sample of SDAIE methods.

Instructional Needs beyond the Classroom

To be successful in their academic courses, English learners often need assistance from organizations and volunteers outside of the classroom. This assistance can come from academic summer programs, additional instructional services such as after-school programs and peer tutoring, and Dial-a-Teacher for homework help in English and in the primary language. Support in the affective domain may include special home visits by released time teachers, counselors, or outreach workers and informal counseling by teachers. Monitoring of academic progress by counselors also helps to encourage students with language needs.

TABLE 5.15 Strategies for Adapting Curricula in Secondary Social Studies

Strategy	How It Helps
Identify similarities and differences	Helps students compare, create metaphors, and use analogies (comparing the U.S. Cabinet to a school can clarify the concept of analogy); builds vocabulary, comprehension.
Historical investigation	Gives students an active role in understanding history and allows them to pursue a question using strategies that work for them; focuses on students' interests; allows students flexibility; encourages self-monitoring of progress.
Inventions	Inventions are/have been an important part of U.S. history; students are able to demonstrate comprehension, knowledge, and creativity within a historical framework while reliving history.
Role-playing	Adolescents are quite dramatic and like to be in "someone else's shoes"; students learn about others' perspectives while using language, gestures, and body language to show their understanding.
Group work	Collaborative projects or assignments help students to solve problems together as they hear and use history-related CALP in a low-anxiety environment; structured group work addresses status issues so that "everyone participates, no one dominates" and English learners have chances to talk.
Decision making	This provides for contemplation and discussion of concepts central to many historical issues; provides students a chance to hear and use language to make decisions.
"What if" stories	Help students use language to create hypothetical predictions about history: for example, what if Columbus had not sailed to America?
Puzzles, riddles	Students see representations of historical concepts in different formats that engage and incorporate multiple intelligences.
Explanations with concrete referents	Help students understand abstract concepts.
Alternative representation formats	Different ways of presenting facts; for example, graphic organizers, maps, tables, charts, and graphs can reduce verbiage and identify key concepts in a lesson; this also models the different means historians use to gather evidence.
Summarizing and note taking	An important skill of historians; allows students to make sense of extensive text and lecture by listening for key words and identifying relevant information.
Preteach assignments	Helps students anticipate key concepts before reading assignment.
Prepare for exams	Teacher can model how to use textbook features such as chapter goals and overviews, summaries, and glossaries; this also helps students self-monitor comprehension and progress.
Provide learning, reading, and study support	Helps students process text and use language to voice their ideas; puts them in role of experts. Teachers arrange jigsaw groups to read text, assigning students to groups and making groups of students experts on specific portions of reading; students read and discuss together; teacher reviews and addresses specific issues with the entire class.
Word association	Vocabulary enrichment; teaching students to hear a word and associate it with an image helps comprehension and retention.
Listen for specific information	Teaches students explicitly what is important in a lecture, text, or historical document; students use teacher-created graphic organizers or fill-in-the-blank lecture notes.

Best Practice	MEETING INSTRUCTIONAL NEEDS BEYOND THE CLASSROOM

Escalante and Dirmann (1990) explicated the main components of the Garfield High School advanced placement (AP) calculus course in which Escalante achieved outstanding success in preparing Hispanic students to pass the AP calculus examination. Escalante's success was not due solely to outstanding classroom teaching; he was the organizer of a broad effort to promote student success. In his classroom, he set the parameters: He made achievement a game for the students, the "opponent" being the Educational Testing Service's examination; he coached students to hold up under the pressure of the contest and work hard to win; and he held students accountable for attendance and productivity. But beyond this work in the classroom was the needed community support.

Community individuals and organizations donated copiers, computers, transportation, and souvenirs such as special caps and team jackets. Parents became involved in a campaign against drug use. This helped Escalante emphasize proper conduct, respect, and value for education. Past graduates served as models of achievement. They gave pep talks to students and acted as hosts in visits to high-tech labs. The support from these other individuals combined to give students more help and encouragement than could be provided by the classroom teacher alone. Students saw concentrated, caring, motivated effort directed toward them—something they had rarely before experienced. The results were dramatized in the unforgettable feature film *Stand and Deliver*.

Teacher Commitment

Although technological tools and techniques for ELD and content area teaching are changing rapidly, what remains constant is the need for English learners to receive high-quality instruction that permits them access to the cognitive academic language they need for school success. Teachers who are dedicated to student achievement are key.

In SDAIE classrooms, it is not only the students who are learning. Successful teachers themselves are open, not only *willing* to learn but also *expecting* to learn.

English-language development and content learning go hand in hand in classrooms that support high-quality instruction for English learners. These classrooms feature multiple modalities for instruction and a rich mix of stimulating materials and linguistic interaction. Most of all, classrooms that foster high achievement have teachers who are committed to enriching language and promoting a high level of content learning using SDAIE to make instruction comprehensible and meaningful.

Go to the Topics Building Background Knowledge, Content Area Learning, Instructional Strategies, and Differentiating Instruction in the MyEducationLab (www.myeducationlab.com) for your course, where you can:

- Find learning outcomes for Building Background Knowledge, Content Area Learning, Instructional Strategies, and Differentiating Instruction along with the national standards that connect to these outcomes.
- Complete Assignments and Activities that can help you more deeply understand the chapter content.
- Apply and practice your understanding of the core teaching skills identified in the chapter with the Building Teaching Skills and Dispositions learning units.
- Examine challenging situations and cases presented in the IRIS Center Resources.
- Check your comprehension on the content covered in the chapter by going to the Study Plan in the Book Resources for your text. Here you will be able to take a chapter quiz, receive feedback on your answers, and then access Review, Practice, and Enrichment activities to enhance your understanding of chapter content.

Go to the Topic A+RISE in the MyEducationLab (www.myeducationlab.com) for your course. A+RISE® Standards2Strategy™ is an innovative and interactive online resource that offers new teachers in grades K–12 just-in-time, research-based instructional strategies that:

- Meet the linguistic needs of ELLs as they learn content
- Differentiate instruction for all grades and abilities
- Offer reading and writing techniques, cooperative learning, use of linguistic and nonlinguistic representations, scaffolding, teacher modeling, higher order thinking, and alternative classroom ELL assessment
- Provide support to help teachers be effective through the integration of listening, speaking, reading, and writing along with the content curriculum
- Improve student achievement
- Are aligned to Common Core Elementary Language Arts standards (for the literacy strategies) and to English language proficiency standards in WIDA, Texas, California, and Florida.

Words and Meanings: English Learners' Vocabulary Development

Lindfors Photography

Words and Meanings: English Learners' Vocabulary Development

> " How beautiful that first slow word
> To those who found it,
> To those who heard,
> Back in the shadowy dawn of Time. "
>
> —Author Unknown

In this chapter, we discuss research on vocabulary learning and teaching, and provide suggestions for promoting vocabulary instruction for English learners. The following questions are discussed:

1. What does research have to say about learning and developing vocabulary in a second language?

2. What does it mean to "know a word"? What words do students need to know?

3. What are some considerations for differentiating vocabulary instruction for English learners? How may such differentiation be accomplished?

4. Which classroom contexts and teaching strategies can best promote vocabulary growth for English learners?

5. How may second language vocabulary be assessed?

R ecently, an elderly friend of ours, Mimi, whose eyesight was failing, asked us if we would read to her. We chose favorite books this retired librarian loved such as Jane Austen's *Pride and Prejudice*. One day when we were reading, she told us that she was having trouble sleeping because a word was crowding her out of her bed. "What was the word?" we asked. **"Nomenclature!"** she exclaimed loudly.

We don't all have words crowding us out of our beds, but through words we weave the tapestry of our lives. On school entry and throughout our education, our vocabulary represents one of the most important determinants of our success in reading, writing, and conversing in and out of school. Similarly second language learners' English vocabulary, upon entering school and throughout, will have a large influence on their ability to navigate their coursework in English and communicate broadly in the English-speaking world.

What Does Research Tell Us About Vocabulary Development in a Second Language?

It has been estimated that native English speakers growing up acquire about 1,000 words per year. Thus a kindergartener starts school with about 5,000 words; enters fifth grade with about 10,000; and graduates high school with about 18,000 (Goulden, Nation & Read, 1990; Nation, 2001; Nation & Waring, 2002). There are, of course, differences among English native speakers. For example, research suggests that higher socioeconomic status (SES) first graders know about twice as many words as lower SES children (Graves, Brunetti, & Slater, 1982; Graves & Slater, 1987). Clearly students new to English have their work cut out for them if they are to approximate the vocabulary level of their native English-speaking peers. We also know the critical role of vocabulary for academic literacy, and research has shown that unknown words place a particular burden on English learners' (ELs') English reading comprehension when com-

 INTERNET RESOURCES

One excellent site on vocabulary is the Second Language Vocabulary Resources page: **www1. harenet.ne.jp/~waring/vocab/index.html**.

The site contains lists of some of the more common words in English as well as other lists. In addition, it contains a bibliography of second language acquisition and learning as well as many references to vocabulary. You might go to the various lists such as a list of the 2000 most frequent words from a variety of sources, or Paul Nation's list for the Range program, or lists for academic

study. After considering the various lists discuss with fellow students which list or lists would be most appropriate for your students and discuss how you would test your students for word knowledge and have them learn the words on the list. The Ohio University site on Vocabulary for English Language Learners (**www.ohiou.edu/esl/ English/vocabulary.html**) contains links ranging from K-University level vocabulary lessons, activities, and games. You could run a class on vocabulary alone using this site.

pared to their monolingual English counterparts (Jiménez, Garcia & Pearson 1996; Cheung & Slavin, 2005; Dressler & Kamil, 2006). What do we, as teachers, need to know and do to help our students narrow the vocabulary gap as they work toward English language proficiency?

First, let's take a closer look at what you know when you "know a word." Consider a rather common word like *catch*. If *catch* is in your **receptive oral vocabulary**, you will recognize and understand it when you hear it; if it's in your **productive oral vocabulary**, you will be able to use it when speaking. Similarly, if *catch* is in your **receptive written vocabulary**, you will recognize and understand it if you come across it while reading; if it's in your **productive written vocabulary**, you will be able to use it when you write. Thus, we have word knowledge in the four language domains: listening, speaking, reading, and writing. It is worth noting here that we know more words receptively than productively.

To use the word *catch* effectively, you need to know its **form**. What does it sound like; how is it pronounced? What does it look like; how is it spelled? What word parts are there to help you recognize or convey meaning? What is the **meaning** of the word? Now here's the catch. As you know, most words have multiple meanings, and the specific meaning of any word depends upon its **use in context**, including its grammatical function in the sentence or utterance. Consider the following:

Let's play *catch*.

That fellow's a great *catch*.

Alexandra didn't *catch* a single fish today.

I don't want to *catch* your cold.

In the first two examples, *catch* functions grammatically as a noun; in the third and fourth, it's used as a verb. Knowing the word *catch* as a noun also entails knowing how to make it plural (add *–es*) and whether and when it takes an article (*a, an, the*). Similarly, knowing *catch* as a verb entails knowing how it changes form in the various verb tenses. In this case, you have to know that the past tense takes an irregular form, *caught*. Word knowledge therefore includes knowing its grammatical functions and how it "morphs" or changes form to modify meaning.

We offered only four different uses of *catch* in our examples above. In our *Encarta World English Dictionary* (1999), *catch* and its derivatives (e.g., catch-as-catch-can; catch phrase) take up all three columns of an entire page with 30 different meanings as a verb, 10 different meanings as a noun, and 24 different derivative words, phrases, and idiomatic expressions. And we are talking about just one word! Learning the variety of meanings and uses of a word like *catch* requires a great deal of exposure to the word as used in various contexts. Furthermore, breadth and depth of word knowledge are acquired incrementally over time as varied meanings are encountered in different contexts, with wide reading representing a major source of word learning. That said, it remains important to focus on vocabulary as part of daily instruction. How can we do so? We start by narrowing our focus to those words students most need to know, followed by a discussion of how words are learned.

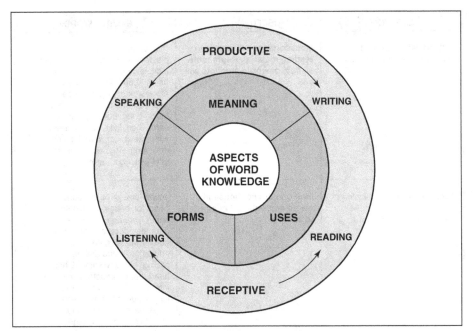

FIGURE 6.1

ASPECTS OF WORD
KNOWLEDGE

What Words Do Students Need to Know?

English learners need to develop a vocabulary that includes general **high-frequency words** along with specific **academic content words** that may occur less frequently but are crucial for learning science, math, history, literature, and so forth. Word frequency estimates point us to those words that occur most often and are therefore important for students to know. For example, the first 1,000 highest frequency words account for about 84 percent of the words used in conversation, and about 73 percent of the words that occur in academic texts (Nation, 2001). When you add the next 1,000 highest frequency words, you now account for about 90 percent of words used in conversation and about 78 percent of words in academic texts. To comprehend a text without help, a student needs to understand about 95 percent of the words. Thus, while a 2,000-word vocabulary works fairly well for *social purposes*, it leaves a student groping in the dark when trying to read or write for *academic purposes*. Interestingly, these figures corroborate Cummins' (1980) distinction between BICS and CALP. These statistics on word frequencies in conversation vs. academic texts underscore the importance of instruction on both low-frequency **academic content vocabulary** and **high-frequency words**.

High-frequency word lists are readily available on the Internet. Figure 6.2 provides websites for the Dolch list and the first 2000 words list. By looking at the examples provided, you should be able to get a feel for the difficulty level of the lists. Based on words in children's books, the 220-word Dolch list was compiled in the 1930s and 1940s for the purpose of teaching beginning reading to native English speakers. When you look at the Dolch list, you will find that many of the most frequent words are **function words**, for example, *the, to, and, he, a, I, of, in*. Function words (articles, pronouns, conjunctions, prepositions) serve to

FIGURE 6.2

SAMPLE HIGH-FREQUENCY WORDS

LIST TYPE	USEFULNESS	SAMPLE WORDS
DOLCH list available at: http://literacyconnections.com/Dolch1.html	**Most common 220 words in reading material: Represents 50-60% of words students will see**	the, to, and, he, you, was, said, his, that, she, on, they, him, with, look, is, her, there, some, out, have, about, after, again, all, always, and, any, because, been, before, best, better, big, black, bring, but, buy, came, carry, then, little, could, when, what, were, get, would, come, now, long, very, ask, over, yours, into, just, good, around
First 2000 words available at: http://www.harenet.ne.jp/~waring/vocab/index.html	**First one or two thousand words students will need to know**	action, award, background, beautiful, bridge, candidate, central, change, complete, daughter, decision, definition, democratic, ear, easy, education, entire, father, feeling, girl, government, happy, heart, heavy, important, include, introduce, job, journey, know, lady, language, lunch, manage, meal, national, necessary, objective, office, package, partner, rain, read
Content area words Although there is an academic word list, recent research indicates it has limited use for students (Hyland & Tse, 2007). We recommend concentrating on specific words needed to understand content areas.	**Words used in specific content area** If you use Google and type in your area you can get a content area dictionary for example, science dictionary, social science dictionary, mathematics dictionary, and so forth:	metaphor, angle, ecology, ratio, simile, integers, false positives, experiment, theorem, capitalism, magical realism, anaphoric reference, biology, division, infrastructure, subtraction, identification, taxonomy, acculturation, heredity, anatomy,

show relationships among other words within a sentence. Sometimes, their meaning will depend on a previous sentence or phrase, as is the case with pronouns. In addition, function words such as *nevertheless, moreover,* and *however* show relationships across phrases and sentences. Therefore, function words are best learned through exposure to natural language use, and must be assessed and taught in the context of a sentence or paragraph. Other words on the Dolch list convey relatively concrete meanings, such as *see, ask, good, blue, red, yellow, brown.* These words are referred to as **content words** (different from *content area words*), and consist of nouns, adjectives, verbs, and adverbs. High-frequency content words are good candidates for explicit instruction because they pack so much meaning, even when presented in isolation. Bearing in mind its focus on the simpler language of children's books in an earlier era, the Dolch list remains useful as a guide to words needed in English.

The first 2,000 words website is especially helpful because it also lists the first 500, the first 1,000, and the first 1,500 most frequent words. Unlike the Dolch list, which was based on children's books, these lists are based on materials for older learners and adults. Thus, even the first 500 list includes perhaps 10 words you would not teach in the primary grades, such as *policy, economic,* and *management.* Word frequency lists may help you choose more basic words to use for paraphrasing and defining technical vocabulary for your students.

The lists also provide one source for selecting words to teach, along with your curriculum content, including text materials, literature, and any other material you are using, oral and written.

How Do Students Learn New Words?

Learning a new word is a gradual process that depends on multiple exposures to the word over time. In the process, students move from not knowing the word at all, to recognizing it on hearing or seeing it, to knowing it in limited contexts, to knowing it more fully in a variety of contexts (Allen cited in Tompkins, 2003). Full word knowledge includes both **breadth**, knowing its varied uses and meanings in different contexts; and **depth**, fully understanding the concept represented. When you teach academic content, you are usually introducing new concepts along with corresponding technical vocabulary. These concepts are often fairly complex and abstract, such as *acculturation, fission, integer, magical realism, photosynthesis, simile,* and *quadrilateral.* If a student has studied the topic before and knows the word in the primary language, a foundation for the concept already exists. If not, you may need to spend more time helping students develop and understand the concept. The following guidelines for teaching new words apply in either case:

1. **Relate the "new" to the "known"** by tapping into students' prior knowledge, including primary language equivalents of the new word and its meaning.

2. **Offer repetitions of the new word in meaningful contexts**, highlighting it with verbal emphasis, underlining it, or pointing to it on a word wall.

3. **Provide opportunities for deeper processing of word meaning** through demonstrations, direct experience, concrete examples, and applications to real life.

4. **Engage students in using newly learned words** as they explain concepts and ideas in writing and speaking.

5. **Provide explicit instruction on strategies** for students to use independently for understanding and using new words.

It's important to remember that your students will learn many new words incidentally through conversations as they interact socially with English speakers in school and out. In addition, they will build and consolidate their vocabularies through your carefully designed curriculum that provides (1) exposure to new words during academic instruction supported

Source: Paul Gruwell.

175

by cues to meaning and opportunities for concept development; (2) experiences reading a variety of material independently and under your guidance; (3) opportunities to write frequently for an audience; (4) explicit instruction on words and word parts; and (5) instruction on vocabulary strategies, including dictionary use, to help students read and write new words independently. Instruction described in items 1–3 above is based on naturally flowing language used in lesson delivery, instructional conversations, books, essays, journal entries, and the like. In other words, in items 1–3 new words are learned in communicative contexts, oral and written. In contrast, instruction described in items 4 and 5 uses words pulled out of context for in-depth study and strategy development aimed at helping students independently deal with new words later on. All of these activities and strategies will help students develop **word consciousness** that will help them recognize, understand, and use new words. Figure 6.3 illustrates the dynamic interactions among the key elements of vocabulary instruction. We'll take a closer look at these interactions next.

When we talk about academic instruction, we are referring to everything you do to teach content, including the texts you assign, your own teacher talk, and the talk among students during group work. The rich, natural language that is part and parcel of academic instruction facilitates vocabulary development provided you use sheltering strategies to develop concepts and make meaning accessible. You will also want to follow up with explicit instruction on selected words you judge most important for learning the material under study, using strategies we offer subsequently in this chapter. When you help students develop and apply new concepts and generalizations in any area of study, you simultaneously help them retain the corresponding vocabulary.

FIGURE 6.3

SOURCES OF WORD LEARNING

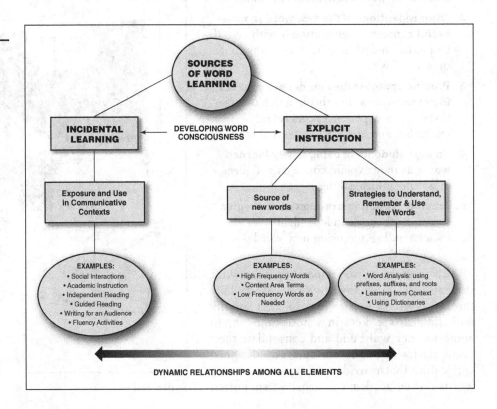

When reading independently or under your guidance, students are dealing with the more or less natural language found in trade books, textbooks, and other materials. During **independent reading**, it is important for English learners to read material geared to their English proficiency and reading ability. As noted previously, if students can't understand most of what they read, about 95 percent of the words in a given text, they will have difficulty inferring the meaning of new words they encounter. If you are on hand to *guide* their reading, students can deal with slightly more difficult texts, and trouble spots offer you the chance to help them apply strategies for dealing with unknown words. Finally, as students write with opportunities for others to respond, they produce text for communication purposes and get feedback on how well their word choices convey the desired message. To summarize, academic instruction, independent and guided reading, and writing for an audience represent three important avenues to vocabulary development within natural, communicative contexts.

In addition to exposure to new words in context, students benefit from **explicit instruction** that focuses their attention on individual words and word parts, such as prefixes, suffixes, and roots (Folse, 2004; Graves, 2004; Nation, 1990, 2005, Schmitt & McCarthy, 2005). Here we are pulling words out of the ongoing flow of oral or written discourse to highlight how they look, how they sound, and what they mean. Analysis of word parts shows students how words are built in English. This knowledge can help them figure out the meaning of new

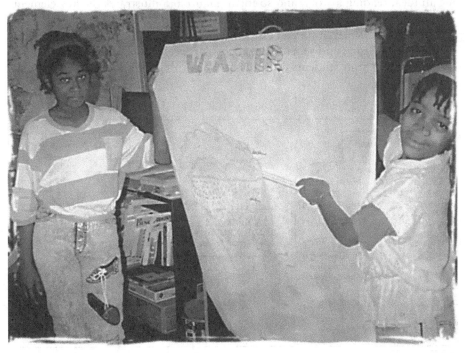

These girls are using new vocabulary as they explain cloud formation and weather.

Suzanne F. Peregoy

177

FIGURE 6.4

MODEL FOR
INSTRUCTING STUDENTS
ON STRATEGIES

Source: N. K. Duke and P. D.
Pearson, "Effective Practices
for Developing Reading
Comprehension," in S. J.
Samuels and A. E. Farstrup,
eds., *What Research Has
to Say About Reading
Instruction*, 3rd ed.
(Newark, DE: International
Reading Association, 2002),
pp. 203–242.

1) Begin with an explicit description of the strategy	1) Tell students what the strategy is and why it is important for them to learn the strategy
2) Model the strategy in action	2) Teacher and/or students may model the strategy
3) Collaborative use of the strategy	3) Ask students to use the strategy with you as you speak aloud and give them your thoughts
4) Continue with guided practice of the strategy	4) Guide students through the use of the strategy while gradually releasing responsibility to them
5) Finish by having students use the strategy independently	5) Ask students to use the strategy with a specific reading or writing assignment

words they encounter, particularly in reading. Through repeated exposure and review of new words, students gain instant recognition of their form and meaning, or **fluency**, and the ability to use them in communication.

In addition to word study, explicit instruction on **vocabulary strategies** will help your students (1) unlock the meaning of new words they come upon in reading and conversation and (2) choose appropriate and precise words to convey messages when writing and speaking. For teaching particular strategies, you may want to use the scaffolding procedure (Duke & Pearson, 2002) shown in Figure 6.4.

By addressing vocabulary both in and out of natural communication contexts, you provide a **balanced approach** to vocabulary instruction (Decarrico, 2001). The ultimate aim, of course, is for students to be able to use words effectively to achieve their communicative goals across a wide range of communication events; for example, listening to a speech, writing a letter, explaining an idea, reading a story, and so forth. Figure 6.5 illustrates the key elements of an excellent vocabulary program. In later chapters we also present strategies that help students elaborate and deepen their knowledge of words; for example, mapping, clustering, and semantic feature analysis. These elements together will assure you that your students are gaining the vocabulary knowledge they need.

FIGURE 6.5

KEY ELEMENTS OF
SUCCESSFUL VOCABULARY
PROGRAMS

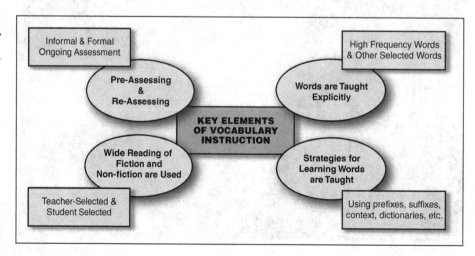

How Do We Differentiate Vocabulary Assessment and Instruction?

To differentiate vocabulary assessment and instruction, you first need to consider each student's: (1) age and grade, (2) English language proficiency (oral and written), (3) primary language proficiency (oral and written), and (4) educational experiences. You already know the age and grade of your students, and that's important for selecting words that are age appropriate and essential for learning grade level curriculum content. Hopefully, you will also have some idea of how much education your student has had both in the primary language and in English as a second or foreign language, as that information gives you a clearer picture of your student's linguistic and conceptual resources, which we talk about next.

English Language Proficiency Considerations

To assess vocabulary and choose words for study, you need to consider each student's English language proficiency. For example, a student new to English might concentrate on words you select from the Dolch list or the first-500 list. On the other hand, an intermediate English learner may benefit more from words on the first-2,000 list. You also need to know whether your student can decode in English. If not, it would be fruitless to assess using a list of written words. Instead, you would need to use pictures or actions to elicit knowledge of a particular word. For instruction, though, it's useful to present both the oral and written forms of a word together for simultaneous acquisition.

Some English learners have studied English formally in their home country. If so, they might display their English proficiency, including vocabulary knowledge, more effectively through writing than through speaking. For these students, you may present a list of words for which the student gives a synonym or a short definition. Students with previous English language study might have developed effective strategies for learning new words, such as memorization and word association. If so, they can use those strategies and share them with their classmates as well. By considering your students' prior knowledge and experiences, you will be able to tailor assessment and instruction accordingly.

Primary Language Proficiency Considerations

Learning about a student's home language use can be helpful, even if you are not teaching bilingually, because aspects of first language knowledge transfer to the second language (Odlin, 1989; Swan, 1997). The extent to which transfer occurs, and whether it helps or hinders, depends on the particular language. For example, the decoding ability in Spanish transfers fairly well to decoding in English, with the notable exception of the vowels. That is because both Spanish and English use the Roman alphabet, with consonants (but not vowels) representing similar sounds in the two languages. On the other hand, literacy in a logographic language such as Chinese offers minimal transfer for decoding purposes, positive or negative, because the Chinese writing system is so different from the English alphabet.

For vocabulary, transfer potentially occurs with cognates, words that look and sound similar in two languages, such as *telephone* in English and *teléfono* in Spanish. Because the two words share the same meaning, they are called "friendly cognates." Knowing the word in one language makes learning fairly easy in the other. On the other hand, there are also "false cognates," that is, words with different meanings in two languages even though they look and sound similar. A good example is *embarrassed* in English and *embarazada* in Spanish, which means "pregnant." You can just imagine the potential for confusion there! Cognates, false or friendly, often occur when two languages share the same source language. For example, the Romance languages share many cognates with English due to the influence of Latin and Greek as a source language in their respective histories. As a Germanic type language, English also shares cognates with other Germanic languages, for example, in English and German: house— *Haus*; water—*Wasser*; brother—*Bruder*; sister—*Schwester*. You probably are aware that cognates with non-European languages are much less prevalent. Where they do exist, they tend be loan words to or from English. The point here is that it is helpful for you to learn about your students' primary language proficiency in order to build upon areas of positive transfer, and understand areas of negative transfer when they occur. In so doing, you will be able to further differentiate vocabulary instruction.

We know that in some classes serving English learners, there may be numerous primary languages represented. Learning about all of them can be an onerous task. One way to make use of your students' home languages and promote linguistic awareness is to create a multilingual wall dictionary. For each word you post in English, your students offer the corresponding word in their primary language. From time to time, you and your students may examine the dictionary to identify cognates and other similarities and differences among words in the various languages. In so doing, you demonstrate recognition and respect for students' home languages while motivating interest in cross-linguistic study.

Vocabulary Assessment For Planning Instruction

Broadly speaking, there are two types of words to be concerned with for English learners' vocabulary development: content area words and high-frequency words. Assessing students' word knowledge ahead of time helps you choose study words, based on what they already know and what they need to learn. For important content area vocabulary, you can engage students in brainstorming a topic before teaching about it to assess both prior knowledge and vocabulary. In addition, or alternatively, you might ask students to work in pairs or triads to write anything they know or can guess about a list of words you provide. They write or draw their responses. You may share ideas from these responses with the whole class as a way to generate interest and pave the way for learning about the topic.

Another way you can assess vocabulary is to give students a short list of words you judge to be at about their instructional level. You may select the words from a word frequency list, a teacher's guide, your curriculum standards, or other resource. Next, ask your students to indicate whether they know the word, and if so how well they know it, using the categories in Figure 6.6: (1) I recognize the word, (2) I can define the word, (3) I can use the word in a sentence, and (4) I can use the word in several different contexts. After briefly describing and giving examples of each of the four categories, you might ask them to place

I Recognize the Word	I Can Give a Definition of the Word	I Can Use the Word in a Sentence	I Can Use the Word in Several Contexts

FIGURE 6.6

INFORMAL ASSESSMENT OF VOCABULARY USING WORD LISTS

words under each category of knowledge. For students just starting to learn English, simple pictures are helpful for eliciting word knowledge. For slightly more advanced beginners, you may use more complex, detailed pictures for students to describe. Wordless books, may also be used to elicit narratives to informally assess students' vocabulary knowledge. From quick, informal assessments such as these, you can begin to identify different student's word knowledge, and differentiate instruction accordingly.

A Word About Dictionaries

There are many vocabulary resources available, including Internet sites and published materials. One important resource, of course, is dictionaries, and there are many to choose from. To meet your students' varied needs, you will want to consider different types of dictionaries and choose the ones that best suit your students, your grade level, and teaching assignment. In addition to standard English dictionaries you use with native English speakers, publishers offer three types of dictionaries that are especially useful for English learners: (1) picture dictionaries; (2) monolingual, learner dictionaries; and (3) bilingual dictionaries.

Picture Dictionaries

There are a number of picture dictionaries designed for elementary school students such as the *Longman Children's Picture Dictionary* (Longman, 2003) and the *Harcourt Brace Picture Dictionary* (Kelly, 2004). Harcourt Brace also offers a Spanish-English bilingual picture dictionary (Crane & Vasquez, 1994). All of these dictionaries provide colorful illustrations of high interest, high-frequency words. Although designed for younger students, they can be useful for older beginning English learners.

Sophisticated picture dictionaries appropriate for older, intermediate to advanced and fluent English speakers are also available, such as the *Ultimate Visual Dictionary* (Evans, 2006). This dictionary contains high quality, color illustrations and diagrams in 14 topic areas, such as the universe, prehistoric earth, physics and chemistry, the visual arts, music, and sports.

Bilingual Dictionaries

For students who are literate in their primary language, bilingual dictionaries can be helpful. As the name implies, these dictionaries are two-way resources in which you can look up the word in English and find its equivalent in the other language and vice versa. One example is *Simon & Schuster's International Spanish Dictionary* (Gamez & Steiner, 2004).

Monolingual, Language Learner Dictionaries

These dictionaries present all definitions in English, therefore offering no recourse to a student's primary language. Geared specifically to non-native speakers, definitions use restricted vocabulary, some relying on only 2,000 common words in their definitions. They also may include information on grammar and usage. Two examples are the Collins *Cobuild Learner's Concise English Dictionary* (HarperCollins, 2006) and the *Longman Dictionary of Contemporary English* (Longman, 2006*)*, which is also available online www.ldoce.com. Although these two dictionaries are designed for older English learners, you can also find monolingual learner dictionaries for children and teens.

In summary, English vocabulary development looms large in the lives of English language learners. The joint dedication of teachers and students is needed to make word learning effective, efficient, and fun. Students will acquire a large number of words through natural communication, oral and written. In addition, they will learn new words through explicit word study. Next, we offer word learning activities and strategies for beginning and intermediate English learners.

Beginning Level Vocabulary Learners: Characteristics and Strategies

Beginning level English learners possess a rudimentary English vocabulary and are likely to benefit from instruction using words you select from the first 500 to 1,000 high-frequency list. Your content area instruction is also a major source of new English words, as these tend to be highlighted and repeated in meaningful contexts over a period of weeks, thus providing for depth of word learning. At this stage, students will also learn many words during the course of day-to-day classroom activities, provided that sheltering strategies are used to support comprehension. In addition, words associated with daily routines are essential and readily learned. The activities that follow are especially helpful to beginning readers because they give them opportunities to learn new words in a variety of ways.

Total Physical Response (TPR)

Total Physical Response is an approach to language teaching which pairs actions with words to convey meaning (Asher, 2000). Typically, you begin with action words, such as "stand up," "sit down," and "wave good-bye." After saying the word and demonstrating its meaning with gestures and dramatization, the teacher uses it in a command. For example, you say, "Stand up!" and your students respond by standing up. This routine is repeated with other actions words. Through active participation, students learn new action words by watching, imitating and responding to the teacher's commands (Schunk cited in Facella, Rampino, and Shea, 2005). As students progress, the teacher uses more elaborated commands, such as "Put your book on the table." In this way, students learn additional words, including nouns, verbs, adjectives, adverbs, and function words. Not least important, the words are learned in meaningful, grammatical contexts.

A variation on TPR is the game Simon Says. To get ready to play, all students stand up. Then the teacher gives a command while gesturing, such as "Simon Says wave your hands in the air." Students are only supposed to carry out the action if the command is preceded by the words, "Simon Says." Otherwise they have to sit down. The teacher tries to "trick" the students by occasionally giving commands and gesturing, but without first uttering "Simon Says." Both TPR and Simon Says are useful for beginners because (1) actions demonstrate word meaning, (2) students show comprehension by responding, and (3) speaking is not required. However, students eventually may take on the role of the teacher, thereby gaining speaking practice as they give the familiar commands.

We experienced TPR ourselves when James Asher, the originator of the technique, generously agreed to come into our classroom to demonstrate. He gave us commands in Arabic such as "sit, stand, walk over here, walk over there, hold your hands up in the air." Amazingly all of us were able to perform the actions almost right away. One student was even able to take the role of leader, giving commands in Arabic. A week later, an Arabic speaker in our class gave some of the same commands and, remarkably we still remembered the words! We saw for ourselves that TPR offers a fun, effective, low-pressure way to learn new words. Experience is the glue that makes learning stick, and TPR illustrates this concept very well!

Read Alouds

We can't emphasize enough how important it is to read aloud to students at all grade levels, K-12. Through listening to selections read aloud to them, English learners gain exposure to various genres: stories, poems, essays, articles, and more. They also gain familiarity with the sounds and cadences of the English language. Moreover, listening to read alouds introduces students to the organization and flow of written English.

For beginners, short selections usually work best, including poems, song lyrics, and brief stories. Choose selections on familiar topics. Before reading, tap into and build students' prior knowledge by briefly discussing the title or main ideas in the piece as a whole; because building background before reading has been shown to promote vocabulary acquisition (Ulanoff & Pucci, 1999). In addition, consider how you will support comprehension through pictures, actions, and other sheltering assistance as you read. Finally, depending on your students' enthusiasm for the pieces you choose, read them again from time to time. Subsequent readings will be easier for students to understand, and vocabulary knowledge can be consolidated.

It's always important to remember, of course, that listening to any extended stretch of oral language is a demanding task, especially for those new to the language. I (Owen) recently became the godparent of a Oaxacan Mexican baby boy.

To prepare for my new role as *padrino*, I was required to attend a two-hour class of religious instruction in Spanish, a language in which I am perhaps an advanced beginner at best. Even though I was already familiar with the content of the class, I found that I could not concentrate for more than about 10 minutes at a time, making me painfully aware of my beginning status.

Word Cards

Word cards are used to help students consolidate and remember words for which they already know the meaning. To create word cards, students write the English word on one side with a picture, short definition, or translation on the other side. By creating their own cards, your students develop a personal collection geared to their own particular needs and interests. In addition, you can supply important content vocabulary for them to add. Because they keep the cards with them, your students can review their words individually or with a peer when they have a spare minute or two. Once they know the basic meaning of their words, they can consolidate their learning through various games and activities. For example, your students can do **word sorts**, such as grouping their words by meaning, by grammatical category, or alphabetically (for more ideas, see also Cunningham (2005); and Bear, Helman, Templeton, Invernizzi & Johnston, 2007). As your students gain fluency with words and their meanings, they can set them aside as learned, making room in their collections for new words. Word cards can be used with students at any level to help them learn and remember general high-frequency words and specific content area vocabulary.

Word Wall Dictionary

One strategy you can use with beginning students is a word wall dictionary on which you post words for students to learn and review. These words may come from your current theme study, a story you are reading, or any topic you are teaching. You may also use your own judgment and knowledge of your students to select words from an appropriate word frequency list. Next to each word, you may post a short definition or a picture to convey meaning. Lisa Fiorentino uses the wall dictionary throughout the year to help her fourth graders learn new words and review them over time. Each morning after roll call, she takes a few minutes to go over the newest words with students and invites them to evaluate which words they know well enough to take down. Word wall dictionaries can also be used to demonstrate the use of ABC order in finding words in published dictionaries, including picture dictionaries (described previously) that are helpful to beginners.

Working with Idioms

Idiomatic expressions are difficult for English learners because their meanings are not literal, but figurative, as you can see in the Peanuts cartoon about "reading between the lines." The best approach is to discuss idioms as they come up in reading material, instruction, or conversation. For a more focused study of idioms, a good starting point can be the Amelia Bedelia books by Peggy Parish and Herman

Source: Peanuts: © United Syndicate, Inc.

Parish. These fun books illustrate humorous situations in which Amelia interprets various words and idioms literally, instead of figuratively, as they are meant to be. For example, to "dust the curtains," she throws dust on the curtains; to make a sponge cake, she uses kitchen sponges. Students have fun in class reading and listening to the books, especially when they already know what the idioms mean before reading. By exposing students to a few idioms, you can alert them to figurative uses of language and help them recognize idiomatic expressions when they come upon them in their reading. Your class may want to compile an idiom book for which each student takes an idiom, illustrates the literal meaning, and describes the figurative one. One handy and comprehensive internet site is www.idiomconnection.com, which lists idioms alphabetically and by topic, such as animals, sports, clothes, colors, food, and money. It also lists the 80 most frequent idioms.

Using strategies such as TPR, read alouds, word cards, word wall dictionaries, and picture dictionaries you can help your students move to up to the intermediate levels.

Intermediate Level Vocabulary Learners: Characteristics and Strategies

Intermediate English learners may know many of the first 2,000 high-frequency words. In addition, many will be competent readers of graded texts and natural authentic texts, depending on their prior educational experiences using English. As with beginning-level learners, you will want to spend the bulk of focused teaching time on the high-frequency words and specific content area words that they need to comprehend their texts. The activities here should be most useful to your intermediate English learners.

Word Wheels

Word wheels can be used to visually portray words that are related in some way, such as synonyms. For example, to help students use more precise terms instead of *said*, a word wheel can be created to show synonyms such as *says, exclaimed, stated, affirmed, related, shouted,* or *yelled* as shown in Figure 6.7. After making sure students know the central word, discuss the different meanings of the

FIGURE 6.7 • WORD WHEEL

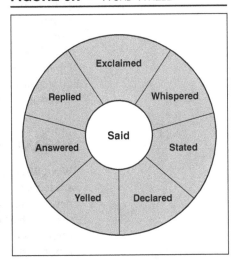

FIGURE 6.8

LANGUAGE WHEEL FOR IRREGULAR VERBS

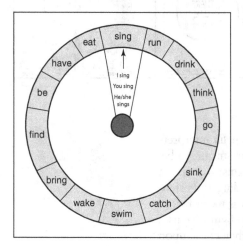

words around the wheel. Your students will enjoy using vivid synonyms for greater precision in their writing and speaking, and they will come to know them receptively as well.

Language Wheels for Verb Conjugations, Adjectives, Adverbs, and Cognates

Language wheels, which are commercially available, can come in handy for English Learners in middle and high school, particularly when writing and preparing for oral presentations. Originally language wheels focused on verb conjugations. Later they were adapted to help students with adjective and adverb forms. In addition, language wheels are available to alert students to false cognates. Made of lightweight tag board, language wheels consist of a bottom circle, about 6 inches in diameter, with a slightly smaller tag board circle attached on top, which you can turn like a dial. Figure 6.8 illustrates how they work with irregular verbs. You simply turn the top wheel to the word you want—*sing*—and the window exposes various conjugated forms: *sing, sang, has sung*.

The same dial-a-word format is used for adjective and adverb forms and false cognates. These tools take us back to our own high-school days learning German and Spanish, and that's a long time ago! For online information about how to find language wheels, type in keywords *language wheel* or *verb wheel*.

Vocabulary Self-Collection Strategy

In the **Vocabulary Self-Collection Strategy** (Haggard, 1986), students select one word they consider important in an assigned reading, pooling their words with those of their classmates to form a study list. The teacher also adds words to the list. Once words are selected from a reading, you and your students work together to define and discuss the words in some detail. Next, you and the class narrow the vocabulary list by eliminating words they already know and selecting words they feel are most important and interesting. Now that you have a study list, you help your students decide on various ways to learn the words, such as testing each other in pairs. In addition, you may wish to post words and definitions on a wall dictionary for reference. Finally, you may wish to test students periodically on words they have studied. The strategy is beneficial in that: (1) students actively participate in selecting in the words for study; (2) it develops a strong sense of word consciousness or awareness; and (3) students learn to take charge of their own vocabulary development.

Word Wizard

Word Wizard (McKeown & Beck, 2004), a research-based strategy, encourages students to actively tune in to new words used in various contexts. After learning new words in class, students take note of their use outside class in different contexts such as conversations, television, radio, magazines, or newspapers. Students then report on their findings when they next meet in class. In sharing their reports, students are encouraged to explain the different ways in which the word was used. One follow-up might be to create a chart summarizing the various ways the word was used along with a tally of how many times a particular use was reported. In the research study by McKeown and Beck on Word Wizard, students were rewarded with points for each new word along with certificates at the end of the week.

Word Wizard focuses your students' attention on new words and opens their eyes to nuanced meanings in different contexts outside class. Perhaps you have noticed how a word you have just learned seems to pop up everywhere thereafter. Word Wizard builds upon this phenomenon and creates enthusiasm among students as they collect words to share in class. Finally, Word Wizard makes a nice complement to the vocabulary self-collection strategy discussed previously.

Contextual Redefinition

Research shows that it is difficult to learn new words from context, even for intermediate and advanced learners (Folse, 2004; McKeown & Beck, 2004; Nagy, Anderson, & Herman, 1987; Nation, 2007). **Contextual redefinition** (Readance, Bean, & Baldwin, 1998; Tierney & Readance, 2000) is a strategy students can apply to figure out the meaning of an unknown word they come upon while reading. For students to be able to determine word meanings from context, they need to have some background knowledge on the topic. In addition, the text should be rich enough in meaning clues to enable reasonable guesses, and those clues are most useful when they stand in close proximity to the unknown word (Schmitt, 2007). Given texts that meet those criteria, contextual redefinition provides a strategy that enables students to figure out unknown words from context by making informed rather than haphazard guesses.

To teach contextual redefinition you use sentences containing words that are important to understanding a passage, and that your students are not likely to know. Your first step is to select such words from an assigned reading, maintaining the entire sentence as context. If the original sentence lacks sufficient context clues, you may need to rewrite the sentence to enrich it. The sentences here illustrate recreated sentences using the words *adamant* and *cachinnation*.

(a) The professor was *adamant* about how students should complete the assignment; he told them he would not accept any other approach.

(b) After she told her joke, there was a great deal of *cachinnation*; everybody laughed a lot.

Without showing the sentences to your students, you present the words *adamant* and *cachinnation* in isolation, pronouncing the words as you do so. Next ask your students to guess the word's meaning and explain their rationale for their ideas. Some guesses may be far from correct, but that's okay because the purpose of this phase of the strategy is to illustrate that it's difficult to guess a word out of context.

Next, you show students the words in context as shown in sentences (a) and (b). Students again guess the meanings of the words, noticing how helpful it is to have the context. At this point, you may want to present another sentence, for which you model your process by "thinking out loud" as you generate possible meanings based on context. In the final step of the strategy, students check the dictionary meaning of words both in isolation and in context to experience the power of context.

Contextual redefinition teaches students how to generate plausible word meanings from context when they are reading on their own. It is rather time consuming, but if your students learn to use context with caution and sophistication, your time will have been well spent.

Vocabulary Journals

You can think of vocabulary journals as an extension of word cards. As students are assigned or come upon new words, they note them in their vocabulary journals along with a definition, a sentence using the word, and any other helpful hint for remembering the meaning. They can also use the journal for reviewing words and becoming fluent with the words. Moreover students can add new sentences when they come across the words again. Thus, the vocabulary journals become a personal dictionary, stimulating interest and building awareness for new words and their meanings.

Dictionary Use

Most of us have used dictionaries often enough to make looking up a word fairly automatic. However, finding the information you need in the dictionary is actually a complex process. To help students out, a seven-step procedure has been developed (Scholfield, 1982) shown in Figure 6.9. As you examine the procedure, consider whether to shorten or simplify it based on your students' age, maturity, and English language development levels. To introduce the procedure, we recommend giving your students a handout of the chart or displaying it on an overhead projec-

FIGURE 6.9

USING A DICTIONARY FOR COMPREHENSION

Source: P. Schofield, "Using the English Dictionary for Comprehension," *TESOL Quarterly* 16(2), pp. 185–194.

STEPS IN DICTIONARY USE	EXAMPLE
Locate word(s) or phrases not understood.	Joe didn't **catch** the drift of the conversation. Student may not recognize he or she didn't understand a word.
If unknown word is inflected, remove inflections to find word to look up.	Example: jump(ed), jump (ing), jump (s); remove the inflections such as -*ed*, -*ing*, -*s*, to get the basic word you want to look up.
Search for unknown word in alphabetic list.	Some students may have to learn the alphabet to do this, especially those with a different writing system.
If you can't find at least one entry for the unknown word, try procedures in the example.	If word seems to be an idiom or set phrase try looking up each main element. If unknown word has a suffix, try the entry for the stem.
If there are multiple senses or homographic entries, reduce them by elimination.	Scan all senses of the word until you find the one that makes the most sense.
Understand the definition and integrate it into the context where the unknown word was found.	Students may also have to look up unknown words that were used in explaining the original definition.
If senses of word don't seem to fit, look for further contextual clues.	Student may have to infer meaning in order to understand.

tor or PowerPoint® screen. Next, model how you would personally use each step, and then have students use the steps to look up words, working in pairs or triads. Learning the strategy takes time and effort, but if students learn to use dictionaries efficiently, they will comprehend more in their reading and will build their vocabulary.

Teaching Prefixes and Suffixes

Prefixes and suffixes (i.e., affixes) are worth teaching if you start out with a small number of the most useful ones. Research has shown that a small number of prefixes can be found in a great number of words students will be reading, and the most common ones may be taught in the early grades with beginners (White, Sowell, and Yanagihara, 1989). For English learners, suffixes for regular verbs are important, such as the *-ed* and *-ing* endings. Your English language development standards, language arts standards, and grade-level curriculum materials will help you choose specific prefixes and suffixes to teach.

Just as you'll want to teach high-frequency words, you'll also want to focus on high-frequency prefixes. For example, the prefixes *un-* and *re-* are used most frequently and begin to occur at about the fourth grade level of reading. Some of the other most common prefixes are *in-*, *im-*, meaning "not". The other most common prefixes on the list are *dis-, en-, in-, im-*.

Once you have selected the affixes most useful to your students, you can begin to think about how you will teach them. Using the model presented by Duke and Pearson (2002) we suggest several steps for teaching prefixes. The same procedure may be used for teaching suffixes.

1. Start by telling students what a prefix is and how they contribute to a word's meaning. Show students several examples of words with prefixes.

2. Provide examples of prefixes such as *un-, dis-,* or *en-* and show how the prefix affects word meaning with several words. For example, explain that *un-* means not, and when it is in front of a word, it changes the meaning: for example, *uninterested* means not interested, *unhappy* means not happy, and so forth. You might also show students that when you take a prefix away you still have a base word (Graves, 2006).

3. Offer examples showing students how you might guess the meaning of a word based on the prefix.

4. Guide students through the process of using prefixes to unlock the meaning of words they find in reading.

5. Ask students to take a list of words with prefixes and figure their meaning and give them reading samples containing words with prefixes.

As a follow-up to explicit instruction, you may wish to make card sets with prefixes on one set of cards and base words on another set. Working individually or in pairs, students match cards from the two sets to create their own words, consolidating vocabulary learning. They may also then write the words in their vocabulary journals. Similar strategies may be used with suffixes.

FIGURE 6.10

STRATEGIES OLDER
STUDENTS FOUND MOST
USEFUL

Source: Based on
Schmitt (2000).

DETERMINATION	SOCIAL	MEMORY	COGNITIVE	METACOGNITIVE
Strategies for the discovery of a new word's meaning	Strategies for the discovery of a new word's meaning	Strategies for consolidating a word once it has been encountered	Strategies for consolidating a word once it has been encountered	Strategies for consolidating a word once it has been encountered
1) bilingual dictionary 2) analyze any available pictures or gestures 3) monolingual dictionary	1) ask teacher for paraphrase or synonym of new word 2) ask teacher for a sentence including new word	1) say new word aloud when studying 2) connect word to its synonyms and antonyms 3) study the spelling of word	1) written repetition 2) verbal repetition 3) take notes in class	1) continue to study word over time

Word Learning Strategies Identified as Useful by Older Learners

We have emphasized the importance of guiding students toward independent use of word learning strategies. You might be interested in the results of one study that attempted to identify strategies that students themselves found most useful, in this case Japanese students learning English in Japan (Schmitt, 2002). Figure 6.10 summarizes the strategies using the researcher's five categories: determination, social, memory, cognitive, and metacognitive. Determination and social strategies help students understand a word's meaning. Determination strategies are used independently, while social strategies involve asking the teacher for help. Memory, cognitive and metacognitive strategies help students consolidate word meanings. If you work with older students, you might share and discuss these strategies with them. Let them choose strategies to try out and then evaluate their usefulness. If you are especially curious, you might want to get the article and replicate the study yourself.

One often mentioned strategy not cited by the students in the study (Schmitt, 2002), is the keyword method for memorizing new vocabulary. In this multistep mnemonic procedure, students select and memorize associations between a target word (L2) and its translation (meaning) and a similar sounding word in the L1. Some older students may find the technique helpful. However, we suggest that vocabulary learning time is better spent hearing and using new words in meaningful contexts, such as theme studies. One caveat we offer about teaching any strategy is the learning payoff in relation to the time spent teaching it.

Assessing Second Language Learners Vocabulary Progress

You may assess your student's vocabulary learning informally in several ways. First of all, you may observe and jot notes as students work in small groups while reading or working in cooperative groups on content area tasks. In addition, you may collect their personal dictionaries periodically, analyze their entries, and make a note of strengths and needs to discuss in an individual conference. When you ask students to write or present their understandings as part of your content area teaching, you may watch for and note correct use of technical vocabulary you have taught. Another way to assess vocabulary during instructional time is to engage students in discussion of word meanings (Simpson cited in O'Malley & Pierce, 1996). For example, you may assess how well students recognize and infer relationships by asking how a pair of words do or do not relate, for example, how *football* and *soccer* are alike or different. Or you may ask students to take a list of objects, classify them by common attributes, and name the class to which they belong, for example, *duck, zebra*, and *frog* may be classified as animals. If rock is in the list, it has to be set aside as an outlier. Each of these alternative strategies asks students to do something more elaborate with a word which may reveal a deeper level of word knowledge.

In addition to assessing vocabulary as part of instruction, you may also use traditional means such as multiple-choice tests and matching items. The benefit of these traditional assessments is that they are quick and easy, and may be administered to the whole class at one time.

Looking back, most of us can remember an influential teacher in our lives. One such influential teacher was Professor Featherstone, who gave the freshmen literature class about 25 key terms we should know in order to appreciate and discuss English literature. We knew we would be tested on those terms, so we studied them well. By the end of the semester, we were all rather impressed by the level of sophistication we had achieved in our literary discourse! Starting with those key terms, I (Owen) ended up majoring in English literature. Professor Featherstone, by teaching important literary terms, provided us with the words and ideas we needed to understand literature and literary criticism. And knowing that he would be testing us on those terms motivated us to study!

Differentiating Vocabulary Instruction

Differentiating vocabulary instruction requires us to consider each student's word knowledge in relation to grade level curriculum standards, goals, and objectives. Student contributions to K-W-L charts and your other observations during instruction provide first steps in assessment. Short word lists of important content area terms are another way to assess student word knowledge prior to instruction. Word frequency lists can help you determine other words your students may need. Finally, each student's personal dictionary entries offer an ongoing record of individual vocabulary levels and growth. With this information in hand, you will be able to make use of several features of this chapter to differentiate instruction. One feature is the division of strategies into beginning and intermediate categories. Another feature is the chart in Figure 6.11, which suggests grade levels at which each strategy may be used. Finally, you will be able to assess student learning after instruction using the various techniques suggested.

Consider a scaffold for planning differentiated instruction that calls your attention to who, what, how and how well. We use that scaffold now to describe differentiated vocabulary instruction related to a theme study on **travel** and **distance** in a fifth-grade class. The lesson is based on a fifth-grade science standard that requires all students to demonstrate knowledge and understanding of the planets in our solar system, their size, distance from the earth, temperature, and the composition of their atmospheres.

Who: Fifth-grade students who are beginning, advanced beginning, and intermediate English language learners. They represent a variety of primary language backgrounds. They have all enjoyed looking at the night sky and are familiar with the words *moon*, *stars*, and *sun*.

What: The opening lesson focuses on the initial concepts for the theme study and corresponding vocabulary: **solar system, sun, planet**, and **distance**. The next part of the theme study will add: **diameter, temperature, atmosphere, surface, gas**, and **oxygen**

How: Showing a large, colorful picture of the solar system, the teacher points out the sun, the Earth, and the planets, inviting students to offer corresponding words in their primary language for the multilingual wall dictionary. A **K-W-L chart** is created to elicit and develop background knowledge on the topic. Students then work in triads to create an illustrated poster on an assigned planet, using textbooks and other resource materials the teacher has gathered. Each triad will include a **beginning**, an **intermediate**, and an **advanced** English learner. The project involves drawing the planet, labeling it, and writing its distance from the sun. The poster will later become the opening page of a short report on the planets covering subsequent information on the planets, including size, position in the solar system, atmosphere, and other facts.

How well: Beginning English learners will be able to point to the sun and the planets as they are named and state their distance from the sun when asked; **intermediate English learners** will be able to orally describe their planet's location in the solar system and its distance from the sun, using target vocabulary; **advanced English learners** will be able to use facts to explain generalizations about their planet, such as how its distance from the sun affects its temperature. All students will record target vocabulary in their science journals, along with any additional words they wish to include. Next to their words they note the meaning in words, pictures, or translations. Just before students present their posters, the teacher meets briefly with homogenous groups (based on English language proficiency) to provide additional vocabulary reinforcement and assistance, differentiated for beginning, intermediate, and advanced English learners.

Summary

In this chapter we discussed vocabulary acquisition and its relationship to reading comprehension, academic literacy, and general communication in and out of school. With a focus on high-frequency words and content area vocabulary, we explained three major sources of word learning (1) incidental learning of words in context including oral communication, reading, and writing; (2) explicit instruction on specific words; and (3) explicit instruction on strategies to unlock word meaning and help students become independent word learners. Explicit instruction on words and word learning strategies also helps students develop word

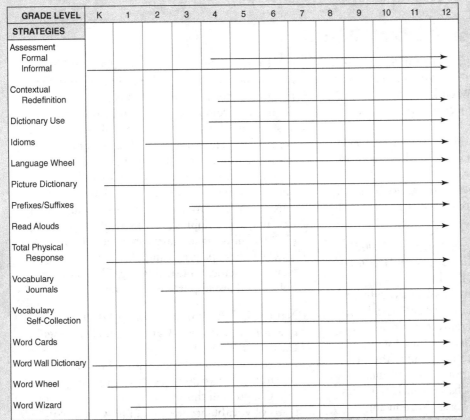

FIGURE 6.11

GRADE LEVELS AT WHICH STRATEGIES MAY BE USED

consciousness so that they become more aware of words, word parts and their meanings, new words they come across, and different forms or uses of learned words. Through this awareness and wide reading, students develop fluency in recognizing and understanding words in oral and written communication.

This chapter has concentrated on teaching specific selected words and on teaching students strategies that will help students learn words independently.

Figure 6.11 presents the grade levels at which we have seen teachers use the various strategies.

Suggestions for Further Reading

Bear, D. R., Helman, L., Templeton, S., Invernizzi, M., and Johnston, F. (2007). *Words their way with English Learners: Word study for phonics, vocabulary, and spelling instruction*. New Jersey: Pearson/Merrill Prentice Hall.

The title says it all; this is a resource every teacher of English learners should have. Everything you could possibly want to know about word study is here with a great variety of activities and strategies for working successfully with English learners.

Beck, I., McKeown, M., and Kucan, L. (2002). *Bringing words to life: Robust vocabulary instruction*. New York: The Guilford Press.

This book, written by important vocabulary researchers, focuses on native English speaking students. However, it contains many ideas and strategies that can and have been used with second language learners successfully. After a lucid presentation of a rationale for "Robust vocabulary instruction," chapters include topics on choosing vocabulary words, introducing vocabulary, and teaching vocabulary in earlier and later grades.

Folse, K. (2004). *Vocabulary Myths: Applying Second Language Research to Classroom Teaching*.

This book, clearly based on research, may change your mind as it did our's on vocabulary teaching. When you read the various ideas about teaching vocabulary, you may be surprised to discover that the following are myths: "Using word lists to learn second language vocabulary is unproductive;" the use of translations to learn new vocabulary should be discouraged; and guessing words from context is an excellent strategy for learning second language vocabulary. The book discusses research on each topic and suggests appropriate activities and strategies based upon research. An excellent starting place to learn about teaching second language learners and vocabulary.

Krashen, S. (2004). *The Power of Reading: Insights from the Research* (2nd Ed.). Portsmouth, NH: Heinemann.

Krashen's book presents evidence in favor of free voluntary reading (FVR). By free voluntary reading he means reading that is selected by students who are not asked to make book reports or answer questions from a teacher about what they are reading. He states that: "Free voluntary reading is the foundation of language education." He says: (1) "Language is too complex to be learned one rule or word at a time"; (2) "Language users must acquire many words with many nuances of meaning and complex grammatical properties"; (3) "Teaching vocabulary lists is not efficient. The time is better spent reading" (p. 19). Krashen's views on incidental learning are different from Folse's and are important to know.

Nation, I. S. P. (2005). *Learning Vocabulary in Another Language*. Cambridge: Cambridge University Press.

Nation is one of the major scholars and researchers on vocabulary acquisition and teaching. Chapters in this excellent book include: the goals of vocabulary learning, knowing a word, teaching and explaining vocabulary, vocabulary and listening and speaking, vocabulary learning strategies and guessing from context, word study strategies, testing vocabulary knowledge and use, and designing the vocabulary component of a language course. This comprehensive book is a valuable resource for any teacher, but especially for teachers of older students.

Nation, P. (Ed.). (1994). *New ways in teaching vocabulary*. Alexandria, VA: Teachers of English to Speakers of Other Languages, Inc.

This is a resource book with over one hundred activities for use with various levels of English learners. Each activity contains a description of the level of the activity such as beginning, intermediate, and advanced, a description of the aim/purpose of the activity, the class time the activity will take, the preparation time, and resources. Activities range from meeting vocabulary for the first time, establishing vocabulary that has been previously learned, enriching vocabulary, and developing vocabulary strategies such as guessing words from context, word building, using dictionaries, and giving learners control. The last section deals with developing fluency with known vocabulary.

Schmitt, N. & McCarthy, M. (Eds.). (2005). *Vocabulary: Description, acquisition and pedagogy.* Cambridge: Cambridge University Press.

This excellent resource book, written by experts, contains sections written by many of the top researchers/educators on second language vocabulary acquisition. Articles cover a range of topics including: vocabulary size, text coverage, word lists, written and spoken vocabulary, vocabulary acquisition: word structure, collocation, word-class, and meaning, what's in a word that makes it hard or easy, some intralexical factors that affect the learning of words, vocabulary learning strategies, and current trends in teaching second language vocabulary. An excellent, sophisticated discussion of many levels of vocabulary acquisition, learning and teaching.

Activities

1. Try reading specific aspects of both Folse's book and Krashen's book. For example, Krashen states that "Teaching vocabulary lists is not efficient. The time is better spent reading" (p. 19). But Folse states that it is a myth that "using word lists to learn second language vocabulary is unproductive" (p. x). Is there a way you can reconcile the two seemingly contradictory views of vocabulary learning? What do Nation and others have to say about learning from lists? How do these various views compare to this chapter's views on the same subject?

2. Look up the different lists recommended for student vocabulary at the beginning, and academic levels. Discuss with a partner or in a group how you might use a list to evaluate student vocabulary levels and to teach students necessary vocabulary. You may want to look at lists on the internet to determine what list(s) would be most useful with your specific students.

3. Describe students in a classroom and explain how you would create lessons for the following lists: the first 1,000 words, the second 1,000 words, or a content area word list. Share your teaching ideas with other students in your class and determine which activities or approaches your group thinks would work best.

4. At the end of this chapter, we suggest giving students a list of words that will provide a foundation for them in a specific content area. Discuss whether you would use this approach or not. In your discussion, talk about how students might learn these words with another approach that may be more interesting or more effective.

5. We shared a specific memory we had learning words in Professor Featherstone's class. Think of your own vocabulary learning in classrooms and beyond. What was most helpful to you? Where and how did you learn most of your vocabulary? How might this knowledge of your own learning inform your classroom teaching?

6. Do you think some students can learn from word lists and that others will not learn as well? How will you adapt your own teaching strategies to meet the needs of students who learn differently from one another, of students who learn well by memorizing lists, and others who do not?

Where the Classroom Comes to Life

Video Homework Exercise

An ESL Vocabulary Lesson (Elementary)

In the video, the teacher demonstrates a vocabulary lesson in which she first pronounces each word, has the children pronounce each word, and then asks students to make vocabulary cards of the words for study. Next, she gives a definition of each word or sometimes she has children act out a word. She also describes each word in ways that will help the children become familiar with them. Finally, they write their own sentences with the words and play the children games with the words to build fluency.

Go to MyEducationLab, select the topic "Vocabulary," and watch the video entitled "An ESL Vocabulary Lesson."

1. Using the model presented in this chapter, how might you develop your lesson for the same words differently?

2. Would this lesson be different for older students who are beginners in English language development? For those who are intermediate in English language development? How?

3. Describe activities from the video that you might use with English learners and activities you might not use? Give a rationale for your decision based on information in this chapter.

Video Homework Exercise

Vocabulary Instruction (Secondary)

In the video, two high school science teachers demonstrate strategies for teaching vocabulary. They try to connect words such as *muggy* and *parasite* to the students' own lives. Finally, they discuss the strategies they are using and the purpose of the strategies.

Go to MyEducationLab, select the topic "Vocabulary," and watch the video entitled "Vocabulary Instruction."

1. In his lesson, is Mr. Gannon teaching students vocabulary that they already know or is he helping students consolidate the meaning of familiar words? What might be the difference between the two approaches?

2. How does the use of absurd sentences, cartoons, and creative writing help students with vocabulary? What can the teacher learn from this student writing?

3. Why does the teacher try to connect a word like *parasite* to the students' own experience? What is the value of this approach?

4. The students in these classes appear to be native English speakers. Would you do anything differently for beginning English learners if you were teaching the same words? What about for intermediate English learners?

Programs for English Learners

English learners enter schooling fluent in a primary language other than English, a proficiency that can function as a resource. In many parts of the world, including Canada, second-language instruction is considered either a widely accepted component of being well educated or a legal mandate in an officially bilingual country. Acquiring a second language is not easy, especially to the level of using that language to succeed in postsecondary education. English learners face that challenge daily.

A growing number of schools in the United States offer two-way immersion programs that help English learners develop academic competence in their heritage language while acquiring fluency and literacy in English—at the same time, native-English-speaking students develop speaking fluency and academic competence in the home language of the English learners. These programs showcase the idea that *multicompetent language use* (Cook, 1999, p. 190) is a valuable skill. Proficiency in multiple languages is also a career enhancement in the modern world of global commerce.

The classrooms of the United States are increasingly diverse, with students coming from many countries of the world. The challenge to any English-language development program is to cherish and preserve the rich cultural and linguistic heritage of the students as they acquire English.

This chapter addresses the history, legality, and design of program models that induct speakers of other languages into English instruction. Although most of these programs take place at the elementary level, an increasing number of students immigrate to the United States at the middle and high school levels, and programs must be designed to meet their needs as well. The program models presented in this chapter vary greatly on one key dimension—how much encouragement is offered to students to maintain their primary language and how much instructional support they receive to accomplish this.

From Chapter 4 of *A Course for Teaching English Learners*, 2/e. Lynne T. Díaz-Rico. Copyright © 2012 by Pearson Education. All rights reserved.

The History of Multilingual Competency in the United States

Bilingualism has existed in the United States since the colonial period, but over the more than two centuries of American history it has been alternately embraced and rejected. The immigrant languages and cultures in North America have enriched the lives of the people in American communities, yet periodic waves of language restrictionism have virtually eradicated the capacity of many U.S. residents to speak a foreign or second language, even those who are born into families with a heritage language other than English. For English learners, English-only schooling has often brought difficulties, cultural suppression, and discrimination even as English has been touted as the key to patriotism and success. This section traces the origin and development of, and support for, language services for English learners in the United States.

Early Bilingualism in the United States

At the time of the nation's founding, at least twenty languages could be heard in the American colonies, including Dutch, French, German, and numerous Native-American languages. In 1664 at least eighteen colonial languages were spoken on Manhattan Island. Bilingualism was common among both the working and educated classes, and schools were established to preserve the linguistic heritage of new arrivals. The Continental Congress published many official documents in German and French as well as in English. German schools were operating as early as 1694 in Philadelphia, and by 1900 more than 4 percent of the United States' elementary school population was receiving instruction either partially or exclusively in German. In 1847, Louisiana authorized instruction in French, English, or both at the request of parents. The Territory of New Mexico authorized Spanish–English bilingual education in 1850 (Crawford, 1999). Table 4.1 surveys the early history of language use and policy in America.

Although there were several such pockets of acceptance for bilingual education, other areas of the country effectively restricted or even attempted to eradicate immigrant and minority languages. In 1879, the federal government forced Native-American children to attend off-reservation, English-only schools where they were punished for using their native language. In the East, as large numbers of Eastern Europeans immigrated, descendants of the English settlers began to harbor resentment against these newcomers. New waves of Mexican and Asian immigration in the West brought renewed fear of non-English influences (Crawford, 1999).

Best Practice EARLY CHEROKEE LANGUAGE RIGHTS

Under an 1828 treaty, the U.S. government recognized the language rights of the Cherokee tribe. Eventually, the Cherokees established a twenty-one-school educational system that used the Cherokee syllabary to achieve a 90 percent literacy rate in the native language. About 350,000 Aniyunwiya (Cherokee) people currently live primarily in Oklahoma and North Carolina, and about 22,000 speak the language (which today is known as Tsalagi). (www.native-languages.org/cherokee.htm)

TABLE 4.1 Early History of Language Use and Policy in America

Date	Event	Significance
Pre-1492	North America is rich in indigenous languages.	Linguistic diversity is a type of biodiversity, encoding millennia of information about the physical and social environment.
16th century	Spain establishes missions in what is now California.	Spanish rulers decree the replacement of indigenous languages by Spanish.
1781	U.S. Articles of Confederation are written in English, French, and German.	Early acknowledgment of U.S. multilingualism on the part of the Founding Fathers.
1800s	European Americans settle Western U.S.	Mexicans and Indians are excluded from Whites-only schools.
1828	U.S. government signs a treaty with Cherokee tribes.	The U.S. government recognizes the language rights of the Cherokee tribes. Eventually, a twenty-one-school educational system achieves a 90 percent literacy rate in Cherokee.
1839	Ohio adopts bilingual education.	Schools could operate in German and English by parental request.
1848	Mexican territory is annexed to the United States in the Treaty of Guadalupe Hidalgo.	Mexican residents of appropriated territory in what are now California, Arizona, New Mexico, Texas, Utah, and Nevada are promised the right to use Spanish in schools, courts of law, employment, and everyday life.
1864	The federal government forces Native-American children to attend off-reservation schools.	Schools are English-only. Native Americans are punished for using their native language.
1888	First antibilingual education legislation is passed.	Wisconsin and Illinois attempt to institute English-only schooling.
1898	U.S. wins Spanish–American War and colonizes Puerto Rico and the Philippines.	Public and private schools are forced to use English as the language of instruction. Submersion in English is a sustained policy in Puerto Rican schools until the 1950s.

The Struggles for Language Education Rights in the Twentieth Century

World War I brought anti-German hysteria, and various states began to criminalize the use of German in all areas of public life. Subsequently, fifteen states legislated English as the basic language of instruction. This repressive policy continued during World War II, when Japanese-language schools were closed. Until the late 1960s, "Spanish detention"—being kept after school for using Spanish—remained a formal punishment in the Rio Grande Valley of Texas, where using a language other than English as a medium of public instruction was a crime (Crawford, 1999).

Although the U.S. Supreme Court, in the *Meyer v. Nebraska* case (1923), extended the protection of the Constitution to everyday speech and prohibited coercive language restriction on the part of states, the "frenzy of Americanization" (Crawford, 1999) had fundamentally changed public attitudes toward learning in other languages. European immigrant groups felt strong pressures to assimilate, and bilingual instruction by the late 1930s was virtually eradicated throughout the United States. This assimilationist mentality worked best with northern European immigrants. For other language minorities, especially those with dark complexions, English-only schooling brought difficulties. Discrimination and cultural repression became associated with linguistic repression.

After World War II, writers began to speak of language-minority children as being "culturally deprived" and "linguistically disabled." The cultural deprivation theory pointed to such environmental factors as inadequate English-language skills, lower-class values, and parental failure to stress educational attainment. On the basis of their performance on IQ tests administered in English, a disproportionate number of English learners ended up in special classes for the educationally handicapped.

Bilingual education was reborn in the early 1960s in Dade County, Florida, as Cuban immigrants, fleeing the 1959 revolution, requested bilingual schooling for their children. The first program at the Coral Way Elementary School was open to both English and Spanish speakers. The objective was fluency and literacy in both languages. Subsequent evaluations of this bilingual program showed success both for English-speaking students in English and for Spanish-speaking students in Spanish and English. Hakuta (1986) reported that by 1974 there were 3,683 students in bilingual programs in the elementary schools nationwide and approximately 2,000 in the secondary schools.

Legal and Legislative Mandates Supporting Language Education Rights

Progress in English-language development services in the United States has taken place on three fronts: cultural, legislative, and judicial. Culturally, the people of the United States have seemed to accept bilingualism when it has been economically useful and to reject it when immigrants were seen as a threat. Legislative and judicial mandates have reflected this ambivalence.

After the civil rights era, the provision of services for English learners has been viewed as a right. This is consonant with the Universal Declaration of Linguistic Rights signed in Barcelona in June 1996, the 1948 Universal Declaration of Human Rights, and the Declaration on the Rights of Persons Belonging to National, Ethnic, Religious and Linguistic Minorities of the General Assembly of the United Nations (1992).

Lau v. Nichols In 1973 a group of non-English-speaking Chinese students sued San Francisco Unified School District officials, claiming that "sink or swim" instruction (denial of language development services) was a violation of their civil rights under Title VI of the Civil Rights Act of 1964. Lower federal courts had absolved the school district of any responsibility for minority children's "language deficiency." But a unanimous Supreme Court ruled as follows: "There is no equality of treatment merely by providing students with the same facilities, textbooks, teachers, and curriculum, for students who do not understand English are effectively foreclosed from any meaningful education"—essentially stating that imposing the requirement that a child must have basic skills in English before effectively participating in the educational program is "to make a mockery of public education" (414 U.S. 563).

Although *Lau v. Nichols* did not specify what type of program a school district must offer, the Chinese parents who sued the San Francisco Unified School District formed an advisory committee, and eventually a program emerged that satisfied the requirements set forth by the court.

The May 25 (1975) Memorandum from the Office for Civil Rights (also called the Lau Remedies) mandated that school districts with more than 5 percent national-origin minority children must offer special language instruction for students with a limited command of English. To be in compliance with *Lau v. Nichols,* the Lau Remedies are still used as the required elements in most states. They prohibit the assignment of students to classes for the handicapped on the basis of their English-language skills, disallow placing such students in vocational tracks instead of teaching them English, and mandate that administrators communicate with parents in a language they can understand.

Because the states reserve the right to dictate educational policy, services for English learners have depended on the vagaries of state law. When the U.S. Congress enacted legislation to begin Title VII of the Elementary and Secondary Education Act, federal funding became available for bilingual education programs. Almost simultaneously, the courts began to rule that students deprived of bilingual education must receive compensatory services. Together, the historical precedents, federal legislative initiatives, and judicial fiats combined to establish bilingual education in the United States (see Tables 4.2 and 4.3).

Best Practice | **INDIGENOUS LANGUAGE RIGHTS**

Times have changed for Native-American-language speakers. In the United States, 281,990 families speak an American-Indian home language (www.infoplease.com/ipa/A0192523. html). The most-spoken Native-American language is Navajo, with 150,000 speakers. In 1990 the U.S. Congress passed Public Law 101-477, which sustains the right of Native Americans to express themselves through the use of Native-American languages in any public proceeding, including publicly supported education programs. Among the goals of this law are the following:

- Preserve, protect, and promote the rights and freedom of Native Americans to use, practice, and develop Native-American languages
- Increase student success and performance
- Promote students' awareness and knowledge of their culture and history
- Enhance student and community pride

Federal and State Requirements for ELD Services

Successive authorizations of the federal Elementary and Secondary Education Act in 1968, 1974, 1978, 1988, and 1989 incorporated federal recognition of the unique educational disadvantages faced by non-English-speaking students. In 1968, Congress authorized $7.5 million to finance seventy-six bilingual education projects serving 27,000 children. In 1974, Congress specifically linked equal educational opportunity to bilingual education, allowing Native-American and

TABLE 4.2 The Early Twentieth Century: Language Use and Policy Are Contested in the United States

Date	Event	Significance
1906	Congress passes English requirement for naturalized citizenship.	First national English-language requirement
1917–1918	The governor of Iowa bans the use of any foreign language in public. Ohio passes legislation to remove all uses of German from the state's elementary schools.	With German speakers as the target, mobs raid schools and burn German textbooks. Subsequently, fifteen states legislate English as the basic language of instruction.
1920s–1970s	Ku Klux Klan members in Maine, numbering 150,141 in 1925, burn crosses in hostility to French Americans.	French is forbidden to be spoken in schools in Maine.
1923	*Meyer v. Nebraska*	The Supreme Court bans an English-only law in a case brought by German Americans.
1930	*Del Rio Independent School District v. Salvatierra*	A Texas superior court finds that the Del Rio Independent school district cannot segregate Mexican students, but a higher court rules that the segregation is necessary to teach English to Mexican students.
1931	*Lemon Grove v. Álvarez*	A state superior court rules that school segregation is against the law in California.
1936	Massive IQ testing of Puerto Ricans in New York is used to justify widespread school placement of Spanish-speaking children two to three years below grade level.	Thousands of New York Puerto Ricans launch a campaign for bilingual education.
1941	Japanese-language schools are closed.	Japanese are incarcerated in internment camps with English-only schools.
1946, 1947	*Méndez v. Westminster School District*	The U.S. Ninth District Court applies the 14th Amendment to schools, insisting "schools must be open to all children . . . regardless of lineage."
1961	Immigrants fleeing the Cuban revolution demand Spanish-language schooling.	Dade County, Florida, implements Spanish–English bilingual education.
1968	10,000 Chicanos boycott schools in Los Angeles demanding bilingual education and more Latino teachers; boycotts spread across U.S.	Leaders of Los Angeles boycott are arrested; two years later charges against them are declared unconstitutional.

TABLE 4.3 Key Legislation and Court Cases in the Struggle for English Learners' Language Rights

Date	Event	Significance
1964	The Civil Rights Act: Title VI	Prohibits denial of equal access to education on the basis of race, color, national origin, or limited proficiency in English in the operation of a federally assisted program. Compliance is enforced through the United States Office for Civil Rights.
1968	ESEA Title VII offers funding for bilingual education programs.	First bilingual kindergarten in New York City; first bilingual education major at Brooklyn College.
Early 1970s	Bilingual programs reach only one out of every forty Mexican-American students in the Southwest.	Based on these data, the U.S. Office of Civil Rights begins enforcing compliance with judicial mandates.
1972	*Serna v. Portales Municipal Schools*	The first federal court enforcement of Title VI of the Civil Rights Act. A federal judge orders instruction in native language and culture as part of a desegregation plan.
1973	*Keyes v. School District No. 1, Denver, Colorado*	Latinos must be covered by *Brown v. Board of Education*—Mexicans cannot be labeled "White" and used to create falsely desegregated schools containing only Blacks and Latinos.
1974	The Equal Education Opportunities Act (EEOA) (U.S. Congress)	"No state shall deny equal educational opportunities to an individual on account of his or her race, color, sex, or national origin by the failure of an educational agency to take appropriate action to overcome language barriers that impede equal participation by its students in its instructional programs."
1974	*Lau v. Nichols* (414 U.S. 563)	U.S. Supreme Court establishes the right of students to differential treatment based on their language minority status, but it does not specify a particular instructional approach.
1975	Lau Remedies—guidelines from the U.S. Commissioner of Education	Standardized requirements for identification, testing, and placement into bilingual programs. Districts are told how to identify and evaluate children with limited English skills, what instructional treatments to use, when to transfer children to all-English classrooms, and what professional standards teachers need to meet.
1977	*Ríos v. Read*	A federal court rules that a bilingual program must include a cultural component.

(continued)

TABLE 4.3 Continued

Date	Event	Significance
1981	*Castañeda v. Pickard*	The Fifth Circuit Court tests the 1974 EEOA statute, outlining three criteria for programs serving EL students. District programs must be: (1) based on "sound educational theory," (2) "implemented effectively" through adequately trained personnel and sufficient resources, and (3) evaluated as effective in overcoming language barriers. Qualified bilingual teachers must be employed, and children are not to be placed on the basis of English-language achievement tests.
1982	*Plyler v. Doe*	The U.S. Supreme Court decides that a state's statute that denies school enrollment to children of illegal immigrants "violates the Equal Protection Clause of the Fourteenth Amendment."
1987	*Gómez v. Illinois State Board of Education*	State school boards can enforce state and federal compliance with EEOA regulations. Districts must properly serve students who are limited in English.
1990	Florida Consent Decree	A federal district court can mandate and monitor statewide teacher preparation and school districts' English learner education.
1994	California passes Proposition 187, which makes it illegal to provide public education to illegal immigrants.	Proposition is overturned in the courts because it violates *Plyler v. Doe*.
1998	California voters approve Unz Initiative Proposition 227 (ED Code 300-340).	Requires that K–12 instruction be overwhelmingly in English, restricting use of primary language as a means of instruction. Subsequent measures pass in Arizona and Massachusetts, but French speakers vote down similar initiative in Maine.
2001	No Child Left Behind Act, Title III	Federal funding is available to support schools in educating English learners.
2004	Individuals with Disabilities Education Improvement Act of 2004 (IDEA), Public Law 108-446	Congress aligns education of children with disabilities with NCLB to mandate equity and accountability.
2004	*Williams et al. v. State of California et al.*	California schools must provide equitable access to textbooks, facilities, and teaching staffs, including teachers of English learners.

Note: See also Crawford (2004, pp. 96–97) for expanded timeline, "Linguistic Diversity in America."

Sources: Cockcroft, 1995; Crawford, 1999; Wiese & García, 1998.

English-speaking children to enroll in bilingual education programs, and funding programs for teacher training, technical assistance for program development, and development and dissemination of instructional materials.

In 1978, Congress added to the definition of bilingual education, stipulating that instruction in English should "allow a child to achieve competence in the English language." Additionally, parents were included in program planning, and personnel in bilingual programs were to be proficient in the language of instruction and English. In 1988, Congress increased funding to state education agencies, placed a three-year limit on participation in transitional bilingual programs, and created fellowship programs for professional training. Developmental bilingual programs were expanded to maintain the native language of students in the reauthorization of 1989.

When the Elementary and Secondary Education Act of 1965 was amended and reauthorized in 1994, it was within the framework of Goals 2000, with the goal to "educate limited-English-proficient children and youth to meet the same rigorous standards for academic achievement expected of all children and youth" ([7102][b]). This emphasis on standards was the linchpin of the 2001 reauthorization, the No Child Left Behind Act, in which all schools are required to provide qualified teachers, and all students are required to pass standardized tests.

No Child Left Behind

Under the No Child Left Behind Act, states must measure student progress on statewide achievement tests. Title III of this act, titled "Language Instruction for Limited English Proficient and Immigrant Students," proposes to measure the progress of English learners against common expectations for student academic achievement by aligning academic assessments, teacher preparation and training, curriculum, instructional materials, and state academic standards.

The purpose of Title III is to upgrade schooling for low-achieving children in the highest-poverty schools, including limited-English-proficient children. The goal is to hold schools, local educational agencies, and states accountable for improving the academic achievement of all students, potentially by closing underperforming schools or providing high-quality educational alternatives to students in such schools.

Because English learners must be tested annually after thirty months of schooling (with few exceptions), and because the continued existence of the school is predicated on annual improvement, English learners experience high-stakes pressure to test well. No second-language acquisition theory in existence makes the claim that the high anxiety of testing furthers language learning. Often, "teaching to the test" leaves little room for teaching English. NCLB, then, appears to be an unfortunate fit with what is known about effective second-language learning.

The Florida Consent Decree

In 1990, a broad coalition of civil rights organizations involved in educational issues signed a consent decree giving the United States District Court, Southern District of Florida, the power to enforce an agreement with the Florida State Board of Education regarding the identification and provision of services to students whose native language is other than English. This remains the most extensive set of state mandates for the education of English learners.

The consent decree settlement terms mandate that six issues be addressed:

- *Identification and assessment.* National origin data of all students must be collected and retained in school districts, which must also form committees to oversee the assessment, placement, and reclassification of English learners.
- *Equal access to appropriate programming.* School districts must provide equal education opportunities for academic advancement and language support to English learners, including provisos for enhancing crosscultural understanding and self-esteem.
- *Equal access to appropriate categorical and other programming for limited-English-proficient (LEP) students.* Schools must provide programs for compensatory education, exceptional students, dropout prevention, student service, pre-kindergarten, immigrant students, Chapter 1, pre–first grade classes, home–school, and discipline.
- *Personnel.* Teachers must have various levels of ESOL endorsement.
- *Monitoring.* Procedures must be followed by the Florida Department of Education to determine the extent to which school districts comply with the requirements of the agreement.
- *Outcome measures.* Mechanisms must be instituted to assess whether student achievement is improved as a result of applying the implementation guidelines.

Proposition 227 in California

In 1998, California, with a school enrollment of approximately 1.4 million limited-English-proficient children, passed Proposition 227, a measure rejecting bilingual education. The proposition stipulates that

> all children in California public schools shall be taught English by being taught in English. In particular, this shall require that all children be placed in English language classrooms. Children who are English learners shall be educated through sheltered English immersion during a temporary transition period not normally intended to exceed one year. . . . Once English learners have acquired a good working knowledge of English, they shall be transferred to English language mainstream classrooms. (California State Code of Regulations [CSCR], 1998, Article 2, 305)

Article 3, Provision 310 of the CSCR provided parents with waiver possibilities if their children met criteria spelled out in the law: "Under such parental waiver conditions, children may be transferred to classes where they are taught English and other subjects through bilingual education techniques or other generally recognized educational methodologies permitted by law." Before parents can ask for a waiver, however, a student must sit through thirty days of structured English immersion (SEI). Potentially one-ninth of a school year could pass before an English learner at the beginning level could comprehend instruction. Unfortunately, expecting children to learn English (along with academic subjects) in a single year flies in the face of contemporary research on language acquisition (Collier, 1987).

Empirical evidence is lacking that indicates any benefit to language-minority students from passage of Proposition 227. A summary of findings from ten studies conducted by research institutes and scholars affiliated with major California universities found that Proposition 227 had shown considerable disruption to the education of language-minority students with no demonstrable benefits in terms of improved teaching and learning conditions or academic achievement (García, 2000).

A study released by the University of California's Linguistic Minority Research Institute (Gándara, Maxwell-Jolly, García, Asato, Gutiérrez, Stritkus, & Curry, 2000) described the implementation of Proposition 227 in sixteen school districts and twenty-five schools throughout the state. The report documents wide variation in the ways school districts have interpreted 227's requirements. School districts with a strong English-only stance before passage showed a mean decrease in primary-language instruction from 17 percent in 1998 to 2 percent in 1999. In contrast, districts with strong primary-language instruction programs experienced only a 2 percent lower rate of Spanish use, from 33 to 31 percent, because parents applied for and were granted waivers.

Language census figures from the California Department of Education show that since Proposition 227 took effect in 1998, three out of five children this law was designed to help remain limited in English, even as the number of English learners statewide has grown nearly 14 percent, to 193,376. Annual redesignation rates remain basically unchanged. Almost one-half million children have been "mainstreamed" to regular classrooms where they receive little or no language support, even though they may still be in need of ELD services. At least 141,428 English learners remain in fully bilingual classrooms at parental request.

Unz's success in California in 1998 led him to fund subsequent propositions in Arizona and Massachusetts (2000) that were successful, as well as one in Colorado (2002) that was defeated. His national organization English for the Children continues to fund antibilingual education efforts (see Stensland, 2003).

Williams et al. v. State of California et al.

In 2000, in a class action lawsuit, a group of plaintiffs, including Eliezer Williams, represented by the Mexican American Legal Defense and Educational Fund (MALDEF) sued the State of California, the California Department of Education, the California Board of Education, and the California Superintendent of Public Instruction on behalf of 75,000 public school students, alleging that substandard conditions in California schools were causing deprivation in violation of the equal protection clauses of the California Constitution. The lawsuit claimed that the students in question had suffered from poorly trained teachers, serious overcrowding, inadequate physical conditions for schooling (filthy bathrooms, leaky roofs, and nonfunctioning heating and cooling systems), and insufficient or outdated textbooks.

A settlement was reached requiring the State of California to pass legislation mandating that every school district provide a uniform process for complaints regarding insufficient instructional materials, unsafe or unhealthy facility conditions, and teacher vacancies and misassignments. Such a law was signed into effect in 2004. Funding was also provided for facilities repair, new instructional materials, upgraded education for teachers of English learners, and phasing out of multitrack schools in the lowest-performing schools. In return for these provisions, the plaintiffs in *Williams v. California* agreed not to initiate lawsuits for redress until a period of four years had elapsed.

This lawsuit should inaugurate a renewed emphasis on the preparation of teachers for classrooms of English learners, as well as improve the learning conditions in California's underperforming schools. For information on the impact of this case, see American Civil Liberties Union (ACLU) Foundation of Southern California (2007).

What Is "Fully Qualified" under NCLB?

It is imperative that teachers are able to understand fundamental principles about second-language acquisition and to communicate, to some degree, with those students acquiring English. Therefore, for teachers to be fully qualified as required by the No Child Left Behind legislation, one might ask, "To be considered 'fully qualified' should teachers acquire at least a basic linguistic competency in the languages that students speak?"

The convenient and widely accepted mythology in the United States that a person can be well educated and remain monolingual is questionable with regard to being "fully qualified." The Hispanic population has become the largest minority in the United States, and educators who are able to augment their teaching using both second-language acquisition principles and Spanish-language skills are increasingly needed. Furthermore, teachers with linguistic competence can enhance the stature of the U.S. educational system in the eyes of the world, as U.S. citizens will no longer be viewed by linguistically multicompetent world citizens as being linguistically handicapped by monolingualism.

The Politics of Bilingual Education

Perceptive teachers realize that the topic of provision of services for English learners is surrounded by political debate. Given the fact that few Americans engage in controversy about second-language acquisition, it is obvious that the underlying arguments for or against bilingual education probably have to do with attitudes about immigration and the role of language in public life. This controversy will continue as Spanish speakers surpass African Americans as the largest minority population in the United States. These arguments treat three main topics: the wisdom of supporting heritage-language proficiency, the role of the native English speaker in bilingual education, and the movement to establish governmental English-only policies. A fourth important aspect, Native-American language revitalization, is less controversial but no less important.

Support for Heritage-Language Proficiency

Developmental bilingual programs are designed for students who enter schooling with a primary language other than English. The goals of developmental bilingual programs are maintenance and full development of the student's primary language; full proficiency in all aspects of English; grade-appropriate achievement in all domains of academic study; integration into all-English-language classrooms; and positive identification with both the culture of the primary- and the majority-language group (Cloud, Genesee, & Hamayan, 2000).

Monolingual English voters outnumber bilingual voters—for example, 61 percent of voters in California are White (presumably monolingual), whereas only 16 percent of voters are Hispanic despite making up 30 percent of the population. Changing the political climate from the current hostility to bilingual education will take a commitment on the part of English-only voters to foster heritage-language skills. Many heritage-language speakers enjoy and seek to preserve their primary language as a cultural and economic resource. Because Spanish is the third most widely spoken language in the world, Spanish–English bilingualism is a distinct competitive advantage in the local and global marketplace, a valuable asset not only for bilingual individuals but also for society as a whole.

Support for Two-Way (Dual) Immersion

For parents of English speakers to start their child's second-language instruction in elementary school, they must seek to maintain or establish two-way immersion (TWI) language programs in conjunction with parents of language-minority students. In this model, English learners from a single language background are taught in the same classroom with approximately equal numbers of English-speaking students. Grade-level-approximate curriculum is provided in both languages. Speakers of each language develop proficiency in both their native and second language, achieve academically through and in two languages, and come to appreciate each other's language and culture (Lindholm, 1994).

One advocate of TWI found that this model promises "mutual learning, enrichment, and respect"; is "the best possible vehicle for integration of language minority students, since these students are grouped with English-speakers for natural and equal exchange of skills"; and is "particularly appealing because it not only enhances the prestige of the minority language but also offers a rich opportunity for expanding genuine bilingualism to the majority population" (Porter, 1990, p. 154). Cummins (2000a) argued that "a major advantage of two-way bilingual programs . . . is that they overcome segregation in a planned program that aims to enrich the learning opportunities of both minority- and majority-language students" (p. 142).

The politics of TWI are such that two distinct types of parents have sought and attained such programs in their communities. The first are the liberal, middle-class Whites who have seen the success of Canadian schools in promoting dual-language competence in English and French and have forged alliances with Spanish-speaking parents (for example, in Long Beach, California; Evanston, Illinois; and Alexandria, Virginia) or French-speaking parents (in the International School of Tucson French Program). The second group comprises parents who are not heritage speakers of a language but who want their children to regain the heritage language (for example, Spanish in Ontario-Montclair School District, California, or in San Antonio, Texas; Cantonese in San Francisco; or Navajo in Chinle, Arizona).

Parents of native-English-speaking children who advocate for the establishment of such a program for their children become advocates for language maintenance on the part of English learners. These parents see advantages in their children learning academic and social skills in two languages, and parents of English learners see that the home language is valued.

English-Only Efforts

The politics of the U.S. English-only movement are driven by an assimilationist model in the belief that for many immigrants the ability to speak English is a necessity for access to the American middle class. However, as Mora (2002) noted, "this outdated image of the assimilation process ignores the multiple patterns of acculturation for different ethnic groups, many of whom enjoy and preserve their bilingualism as an important cultural and economic resource" (n.p.). Therefore, the idea that the majority should enforce monolingualism on a linguistic minority amounts to linguistic authoritarianism.

English-only bills in the U.S. Congress have repeatedly been defeated. Crawford (2006) described English-only efforts as the politics of fear:

> English Only has always been about fear. Fear of demographic and cultural change, as American communities are transformed by immigrants. Fear of strangers speaking Spanish in public places or posting business signs in Chinese. Fear among Anglos about losing their majority status and, with it, their political dominance. Fear of "the other." (n.p.)

Evidence has shown repeatedly that English learners are more successful when given a firm foundation in their primary language (c.f. Ramírez, 1992) and that bilingualism offers a cognitive advantage (Cummins, 1976). To insist that the United States revert to an outmoded model of monolingualism is to attempt to turn back the clock to an era of language restrictionism, a poor move in a world in which bilingual skills are in increasing demand.

Language Revitalization

Many American Indian languages are undergoing revitalization, attempts to preserve endangered languages. Of the more than 800 Amerindian languages, including those in Central and South America, 500 are endangered or worse. In North America even relatively "healthy" languages such as Cherokee—spoken by 22,000 people—are threatened by low percentages of children learning the languages.

American Indian languages in the United States were deliberately destroyed as Indians were separated from their linguistic kin and resettled hundreds of miles away with individuals from other tribes who could not understand each other. Sending Indian children to boarding schools and punishing them for speaking their languages also caused linguistic devastation; for example, the percentage of Cherokee children being raised bilingually fell from 75 percent to 5 percent during the boarding-school-policy days. Other languages with fewer users died entirely. However, without such radical eradication policies, indigenous languages can persist for centuries. (In Paraguay, for example, more than 90 percent of the population is bilingual in Spanish and Guarani.)

Now that the Amerindian languages of North America are in such a precarious situation, simply leaving them alone will not diminish their extinction trends. However, languages can be revitalized by inspiring younger generations to take an interest and pride in ancestral languages and by providing learning opportunities for them. Navajo, for instance, was in steep decline until the 1940s, when the language was used by the Navajo code talkers to thwart the Germans and Japanese in World War II, causing its prestige to soar and numbers of users to increase steadily (Redish, 2001). Ironically, Indian casino gaming has furnished profits for tribes to pay for language classes, a hopeful trend toward language revitalization

Empowerment Issues Related to English Learners

Despite the fact that research has shown the effectiveness of educational programs that support and develop a student's primary language, very few students have ever been fully served with bilingual education programs; for example, in California only 8 percent of students received bilingual education services before Proposition 227 (Mora, 2002). Therefore, one must ask, in a social climate that does not support primary-language programs for students, how can English learners nonetheless be supported? How can communities empower themselves to ensure that language-minority students receive educational equity?

One answer—equivalent to the real estate mantra "location, location, location"—is the political mantra "lawyers, lawyers, lawyers." MALDEF's victory in *Williams et al. v. State of California et al.* has provided school district–based means for families to submit grievances about poor facilities and resources. School authorities can also do much to create a positive affective environment for all students, communicating that school and the family are partners in education. They can respect parent program choices by encouraging parents to seek out primary-language maintenance programs and by staffing such programs in each neighborhood school rather than forcing families to bus their children to magnet programs.

Cummins (1989, 1996) contrasted educational practices that serve as *collaborative* relations of power with those that are *coercive*. Cummins cautioned that children who enter schools in which diversity is *not* affirmed soon perceive that their "difference" is not honored. Often English learners are not encouraged to think critically, to reflect, and to solve problems. This attitude on the part of teachers communicates a sense of reduced worth, resulting in poor motivation to achieve.

Pressuring students to conform to schooling practices that are unfair or discriminatory results in a loss of their identity as human beings. Teachers who are dedicated to social change must help students develop the confidence and motivation to succeed academically; they must also be aware of the ways in which spoken and unspoken language can encourage positive attitudes, building strong personal and social identities.

Equity and Policy Issues Related to English Learners

Achieving high-quality education for English learners has been a centuries-long struggle in the United States. Judging from many measures (e.g., achievement gap, dropout rates, expulsion and detention rates, retention/promotion, tracking, access to AP classes, segregation, length of program, special education placements, gifted education placements, teacher qualifications, teacher retention, and funding and resources), the struggle is by no means over (Donato, 1997; Mora, 2000; Rumbaut, 1995).

Among the indicators that language-minority students have not done well in schools is the fact that nationally Latino students (30.3 percent of whom are limited-English-speaking) are behind their peers in grades 4 and 8, with more than 50 percent below the basic level in reading and math. Latino students are being taught by less qualified teachers, have less access to high-level rigorous classes, are enrolled in fewer college prep courses, and receive fewer state and local funds. More than 40 percent of the teachers teaching English-as-a-second language/bilingual classes are not certified to teach bilingual education or ESL (Gutiérrez & Rodríguez, 2005). Only 9.9 percent of Hispanics/Latinos have a college degree, and 48.5 percent do not have a high school diploma.

Statistics show poor progress as well for Cambodian students (56 percent of whom are limited-English-speaking); only 6 percent of this population have a college degree. Pacific Islanders, however, show a high college enrollment—35.4 percent (compared with 26.1 percent for Whites). Available data show that 31.3 percent of Chinese are not proficient in English, yet

46.3 percent have college degrees; 32.9 percent of Koreans are not proficient in English yet have a 43.6 percent rate of attaining a college degree (www.asian-nation.org).

There is no question that the public climate of support affects the supply of teachers with expertise in educating English learners. Gándara and colleagues (2000) found that between 1997–1998 and 1998–1999, the year of implementation of Proposition 227 in California, the number of credentialed bilingual teachers in California using their bilingual credential in a teaching assignment with language-minority students dropped by 32 percent. In 1998, 10,894 teacher candidates had bilingual certification; in 1999, that number was reduced to 5,670. The number of teacher candidates earning a credential with a crosscultural, language, and academic development (CLAD) endorsement, meanwhile, rose only 11 percent (Gándara et al., 2000). This does not bode well for staffing the classrooms of English learners, at least in California.

Components of ELD Programs

In the widely varied climate of support from area to area in the United States, educational programs range from those that promote additive bilingualism to those that in effect eradicate primary-language proficiency. At the same time as learning English, the language-minority student must gain adequate access to academic content, so a comprehensive program must make

---

Dual-language programs encourage students from two different languages to teach one another their languages.

Lindfors Photography

provisions for both English and academic learning (and, ideally, a primary-language maintenance component to ensure content and language development in L1). The following sections offer a representative set of the main program types, with the acknowledgment that local implementations might result in a mix of program models or in outcomes that are not optimal.

Immersion Bilingual Education

Immersion bilingual education provides academic and language instruction in two languages so students can become proficient in both languages—additive bilingualism. The term has come from program models in Canada where middle-class English-speaking children are instructed in French. In the United States, English-only submersion programs for English learners are sometimes mischaracterized as immersion. This misconception has led to confusion. Canadian immersion is not, and never has been, a monolingual program, because both English and French are incorporated into the programs as subjects and as the media of instruction. In addition, the social context of French immersion is the upper-middle class in Quebec Province, where both English and French have a high-language status for instructional purposes. In contrast, when English learners are submerged in mainstream English classes, instruction is not given in their home language, and they do not become biliterate and academically bilingual.

U.S. Enrichment Immersion   In the United States, a comparable social context to Canadian-style immersion is a program in which a foreign language is highly supported. This program model can be considered "enrichment immersion." This model is distinguished from foreign language programs in elementary schools (FLES) in that academic instruction may be delivered directly in a foreign language, and tutoring and travel abroad are often an integral part of the program.

Dual-Language Development Programs (Additive Bilingualism)   In two-way immersion classrooms (also called two-way maintenance bilingual classrooms), English learners from a single language background are grouped in the same classroom with approximately equal numbers of English-speaking students. Grade-level-approximate curriculum is provided in both languages. Speakers of each language develop proficiency in both their native and second language, achieve academically through and in two languages, and come to appreciate each other's languages and cultures (Lindholm, 1994). This enhances the status of the students' primary language, promoting self-esteem and increased cultural pride (Lindholm-Leary, 2000), leading to increased motivation.

Two-way immersion programs (TWI) had been implemented in 329 schools in the United States by 2006 (www.cal.org/twi/directory), with the number of schools growing yearly. Sites were located in twenty-nine states ranging from Alaska to Florida, with the largest numbers in California and New York. Nearly all schools (308) were Spanish–English in design, although other schools immersed students in Cantonese–English, Japanese–English, Navajo–English, Mandarin–English, and German–English. The grade levels served were predominantly K–6, but thirty-four of these schools were middle schools and nine were high schools.

Careful attention to a high-quality bilingual program in the context of primary-language maintenance is key to the success of dual immersion programs (Veeder & Tramutt, 2000). The

National Clearinghouse for English Language Acquisition has a wealth of information about two-way programs at www.ncela.gwu.edu, as does a website from the California Department of Education (www.cde.ca.gov/sp/el/ip/faq.asp).

Best Practice   MANDARIN DUAL IMMERSION PROGRAM

The Cupertino Language Immersion Program (CLIP) is a K–8 education program located at R. I. Meyerholz Elementary (K–5) and Sam H. Lawson Middle School (6–8) in the Cupertino Union School District (CUSD), Cupertino, California. CLIP's goals are to develop biliteracy, enrich culturally, and achieve academic proficiency that meets or exceeds the district guidelines.

Mandarin was chosen as the target language, and in 1998 CLIP became the first public K–8 two-way Mandarin immersion program in California. In 2007, the first class of immersion students graduated from middle school. CUSD supports CLIP with teachers, facilities, and English curriculum; all aspects of the Mandarin curriculum are financed by grants and donations.

TWI is predicated on beginning literacy instruction for students in both languages. Reading in a foreign language above the level of emergent literacy takes place by using both literature and subject area content, following many of the same principles as reading in the native language. Time is given in class for reading so that students working in groups can facilitate one another's comprehension. To appeal to students' varied interests, all types of content are used (magazines, newspapers, plays, novels, stories, and poems), depending also on the proficiency level of students and the level of language studied. In this way, students are assured of receiving a challenging academic program in both languages.

Critics have alleged that TWI delays English learning and that these programs fail to teach English to English learners. Amselle (1999) argued, "dual immersion programs are really nothing more than Spanish immersion, with Hispanic children used as teaching tools for English-speaking children" (p. 8). Experts concede that the greatest challenge in two-way bilingual programs is to "reduce the gap" between the language abilities of the two groups (English learners and second-language learners [SLLs]). This gap appears when content classes in English are modified (slowed down) for English learners to "catch up," or when content delivery in the primary language is slowed for SLLs. Table 4.4 features program elements of two-way immersion programs.

Best Practice   PROMOTING ADDITIVE BILINGUALISM

Skilled teachers help students build English proficiency on a strong first-language foundation by the following practices:

- Encourage families to preserve the home language
- Stock classroom libraries with books in the home language(s)
- Welcome classroom visitors and volunteers who speak the home language and ask them to address the class about the importance of proficiency in two languages

---

TABLE 4.4 Program Components of Two-Way Immersion

Program Elements	Program Features
Philosophy	Bilingualism as a resource
Goal	Additive bilingualism for English learners and native English speakers
Purpose	Cognitive academic language proficiency achieved through grade-level-appropriate instruction in both languages
Ideal Outcome	Additive bilingualism for English learners and native English speakers
Grade/Proficiency Level(s)	Usually begins in kindergarten, with cohort staying together throughout elementary or middle school
Placement Criteria	Parental exemption waiver
Exit Criteria	Parental choice
Program Length	Parent choice (usually K–6)
Class Composition	Ideally, 50/50 English native speaker and English learner
Language Components	English-language development and primary-language maintenance for English learners; English language arts (ELA) and primary-language-as-a-second-language instruction for native English speakers
Limitations	ELD and ELA must be taught separately, as must primary-language maintenance versus primary-language-as-a-second-language instruction for native English speakers, or both groups will be slowed in achievement in their native languages

Not all primary-language maintenance programs are two-way immersion, but two-way immersion programs featuring native English speakers often enjoy more community support. The following vignette illustrates the public pressure faced by one such school that offers primary-language maintenance.

 Classroom Glimpse

SEMILLAS DEL PUEBLO

A primary-language maintenance charter school in El Sereno (part of Los Angeles), Academia Semillas del Pueblo, found itself in the center of controversy when a local talk radio station and a conservative Internet blog made assertions that the school espoused a covert separatist ethos. Principal Minnie Ferguson said that despite low test scores, other measures of achievement are more encouraging, showing Semillas del Pueblo students advancing to English fluency at a greater rate than Los Angeles Unified students overall.

The Academia held an open house in June, during which groups of children in brightly colored red and yellow shirts sat in circles and played games as others listened intently to teachers reading history lessons in Spanish or sang songs in Mandarin. The curricular emphasis is on multicultural values, with enrollment in 2005–2006 that included White, Black, Latino, Asian-American, American-Indian, and native Hawai'ian or Pacific Islander children. (Rivera, 2006)

Transitional Bilingual Education

Transitional bilingual education (TBE) programs support the use of students' home language in academic settings only during the period in which they are acquiring enough English proficiency to make the transition into English-only education. This supports a subtractive view of bilingualism, in effect requiring that English learners discontinue the use of their native language as they increase their fluency in English (Nieto, 2007). In these programs, students receive initial instruction in most, if not all, content areas in their home language while they are being taught English.

There are numerous problems with a TBE program. It may be perceived as a remedial program or another form of segregated, compensatory education. TBE rests on the common misconception that two or three years is sufficient time to learn a second language for schooling purposes, but in fact this is not long enough for students to build cognitive academic language proficiency (CALP) either in their native tongue or in English. As a consequence, they may not be able to carry out cognitively demanding tasks in English or their home language.

Another shortcoming of transitional bilingual education is the effect that English-only schooling has on home-language use. After transition to English, students frequently switch to English as their primary language of communication, and conversational fluency in the home language tends to erode. This retards rather than expedites academic progress in English, primarily because children and parents lose the benefit of a shared language for such purposes as homework help. For these and other reasons, TBE programs have not led to school success for many students (see Medina & Escamilla, 1992) (see Table 4.5).

It is misleading to think of transition as a brief phase in the life of a bilingual student that happens as they reach a certain grade. As Uribe and Nathenson-Mejia (2008) pointed out,

> Successful transition requires that the entire school have a specific infrastructure in which all the elements and personnel support ELL children in the changes they are facing. The teachers across grade levels and from all content and enrichment areas ensure that students have the cultural, language, and literacy development that helps them meet the academic standards and succeed as new participants in the school. (pp. 3–4)

Structured English Immersion

In structured English immersion (SEI) programs students are taught solely in English supplemented with strategies designed to increase their understanding of the content. Teachers are not necessarily fluent in the L1 of the students. Many of the teaching techniques used for SEI programs were developed for multilingual, often urban, classes where there is not a single primary language shared by the learners and the use of L1 is not feasible.

SEI programs are designed to address the learning needs of English learners whose English is at the intermediate level of fluency or above. Unfortunately, this approach is too often used for beginning English learners. The chief element of "structure" built into these programs is the use of specially designed academic instruction in English (SDAIE), also called "sheltered instruction." SDAIE incorporates specific teaching modifications to make a lesson understandable to students.

TABLE 4.5 Program Components of Transitional Bilingual Education

Program Elements	Program Features
Philosophy	Bilingualism as a bridge to English proficiency
Goal	Bilingualism for English learners only until replaced by English as the language of instruction
Purpose	Cognitive academic language proficiency achieved through grade-level-appropriate instruction in English
Ideal Outcome	Educational parity for English learners and native English speakers
Grade/Proficiency Level(s)	Usually K–2, from beginning through advanced proficiency
Placement Criteria	Parental exemption waiver
Exit Criteria	(See Chapter 3 on Reclassification)
Program Length	Usually three years (K–2)
Class Composition	Usually Spanish-speaking, but in California bilingual teachers have been certified in twenty languages
Language Components	Content instruction in the primary languages, combined with ELD instruction
Limitations	Lack of programmatic support after transition often leads to subtractive bilingualism

English learners obtain access to core curriculum subjects when the content is modified using SDAIE, and thus they can maintain parity with native-English-speaking classmates. Even literature classes can be modified with SDAIE so that English learners are not relegated to ELD programs whose course credits may not be considered college preparatory in nature. SEI programs also have a key advantage in that all teachers are responsible for the education of English learners and must be knowledgeable about language development issues and techniques. However, even with an elaborate set of SDAIE techniques designed to augment verbal explanation, few experts would agree that a student subjected to SEI achieves the same level of comprehension that same student would reach if taught in the primary language.

Also missing in the SEI approach is the opportunity for additive bilingualism. The same drawbacks that can be identified in the TBE model also hold true for SEI programs: There is no development of the primary language, resulting in subtractive bilinguality (see Table 4.6). Moreover, as Lucas and Katz (1994) pointed out, the move toward English-only schooling disadvantages English learners and maintains the advantage of the socially powerful:

> This unspoken and unacknowledged political motivation for allowing instruction only in English is suspect. If all instruction is provided in English, students who are not fluent in English cannot hope to successfully compete with those who are. Thus, this situation perpetuates the power differences that already exist between native-born speakers of standard (middle-class) English and others. (p. 541)

TABLE 4.6 Program Components of Structured English Immersion

Program Elements	Program Features
Philosophy	Academic content acquisition is more important than primary-language maintenance
Goal	Primary-language use for English learners is acceptable only until replaced by English as the language of instruction
Purpose	Cognitive academic language proficiency can be achieved through grade-level-appropriate instruction in English
Ideal Outcome	Educational parity for English learners and native English speakers
Grade/Proficiency Level(s)	Possibility for all grades, all CELDT levels
Placement Criteria	CELDT score level of beginner through advanced
Exit Criteria	(See Chapter 3 on Reclassification)
Program Length	Varies depending on individual progress
Class Composition	Mixed CELDT levels
Language Components	Content instruction in SDAIE-enhanced English combined with ELD instruction
Limitations	Access to core academic content depends on SDAIE skills of teachers

Newcomer (Front-Loaded) English

The goal of newcomer programs is to foster in recent immigrants rapid English learning during the period of early acculturation (Short & Boyson, 2004). Newcomer centers, like Newcomer High School in San Francisco, are more common at the secondary level than in the elementary grades. Newcomer programs may be organized as centers, as separate programs in their own locations, or as programs within a school (Genesee, 1999).

The chief rationale for newcomer programs is that students must learn English before they can be educated in English. A second rationale is that students need social and emotional support during a time in which they may experience culture shock. A third reason is that there are not enough teachers for the number of English learners, so they must be grouped for educational services.

Programs vary in length; some are full day, whereas others are half-day or after school. Students may be enrolled for a year, four years, or only one semester (Short, 1998). The curriculum is designed to help students move into the regular language support program as soon as possible while helping them gain an understanding of U.S. schools and educational expectations. SDAIE techniques predominate in content classes, if offered. Increasingly, however, the newcomer model is called "front-loading." This means that only English-language development is offered, on an intensive basis, during the newcomer period, with students' having limited access to the core curriculum during this time.

However, research has cast doubt on the argument that students must learn English before they can be educated in English (Orfield & Lee, 2005). Major disadvantages of the newcomer approach are, first, the idea that newcomers should be separated from the mainstream

English-speaking population during their period of early adjustment. The U.S. Supreme Court, in the ruling *Brown v. Board of Education* (1954), decided that separate educational programs, however well meaning, are inherently unequal in implementation. The idea that immigrants should be educated separately—at any stage—promotes segregation in a nation whose school facilities are unfortunately increasingly ethnically separate (Orfield & Lee, 2005).

A second drawback is that the newcomer approach is based on subtractive bilingual education. Academic support in the primary language is seldom offered, much less primary-language development. It is probably helpful for students to receive counseling and other assistance to help with culture shock, but no amount of humanistic socioemotional "support" in English during students' adjustment period can realistically take the place of genuine support—receiving mediation in the primary language.

A third drawback is that content vocabulary cannot be learned effectively in a front-loaded manner because it is an integral part of learning content concepts. Unfortunately, students are inevitably slowed in their educational advancement when forced to halt academic learning until their English is developed to some arbitrary point. Moreover, if basic interpersonal skills take two years of exposure to English to develop, and cognitive academic language takes five or more years to develop (Cummins, 1981a; Hakuta, Butler, & Witt, 2000), then theoretically two to five years of "boot camp" English would be required, an inordinate amount of time for newcomers to be segregated. Thus, the newcomer, or front-loading, model is ill advised (see Table 4.7).

TABLE 4.7   Program Components of Newcomer (Front-Loaded) Programs

Program Elements	Program Features
Philosophy	Intensive English is the key to English proficiency
Goal	Intensive English for English learners must take place before English can be used as the language of instruction
Purpose	Cognitive academic language proficiency can be achieved through grade-level-appropriate instruction in English
Ideal Outcome	English learners can participate in SDAIE-enhanced content instruction
Grade/Proficiency Level(s)	Newcomer programs are usually implemented in secondary schools, but front-loading can be done at any grade or level, beginning through intermediate proficiency
Placement Criteria	Varies—CELDT score level of beginner or early intermediate plus parental choice
Exit Criteria	(See Chapter 3 on Reclassification)
Program Length	Varies
Class Composition	Mixed CELDT levels
Language Components	Content instruction in SDAIE-enhanced English combined with ELD instruction
Limitations	Access to core academic content depends on SDAIE skills of teachers; segregative

English-Language-Development Programs

English is taught to English learners in a variety of ways, and studies have shown varying degrees of student success depending on the program model (Thomas & Collier, 1997). Whereas it may be true that extensive exposure to a high-quality English-language development program is a necessity, it is a fallacy to believe that total immersion in English is effective. When students are provided with a solid foundation in their primary language, faster English acquisition takes place. The following four models are the norm for teaching English to English learners.

Pull-Out ELD When English learners must leave their home classroom and receive instruction in vocabulary, grammar, oral language, or spelling for separate half-hour to one-hour-a-day classes with a trained ELD teacher, they are said to be "pulled out." Such instruction rarely is integrated with the regular classroom program, and when students return to the home classroom, they usually are not instructed on curriculum they missed while they were gone. This lack only exacerbates an already difficult learning situation. Of the various program models, ELD pull-out is the most expensive to operate because it requires hiring an extra resource teacher (Chambers & Parrish, 1992).

Researchers who compared the instructional outcomes of a separate ELD oral language development instructional block at the kindergarten and first-grade levels found that teachers in a separate ELD period tended to be more efficient and focused on oral language objectives, but that the oral language instruction that ensued was no more focused on cognitive academic language than was a regular language arts class for English learners (Saunders, Foorman, & Carlson, 2006). Therefore, the particular opportunity was lost for developing CALP in a dedicated ELD period.

ELD Class Period Although pull-out ELD is normally found at the elementary level, students in the secondary school often have separate ELD classes that help them with their English skills. Unfortunately, these classes often focus entirely on the English language and do not help students with their academic subjects. Moreover, in some school districts students who are placed in separate ELD classes at the high school level do not receive college-entrance-applicable credits for these classes. In other words, to be placed in an ELD class is to be denied the chance for college admission. This unfortunate policy is avoided if students are placed in SDAIE-enhanced high school English classes that do bear college-entry credit value.

Content-Based ELD In content-based ELD classes, the ELD teacher collaborates with content area teachers to organize learning objectives around academic subjects in order to prepare students to master grade-level curricula (Ovando & Collier, 1998). Content-based ELD classes develop not only language proficiency but also content knowledge, cognitive strategies, and study skills. Learners receive comprehensible input in systematic, planned instruction that presents vocabulary, concepts, and structures required for mastery of the content (Snow, 1993). The content to be taught, general instructional goals, and time available for instruction are negotiated with the content teacher.

Learning English through content is a worldwide means of English instruction (Brinton & Master, 1997), whether for purposes of business, engineering, medicine, or science. It is most effective when content teachers take an interest in language development and ELD teachers take more responsibility for content.

Universal Access to the Language Arts Curriculum   As described in Chapter 3, the goal of ELD programs is for English learners to make the transition from the ELD standards to the standards outlined in the *Reading/Language Arts Framework* and the ELA standards so they can be instructed in a mainstream classroom. This is accomplished through implementing principles of Universal Instructional Design (UID).

With an augmented emphasis on learning styles and other learner differences, UID promotes access to information, resources, and tools for students with a wide range of abilities, disabilities, ethnic backgrounds, language skills, and learning styles. Burgstahler (2002) noted that "Universal Instructional Design principles . . . give each student meaningful access to the curriculum by assuring access to the environment as well as multiple means of representation, expression, and engagement" (p. 1).

Table 4.8 offers an overview of the principles of UID and some suggested applications of these principles in the education of English learners. UID does not imply that one universal strategy fits all but rather that a diversity of opportunities will work for many different students.

The recommended model for delivery of ELD is to integrate it with content instruction in a classroom in which the English learner has access to native speakers of English as language models. However, because the English learner is still acquiring basic English skills, ELD instruction cannot provide grade-level-appropriate content. To accomplish this, academic instruction and ELD must go hand in hand.

English-Language Development and Academic Instruction

English learners can succeed in content area classes taught in English. If they can follow and understand a lesson, they can learn content material, and the content area instruction—if modified to include English-language development—becomes the means for acquiring English. Basically, specially designed academic instruction in English (SDAIE) addresses the following needs of English learners: (1) to learn grade-appropriate content, (2) to master English vocabulary and grammar, (3) to learn "academic" English, and (4) to develop strategies for learning how to learn.

The SDAIE-Enhanced Content Classroom

Specially designed academic instruction in English (also called "sheltered content instruction"—see Echevarría and Graves, 2011) combines second-language-acquisition principles with those elements of quality teaching that make a lesson understandable to students. SDAIE is, ideally, one component in a program for English learners that includes ELD instruction, primary-language instruction in content areas (so that students continue at grade level as they learn English), and content-based ESL classes.

An SDAIE classroom has content objectives identical to those of a mainstream classroom in the same subject but, in addition, includes language and learning-strategy objectives. Instruction is modified for greater comprehensibility. The distinction between SDAIE and content-based ELD instruction is that SDAIE features content instruction taught by content

TABLE 4.8 Principles of Universal Instructional Design Applied to English Learners

Principle	Definition	Application
Inclusiveness	A classroom climate that communicates respect for varying abilities	Use bilingual signage and materials; welcome and respect aides and assistants.
Physical access	Equipment and activities that minimize sustained physical effort, provide options for participation, and accommodate those with limited physical abilities	Furnish assistive technologies such as screen readers and online dictionaries to assist in translation; make online chatrooms available for students in two languages.
Delivery methods	Content is delivered in multiple modes so it is accessible to students with a wide range of abilities, interests, and previous experiences.	Provide a full range of audiovisual enhancement, including wireless headsets, captioned video, audiotaped read-along books, typed lecture notes, and study guides.
Information access	Use of simple, intuitive, and consistent formats	Ensure that information is both understandable and complete; reduce unnecessary complexity; highlight essential text; give clear criteria for tests and assignments.
Interaction	Accessible to everyone, without accommodation; use of multiple ways for students to participate	Set up both heterogeneous groups (across second-language ability levels) and homogeneous groups (same-language ability level); instruct students on how to secure a conversational turn.
Feedback	Effective prompting during an activity and constructive comments after the assignment is complete	Employ formative assessment for ongoing feedback.
Demonstration of knowledge	Provision for multiple ways students demonstrate knowledge—group work, demonstrations, portfolios, and presentations	Offer different modes to all students so that English learners are not the only ones with alternatives.

Source: Adapted from Burgstahler (2002), Egbert (2004), and Strehorn (2001).

area teachers with English-language support. Content-based ELD, taught by ELD teachers, features the use of content area materials as texts for ELD lessons.

A Model for SDAIE

A model for SDAIE originally developed at the Los Angeles Unified School District in 1993 had four components—content, connections, comprehensibility, and interaction. Often, however, teachers could be technically proficient in many of the SDAIE elements yet not be successful with English learners. Discussion and observation revealed that the teacher's attitude played such a critical part in the success of the class that it needed to be explicitly incorporated into the

Depending on their assessed English level, students can participate in SDAIE-enhanced content lessons.

model. Therefore, teacher attitude was added as an overarching component (see Figure 4.1). This model has been the foundation for the SIOP model (see Chapter 5).

Teachers often find that they do not use every aspect of the model in every lesson, but by working within the overall frame they are more assured of providing appropriate learning opportunities for their English learners. The following sections explain and illustrate each of the five SDAIE components.

Teacher Attitude   Teachers are no different from the rest of the population when faced with something new or different. Many recoil, dig in their heels, and refuse to change. But teachers have also chosen to work with people, and they frequently find delight and satisfaction in their students' work, behavior, and learning. It is this sense of delight that is important to capture in working with all learners, particularly English learners.

Three aspects characterize a successful attitude in working with second-language learners:

- Teachers believe that all students can learn.
- Teachers are willing to nurture language development.
- Teachers recognize that a person's self-concept is involved in his or her own language and that at times students need to use that language.

FIGURE 4.1 A Model of the Components of Successful SDAIE Instruction

Teacher Attitude

The teacher is open and willing to learn from students.

Content

Lessons include subject, language, and learning-strategy objectives.

Material is selected, adapted, and organized with language learners in mind.

Comprehensibility

Lessons include explicit strategies that aid understanding:

- Contextualization
- Modeling
- Teacher speech adjustment
- Frequent comprehension checks through strategies and appropriate questioning
- Repetition and paraphrase

Connections

Curriculum is connected to students' background and experiences.

Interaction

Students have frequent opportunities to

- Talk about lesson content
- Clarify concepts in their home language
- Represent learning through a variety of ways

Best Practice POSITIVE TEACHER ATTITUDES

An ELD teacher observed and interviewed colleagues at her school. She discovered that accomplished teachers set up effective learning environments for the English learners. They understood the needs of their culturally and linguistically diverse students and created an atmosphere in the classroom that helped newly arrived students integrate into the life of the school. For example, they would pair each English learner with a buddy. They encouraged friendships by asking a classmate to stay with the English learner at lunch. They provided appropriate instruction for their English learners and applauded their successes. This environment helped relieve much of the beginners' anxiety. (Haynes, 2004)

Content   *Content objectives* are necessary to guide teaching. A lesson with a clear objective focuses the instruction by concentrating on a particular goal and guides the teacher to select learning activities that accomplish the goal. Teachers may have to be selective in choosing only the most essential content standards to address in the time allotted.

Best Practice ORGANIZING CONTENT FOR THE THEME OF "ACCULTURATION"

Content materials for the social studies theme "acculturation" might include primary documents, personal histories, and literature. Students who research specific concepts related to acculturation, such as immigration assimilation, culture shock, job opportunities, or naturalization, may find that each document features a unique voice. A government document presents a formal, official point of view, whereas a personal or family story conveys the subject from a different, more intimate perspective. In addition, numerous pieces of literature, such as Eve Bunting's *How Many Days to America?* (1988) or Laurence Yep's *Dragonwings* (1975), offer yet other points of view.

Connections   Students engage in learning when they recognize a connection between what they know and the learning experience. Therefore, a critical element of the SDAIE lesson is the deliberate plan on the teacher's part to elicit information from and help make connections for the students. This can be accomplished in several ways: through *bridging*—linking concepts and skills to student experiences or eliciting/using examples from students' lives—and by *schema building*—using scaffolding strategies to link new learning to old.

Comprehensibility   A key factor in learning is being able to understand. Through all phases of a lesson, the teacher ensures that students have plenty of clues to understanding. This is one of the aspects of SDAIE that makes it different from mainstream instruction. Teachers are aware that they need to present concepts in a variety of ways. They increase the comprehensibility of lessons in four ways: *contextualization* (strategies that augment speech and/or text through pictures, realia, dramatizations, etc.); *modeling* (demonstration of the skill or concept to be learned); *speech adjustment* (strategies to adjust speech from the customary native speech patterns); and *comprehension checks* (strategies to monitor listening and reading comprehension). Table 4.9 provides a list of both object and human resources that can help contextualize classroom content.

Interaction   The organization of discourse is important for language acquisition in content classes. In "teacher-fronted" classrooms (Harel, 1992), the teacher takes the central role in controlling the flow of information, and students compete for the teacher's attention and for permission to speak. More recent research (Gass, 2000), however, points to the role of the learner in negotiating, managing, even manipulating conversations to receive more comprehensible input. Instead of English learners being dependent on their ability to understand the teacher's explanations and directions, classrooms that feature flexible grouping patterns permit students to have greater access to the flow of information.

The teacher orchestrates tasks so that students use language in academic ways. Students are placed in different groups for different activities. Teachers themselves work with small groups to achieve specific instructional objectives (e.g., in literature response groups, as discussed in Chapter 7, or in instructional conversations, discussed in Chapters 1 and 6).

In planning for interaction in the SDAIE lesson, the teacher considers opportunities for students to talk about key concepts, expects that students may clarify the concepts in their primary language, and allows a variety of means through which students can demonstrate their understanding.

TABLE 4.9 Media, Realia, Manipulatives, and Human Resources to Contextualize Lessons

Object Resources	Human Resources
Picture files	Cooperative groups
Maps and globes	Pairs
Charts and posters	Cross-age tutors
Printed material:	Heterogeneous groups
Illustrated books	Community resource people
Pamphlets	School resource people
News articles	Parents
Catalogs	Pen pals (adult and child)
Magazines	Keypals
Puzzles	
Science equipment	
Manipulatives:	
M&Ms	
Buttons	
Tongue depressors	
Gummy bears	
Costumes	
Computer software	
Internet	

 Classroom Glimpse

INTERACTION

In one fifth-grade class, the students produced a news program with a U.S. Civil War setting. The program included the show's anchors; reporters in the field interviewing generals, soldiers, and citizens; a weather report; and reports on sports, economics, and political conditions. There were even commercial breaks. The students engaged in much research in order to be historically accurate, but enthusiasm was high as they shared their knowledge in a format they knew and understood. In addition, students were able to work in the area of their particular interest.

SDAIE offers English learners an important intermediate step between content instruction in the primary language, an environment in which they may not advance in English skills, and a "sink-or-swim" immersion, in which they may not learn key content-related concepts. In most effective instruction for English learners, ELD methods and SDAIE are used together to provide language development and achievement of core content standards for English learners, depending on the program model used and the specific needs of the students. SDAIE is covered in more depth in Chapter 5.

Parental Rights and Communicating with Families

"Strong parent involvement is one factor that research has shown time and time again to have positive effects on academic achievement and school attitudes" (Ovando & Collier, 1998, p. 270). Yet, for various reasons on the part of both schools and communities, parent involvement has sometimes been an elusive goal. The growing number of English learners in the school system, however, clearly requires that efforts continue to establish communication, develop partnerships, and involve parents, families, and communities. Fortunately, over the past decade successful programs have been developed and various guidelines are available to help school personnel, parents, and communities work together to ensure parental rights, family involvement, successful programs, and school–community partnerships that benefit students.

Parental Rights

Parents have numerous rights that educators must respect and honor in spite of the challenges they may present to the school. These include (1) the right of their children to a free, appropriate public education; (2) the right to receive information concerning education decisions and actions in the language parents comprehend; (3) the right to make informed decisions and to authorize consent before changes in educational placement occur; (4) the right to be included in discussions and plans concerning disciplinary action toward their children; (5) the right to appeal actions when they do not agree; and (6) the right to participate in meetings organized for public and parent information (Young & Helvie, 1996).

Parents have the right to choose in which language development program options their child will participate (e.g., waiver process) and have the right to be contacted about such rights in an appropriate and effective medium (e.g., bilingual phone calls, home visits, primary-language materials, videos). The *Williams et al. v. State of California et al.* remedies offer several mechanisms by which parents can exert more influence on school procedures.

A fundamental right that all parents have is support in school for the home language. To deny access to native-language literacy exploits minorities (Cummins, 1989). It is important that teachers help families understand the advantages that bilingualism provides to the individual, connecting students to their heritage culture; adding a cognitive dimension by expanding and deepening students' thinking; and, later in life, expanding career opportunities. Family support for bilingualism helps to establish expectations for high academic performance in two languages (Molina, Hanson, & Siegel, 1997). Chapter 9 continues this definition of family involvement.

School–Community Partnerships

In addition to developing partnerships with parents, schools are reaching toward communities for help in educating all children. Community-based organizations (CBOs)—groups committed to helping people obtain health, education, and other basic human services—are assisting students in ways that go beyond traditional schooling. Adger (2000) found that school–CBO partnerships support students' academic achievement by working with parents and families, tutoring students in their first language, developing students' leadership skills and higher education goals, and providing information and support on issues such as health care, pregnancy, gang involvement, and so on.

Communities can foster a climate of support for English learners by featuring articles in local newspapers and newsletters about these students' achievements in the schools and prizes they have won, by sponsoring literature and art exhibitions that feature students' work, and by publishing their stories written in both languages. Students can be invited to the local library to offer their stories, books, and poetry to other students, again in both English and the primary language. In this way, support for bilingualism and bilingual education programs is orchestrated in the community at large. Working with families and communities is further detailed in Chapter 9.

Teaching Collaboratively

Team teaching, peer tutoring, mentors, and bilingual paraprofessionals offer different means of supporting student learning. All individuals working with the teacher provide a challenge in planning activities and monitoring student achievement. Teachers who value the help provided by assistants and peers must be willing to invest time in both planning and supervising for such teamwork to be employed effectively.

Teaching with Peers

Peer collaboration is "a style for direct interaction between at least two coequal parties voluntarily engaged in shared decision making as they work toward a common goal" (Friend & Cook, 1996, p. 6). This definition pinpoints several necessary principles: Professionals must treat one another as equals; collaboration is voluntary; a goal is mutually agreed on (that of finding the most effective instruction for the students under consideration); and responsibility is shared for participation, decision making, and resources, as well as accountability for outcomes. These are predicated on a collegial working environment of mutual respect and trust.

An ELD teacher who is a specialist can act as a helpful colleague with the classroom teacher, sharing expertise about L2 acquisition effects, lesson planning, or potential crosscultural misunderstandings. They collaborate to resolve conflicts, work with translators, and draw on community members for information, additional resources, and parental support. Some schools assign mentor teachers to work with beginning teachers, offering support and feedback.

Working with Paraprofessionals

Paraprofessional educators may be instructional aides, volunteers from the parent community, tutors from other grades, high school students, or senior citizens and other community volunteers. Involving paraprofessionals requires careful organization to recruit skillful helpers and to use them effectively. Prudent planning is needed to maintain high-quality instruction and to ensure that assistants in the classroom feel valued.

A paraprofessional works alongside the teacher to assist in preparing materials, doing clerical work, monitoring small groups of students, giving tutorial help, or providing basic instruction under teacher supervision. The quasi-instructional duties, such as tutoring and assisting small groups of students, provide an extension of teacher expertise. It is the teacher's responsibility to see that the aide is effective in promoting student achievement and that students receive high-quality instruction.

Classroom teachers have responsibility for all instruction and classroom behavior. The tasks carried out by the aide should be planned by the teacher—paraprofessionals should not be expected to plan and prepare materials without teacher supervision. Instruction provided by the aide likewise is valid and important and should be considered as such by the students. Moreover, student achievement should not be evaluated solely by the paraprofessional; this is a responsibility of the classroom teacher.

Paraprofessionals should have a classroom space provided for their tutoring or group work. The number of students for which an aide is responsible may vary, from one-to-one tutoring to supervising the entire class while the teacher is involved in conferences or individual student contact. Should the aide be unavailable, the teacher must have backup plans so that the day's activities can be modified.

Often, paraprofessionals who are brought into the classroom to offer primary-language instruction share the students' cultural background. These individuals can provide valuable linguistic and emotional support for students as they learn English. On the other hand, such aides may subtly modify the teacher's educational intentions.

 Classroom Glimpse

THE AIDE HAS HER OWN IDEAS

Mr. Burns, a fifth-grade teacher in a bilingual classroom, had a Cambodian aide, Sarit Moul, who was the mother of four students in the school. While working in cooperative groups, the students were expected to exchange ideas and information, as well as compose and deliver group reports. Mr. Burns began to notice that the Laotian students did not speak voluntarily but waited to be called on. In observing Ms. Moul work with these students, he found that she discouraged students from speaking unless they received permission to do so. In conferring with her, Mr. Burns discovered, to his chagrin, that she believed that speaking out undermined the teacher's authority. A compromise had to be negotiated that would encourage students to develop speaking proficiency.

Box 4.1 Guidelines for Working with and Supervising a Paraprofessional Teaching Assistant

- Develop a daily schedule of activities.
- Inform your paraprofessional about your expectations of him or her.
- Demonstrate and verbally explain specific teaching tactics to be used for particular lessons and students.
- Be open to suggestions from the paraprofessional.
- Take time to observe the aide's performance, providing praise or corrective feedback for specific actions.
- Provide remedial attention for any documented weak areas and keep a record of effort spent working on these areas.
- Do not criticize the paraprofessional in front of the students.

Source: Adapted from Westling & Koorland (1988).

It is not easy to be a paraprofessional and to work under someone else's supervision. Making the aide feel part of the instructional team is an important aspect of morale. For this to happen, aides need to be engaged in meaningful work from which they can derive a sense of accomplishment and not be relegated to tedious and menial tasks. They need to be given clear directions and understand not only what is expected of them but also what is expected of the students. It is important that they participate in instructional planning and be involved in seeing certain activities through to closure. Aides are also a source of valuable feedback to the teacher on students' needs and accomplishments. For their efforts, paraprofessionals deserve appreciation, whether it is a spoken "thank you" and a pat on the back or an occasional gift or token of esteem. Box 4.1 provides guidelines for teachers who are working with a paraprofessional.

Many people feel that any tolerance of linguistic diversity undermines national unity. However, others hold the view of the United States as a "salad bowl," which features a mixture of distinct textures and tastes, instead of a "melting pot," in which cultural and linguistic diversity is melted into one collective culture and language. The best educational programs for English learners are explicitly bicultural as well so that students' native cultures and heritage languages can be fostered. With these programs in place, the United States will benefit from the rich language resources of all its people.

myeducationlab
The Power of Classroom Practice
www.myeducationlab.com

Go to the Topic Instructional Programs in the MyEducationLab (www.myeducationlab.com) for your course, where you can:

- Find learning outcomes for Instructional Programs along with the national standards that connect to these outcomes.
- Complete Assignments and Activities that can help you more deeply understand the chapter content.
- Apply and practice your understanding of the core teaching skills identified in the chapter with the Building Teaching Skills and Dispositions learning units.
- Examine challenging situations and cases presented in the IRIS Center Resources.
- Check your comprehension on the content covered in the chapter by going to the Study Plan in the Book Resources for your text. Here you will be able to take a chapter quiz, receive feedback on your answers, and then access Review, Practice, and Enrichment activities to enhance your understanding of chapter content.

A+RISE

Go to the Topic A+RISE in the MyEducationLab (www.myeducationlab.com) for your course. A+RISE® Standards2Strategy™ is an innovative and interactive online resource that offers new teachers in grades K–12 just-in-time, research-based instructional strategies that:

- Meet the linguistic needs of ELLs as they learn content
- Differentiate instruction for all grades and abilities
- Offer reading and writing techniques, cooperative learning, use of linguistic and nonlinguistic representations, scaffolding, teacher modeling, higher order thinking, and alternative classroom ELL assessment
- Provide support to help teachers be effective through the integration of listening, speaking, reading, and writing along with the content curriculum
- Improve student achievement
- Are aligned to Common Core Elementary Language Arts standards (for the literacy strategies) and to English language proficiency standards in WIDA, Texas, California, and Florida.

Index